Subtle Citation, Allusion, and Translation in the Hebrew Bible

Subtle Citation, Allusion, and Translation in the Hebrew Bible

Edited by
Ziony Zevit

SHEFFIELD UK   BRISTOL CT

Published by Equinox Publishing Ltd.
UK: Office 415, The Workstation, 15 Paternoster Row, Sheffield, South Yorkshire
       S1 2BX
USA: ISD, 70 Enterprise Drive, Bristol, CT 06010

www.equinoxpub.com

First published 2017

British Library Cataloguing-in-Publication Data
A catalogue record for this book is available from the British Library.

ISBN-13   978 1 781792 66 7   (hardback)
          978 1 781792 67 4   (paperback)

Library of Congress Cataloging-in-Publication Data

Names: Zevit, Ziony, editor.
Title: Subtle citation, allusion, and translation in the Hebrew Bible /
   edited by Ziony Zevit.
Description: Bristol, CT : Equinox Publishing Ltd., 2017. | Includes
   bibliographical references and index.
Identifiers: LCCN 2016007369 (print) | LCCN 2016035975 (ebook) |
   ISBN 9781781792667 (hb) | ISBN 9781781792674 (pb) | ISBN 9781781794555 (e-PDF) |
   ISBN 9781781794562 (e-epub)
Subjects: LCSH: Bible. Old Testament—Extra-canonical parallels. | Middle
   Eastern literature—Relation to the Old Testament. | Bible. Old
   Testament—Sources. | Allusions in the Bible. | Bible. Old
   Testament—Translating.
Classification: LCC BS1184 .S83 2016 (print) | LCC BS1184 (ebook) | DDC
   221.6—dc23
LC record available at https://lccn.loc.gov/2016007369

Typeset by S.J.I. Services, New Delhi
Printed and bound by Lightning Source Inc. (La Vergne, TN), Lightning Source UK Ltd.
(Milton Keynes), Lightning Source AU Pty. (Scoresby, Victoria).

Contents

to

Naomi, Itamar, and Ofri

Chapter 1

Echoes of Texts Past

ZIONY ZEVIT[*]

The American poet Emily Dickinson (1830–86) wrote the following line: "Consider the lilies" is the only commandment I ever obeyed.[1] In this sentence, Dickinson alluded obviously to Matthew 6:28 in the King James translation: "And why take ye thought for raiment? Consider the lilies of the field, how they grow; they toil not, neither do they spin" (KJV).[2] By directing attention to Jesus' lesson in common-sense piety, Dickinson managed—as William Safire explained—to shoehorn a great message into a few words.[3] In fact, without her assumption that the nineteenth-century recipient of her letter would grasp the allusion to the gospel verse, the rest of Dickinson's comment is incomprehensible.[4]

---

[*] Ziony Zevit is Distinguished Professor of Biblical Literature and Northwest Semitic Languages and Literatures at the American Jewish University, Los Angeles.

[1] This form of the citation is widely known though Dickinson did not put it that way exactly (see note 4 below).

[2] It is obvious because by referring to a "commandment" and implying through the use of "only" that it is but one of many, she directs her reader to something prior to and outside of her text, but something accessible within their shared frame of discourse. Moreover, the quotes formally marking a citation from a pre-existing text, the imperative form of the verb, and identical sequence of words support evaluating the allusion as obvious.

[3] Safire 1991; see Farr 2004: 178–79.

[4] Other versions of her sentence exist. In an online blog, Makoto Fujimura, a contemporary artist, writes: "Considering the lilies," Emily Dickinson once stated, "is the only Commandment I have ever obeyed" (nihonganotes.blog-spot.com/p/consider-lilies.html [5/5/2015]). Dickinson's line, in context, appears in a brief letter sent to a Mrs. Frederick Tuckerman following the birth

What happens to her allusion when a twenty-first century reader unfamiliar with the biblical passage thinks instead about *The Lilies of the Field*, a 1962 novel by Edmund Barret, or, more likely, the highly-regarded, 1963 film adaptation of the book? Dickinson's allusion falls flat; in fact, it becomes nonsensical.[5] No meaning is shoehorned into anything anywhere. Moreover, my imagined reader—a callow individual, to be sure—has botched the chronology. Dickinson died more than seventy years before the novel, but she lived long after Matthew and Jesus. Having botched the chronology, my reader is left with a vague idea that there may be a connection between Dickinson's statement and the novel or film, but not with any intelligible allusion.[6]

Allusions belong to the creative side of literary productions and most, not all, authors (of poems, sermons, political speeches, jokes, psalms, prophecies, histories and so on) who make them assume that they will be appreciated by the receiver of the text and experienced aesthetically. Allusions, used this way, are friendly winks of the inner, literary eye that an author directs to her audience. Allusions traffic in insider-information to enrich a work by connecting it to prior works and to create a slight bond between author and reader on the basis of their common knowledge. But allusions need not be obvious to all.

An erudite author may direct them at fellow literati or at a wider group of appreciative cognoscenti, or even to nobody at all, alluding esoterically for his own, private gratification as a form of self-satisfying

---

of a daughter: Let me commend to Baby's attention the only Commandment I ever obeyed—"Consider the Lilies." (The use of capital letters and quotation marks follows Dickinson. See Johnson 1958: 825, #904. I thank Christina Barber, Deputy Archivist at Amherst College for sending me a copy of the autograph [April 21, 2015].) Dickinson's sentiment was that the unnamed baby should grow to appreciate beauty in nature and ponder its ultimate significances (Heit 2013: 80–83). The formulation cited by Fujimura conflates the line in the letter to Mrs. Tuckman with a sentence in a letter to Dickinson's aunt, Mrs. Joseph Sweetser in Spring 1884: Thank you for "considering the Lilies." The Bible must have had us in mind, when it gave that liquid command (Johnson 1958: 821 #897).

5 The title of the book alludes to Matt 6:28, but in the book, the actual "lilies" are German nuns wearing their habits—first seen by Homer Smith, the main protagonist, across a cultivated field—as they try to repair a dilapidated farmstead.

6 In part, the "wit" of the line, when presented out of context, as I do in my first paragraph, lies in its coy suggestion that Dickinson disregarded all other commandments in Scripture. Emily Dickinson was not, however, Dorothy Parker (to whom I have heard the line attributed).

one-upmanship. A famous example of this is T. S. Eliot in *The Wasteland* published in1922. In his complex, allusion-rich poem Eliot, an American transplant to England, voiced dismay at (what he perceived as) the decay and sterility of the elitist European culture that he had adopted as his own. Without Eliot's eleven pages of copious notes explaining many of his allusions, his original, intended audience would have missed them entirely, not to mention his more recent readers.[7]

Biblicists concerned with the historical backgrounds of the Bible, read ancient Near Eastern texts from cultures known only but partially and discern in them lexical, grammatical, thematic, and structural "parallels" to texts in the Bible.[8] On first or second impression, at least one of the two similar items (or grouping of like items) constituting the "parallel" appears to be a candidate for the label "allusion" or "citation." But is it? After attending to the important matter of chronology, contemporary scholars know to ask whether or not what appears to be an allusion would have been comprehended as such by ancient Israelites.[9] The difficulty is not in providing a simple "yes" or "no" but in creating a strong case in support of the seemingly simple answer, an answer best treated as an assertion requiring justifications.

A consideration of adjectives used to describe allusions suggests how useful *allusion* may be as a general term, but how useless it is when referring to a specific type of relationship between an alluding text and its (alleged) earlier target or inspiration: activating, astronomical, biblical, biographical, classical, comic, conspicuous, contemporary, cultural, deliberate, direct/indirect, evocative, explicit, grammatical, hidden, humorous, key phrase, proper name, punning, situational, subtle, superficial, strong/weak, stylistic, thematic, veiled, verbal, and visual.[10] Any single

---

7 Eliot 1930: 54–64.

8 The phrase "and/or" should be inserted between each item listed in this sentence. While one such item in different texts may be declared a parallel, the greater the number of shared features linked by "and" in each text, the greater the likelihood that the parallel will be considered interesting, worthy of discussion and analysis.

9 Katherine Dell and Will Kynes point out how determining the date of Job affects the interpretation of parallels between that book and other biblical sources. Dated very early, it would appear that many books in classical Hebrew were influenced by its vocabulary and that many alluded to it; but dated to the exilic or post-exilic period, it appears that Job itself was influenced by or that it alluded to many earlier books (2013: xv–xvi).

10 Most adjectives on this list are from Leppihalme 1997: 7, 19, 31, 37–39; others I collected from publications in my office skimmed over 60 minutes.

case of allusion might require many such adjectives to encapsulate the relationship.

Because *allusion* lacks the concise, diamond sparkle of clarity, *echo* has been introduced into discussions of these phenomena. (An *echo* is like the original sound, but different; familiar, yet altered, even slightly distorted like a human figure in a fun-house mirror. It is the noun that I use in the title of this article.) *Echo*, in the term "echo verse" refers to the repetition of the final syllable(s) of a word ending the first line of poetry in the final syllable(s) of one or two different words in the following line. With reference to other topics, however, *echo* is used to refer to any close phonological parallel and, by semantic extension, to any repetition or imitation or evocation of a stylistic feature or motif or theme of one text in a later text, be they connected or not.[11] It is used by students responding to the question "Of what does this remind you?" when *what* refers to any of the items listed in my previous sentence. It is the aural equivalent of *recalls/ recollection* in the plastic arts as in the following sentence: The hair on this bronze of a young warrior recalls that on statues representing Alexander the Great. In this statement, *recalls* evokes the sense of a gentle reminiscence, at least in the mind of the beholder. It is not necessarily a statement about the artist and his creation.

Labeling a run of word, or of elements in the structure of a text an *echo* of something similar and familiar in an earlier text suggests mildly either that it may have been intended to evoke a remembrance of something in the prior work or that the feature noticed in the later work draws, defines, and adds texture or clarity to its parallel in the precursor work. Thinking about the connection between texts less benignly, *echo* may imply that the detected similarity signals a case of "light plagiarism."[12] Such thoughts give rise to ponderables: Does the literary structure of some biblical covenants

11 For example, Christopher Beetham (2008: 23–24) suggests that what an author wrote may echo a prior text even when the author is unaware of it and even when he or she may not have intended it. Consequently, as a matter of Beetham's definition, linkages between the older and younger texts in a case of *echo* are significantly weaker and of a different nature than that of *allusion*. This particular understanding of *echo* as a quasi-technical term was tailored for his particular research project. It is neither author-centered nor reader-centered, but researcher-centered and has nothing to do with stylistics or literature per se. Beetham, to be sure, is aware of this and discusses clearly the more conventional understandings of *echo* along with terms such as *allusion* as well (2008: 17–24).

12 Perhaps we should distinguish between what K. R. S. St. Onge (1988: 1–8) calls "grand verbal larceny," the overt incorporation of syntax and extended runs of

echo Neo-Assyrian Vassal Treaties? To what exactly does "echo" refer when applied to (biblical) literature and what criteria can be used to create a strong case for its presence? Is that which we call *echo*, like Juliet's rose, merely *allusion* by another name? When contemporary scholars discover what they refer to as allusions and echoes, are they revealing illusions or delusions of the eye? Is a scholarly article illustrating the presence (or absence) of historical, intellectual, and literary connections between alleged parallels an eisegetical essay about Rorschach inkblots or an exegetical narrative about actual literary links?[13]

Unlike allusions and citations, translations are reproductions of literary works composed in language A that have been recoded into the medium of language B. Translations, to the degree that they are claimed to have been found by researchers, involve changes not only in the language code of the putative original, but possibly in the culture code as well. When identified, scholars confront questions: What do they mean? How do they mean? Is a translation from a precursor text an adaptation or should it be thought of as something completely new? And, if new, new in what way?[14]

Questions about the definitions of these terms and the implications of the answers draw attention to the fact that when scholars are able to establish the presence of true allusions, echoes, citations, and translations—be they overt or subtle—in biblical literature, they are, in fact, mapping parts of the cognitive territory, both local and foreign, of those who listened, read, and wrote in early antiquity.[15]

* * *

In a 1920 collection of critical studies, *The Sacred Wood*, T. S. Eliot published an essay evaluating the debt that Philip Massinger, a seventeenth-century dramatist, owed Shakespeare. A gifted poet, Eliot was also a versatile critic of great acumen. He was capable of distancing himself from his subject in order to maintain a proper perspective while continuing to view literature from within his art. In his essay, Eliot wrote truthfully with a touch of sardonic humor: "Immature poets imitate; mature poets steal; bad poets

---

words, and "petty verbal larceny," a few phrases that don't even amount to an allusion.

13 For this metaphor applied to the recognition of literary patterns, see Fox, 2009: 481; and for its application in a description of how some ancient Near Eastern parallels to biblical texts have been (mis)used, see Walton 2011: 2–4.

14 See Frus and Williams 2010: 3–6 and the discussion in Crouch 2014: 7–11.

15 Walton 2011: 6–8.

deface what they take, and good poets make it into something better, or at least something different."[16]

Eliot's point in this remark about different types of poets was that accomplished practitioners of the verbal arts do assimilate ideas, methods, techniques, themes, motifs, structural principles, along with metaphors, turns of phrase, and appealing, ear tingling vocabulary from the works of their predecessors and living peers. This fills part of their tool-box. The remainder of each poet's box contains private, innate talent with words, power of imagining, and deftness at enabling contemporaries to hear incubated ideas and experience images shaped by a personal, inner voice.

In a second essay, "Tradition and the Individual Talent," appearing in the collection mentioned above but published originally in 1917, Eliot wrote: "No poet, no artist of any art, has his complete meaning alone. His significance, his appreciation is the appreciation of his relation to the dead poets and artists. You cannot value him alone; you must set him, for contrast and comparison, among the dead."[17]

Considered together with Eliot's description of how he mined the works of others, living and dead, in *The Wasteland*, these two citations do not defame those who deface, steal from, or improve the works of others. Rather, they indicate concisely that filiations between literary works are to be expected and adjudged normal, whether or not they derive from conscious or unconscious choices. That is why, as a critic, Eliot opines that the work of a poet finds its meaning and critical appreciation only after it has been compared and contrasted with other works by skilled reader-critics such as himself.[18]

16 Eliot 1950: 125. Writers made similar observations long before Eliot. For example, in the eleventh century, poets writing in the literary context of Arabic speaking, Muslim civilization reached similar conclusions. See Dana 2014: 95–98.

17 Eliot 1950: 49.

18 A generation later, Roland Barthes developed these notions and spoke about the death of the author as the sole creator of meaning, that is, the text created by the author is no more than a structured constellation of its sources as interpreted by each individual reader. For Barthes, "text" included "the activity of reading...and not only the activity of fabricating the written" (1981: 42). W. Irwin argues that the theorizing of Barthes and of others about inherent ambiguities or semiotic instabilities in written texts that are resolved differently by different readers was a post-war reaction against the rigid French academic tradition that insisted on clarity in writing (2004: 229–30, 231–37). Barthes describes how "text" was misunderstood in the French education of his day at the bottom of the page in 1981: 41.

Eliot indicates that poets and, by extension, other producers of literary texts such as those that we study in the Bible, require not only an audience, but also predecessors. To put it more bluntly, all who produce literary texts have literary predecessors whether or not they want them, acknowledge them, or are even aware of them. This fact does not necessarily bear on the originality of their work, but it is relevant when critics in the author's period or in a later one evaluate the quality of their originality.

Edward P. J. Corbett and Robert J. Connors describe the significance of imitation through copying, memorizing, rewriting, and analyzing master texts in the training and formation of good writers.[19] The work of Corbett and Connors is of particular interest in that it draws insights from many sources, not the least from the testimonials of well-known writers of the eighteenth, nineteenth, and twentieth centuries. Although these authors learned their craft through imitation, they went on to develop their own styles by innovating in their vocabulary, diction, figures of speech, and rhetoric.[20]

Contrasting and comparing a poet's work with those of his dead predecessors and discovering its sources, may indeed reduce the poet's work to its sources, at least part of it, particularly if he or she is not particularly talented.[21] It does not, however, justify a claim that a work, even if a bricolage, is nothing other than the sum of its parts. Rather, the exercise of comparing and contrasting provides data that enable us to study the historical process of "emergence." This is the process by which an "emergence," something new and different, was created from something else or from many something-elses.[22] Michael Fishbane, focusing on biblical literature alone, refers to this as a "transformative" process. [23]

* * *

19 Corbett and Connors 1999: 75–88.

20 Other examples of training through imitation are provided in Lindey 1952: 41–43. In this context, it is interesting and, perhaps, even worthwhile, to consider that text is derived from Latin *texere* (to weave, braid together), itself derived from a proto-Indo-European **teks* (to weave, make).

21 On lusterless poets in biblical Hebrew, see Zevit 1986. The original paper on which this article is based was entitled "Sloppy Psalms."

22 "Emergence" is philosophical concept whose popularity has waxed and waned in England since 1875. It refers to the observation that, in material and biological sciences at least—and I argue also in the humanities—the whole is often more than the sum of its parts. Accordingly, water may be described as wet, but it would be meaningless to ask whether a molecule of H_2O is wet. See P. C. W. Davies, 2006: x; and P. Clayton 2006: 4–8. (I thank Prof. Steven Fink for a discussion about how the concept is used in biology [April 2015].)

23 Fishbane 1985: 318–407.

An additional factor must be considered when studying literary emergences, particularly in ancient Israel. Not all Israelite authors whose texts we read may have sought to be creatively innovative in a modern sense, to stand out from their peers and predecessors, to leave their personal stamp, so to speak, on what they (said and) wrote. They may not have consciously cited from or alluded to or translated prior texts, even when it appears so to contemporary scholars.

Israelite society valued memorization in learning and may have preferred imitation in the crafting of its literature. It may have esteemed conservatism and shunned overt creative innovation.[24] D. Z. Bannet describes this phenomenon in medieval Arabic poetry: "[O]ne feature of [Arabic] literature is a conservatism that reaches astounding proportions. Once a literary form has been created, and considered beautiful in its time, it is not relinquished...."[25]

Under such circumstances, originality in ancient Israel may have consisted in drawing liberally from stores of memorized, partially memorized, and incompletely recalled materials deemed traditionally acceptable. Among the accessible material would have been stories, liturgical texts, and prophecies. From these, the sensitive listener would have garnered knowledge of repeated word pairs, well turned phrases, lyrics, aphorisms, snatches of clever speeches, patterns of story-telling, and even stylistic devices such as the use of assonance and alliteration.[26] All this would have been common knowledge in the public domain. New authors, if talented, altered old templates for better, or for worse, if they were not. They attired their thoughts in literary and stylistic hand-me-downs, very much aware of the cultural attitudes affecting their use of generic patterns and language.[27]

If, indeed, such was the tendency in some quarters within Israel from the tenth through the fifth century BCE, then the significance attributed by contemporary researchers to literary connections between early and later biblical compositions requires reevaluation. (Note the conditional *if* at the beginning of my previous sentence.) What we, operating with our

---

24 See Carr 2005: 3–8, 124–56.

25 Bannet 1979: 2–3; cited in Dana 2014: 93–94.

26 On alliteration, see now Yogev and Yona 2015: 108–115.

27 Eliot records some insights that can be readily applied to such writing within a conservative tradition, in his essay "Tradition and the Individual Talent" (see 1950: 48–49). I liken what I have in mind to a rigid type of art called "Soviet Realism."

contemporary presuppositions about how literature is formed, consider artful and assign to the artistry of ancient authors may turn out after investigation to be an expression of Israelite writers' cultural awareness that their production should sound/read very much like other texts of the same genre.[28] They need not have been aware of the source(s) of the well-turned phrase or infrequently used words fished out from their lexical pool and dropped into their compositions. Their alleged allusions and citations may owe their existence to random coincidence.

In Israel, this may have been owing to the communitarian orientation of its mainly rural society that inclined toward social and literary conservatism. Speakers and authors conformed their innovative utterances and texts to accepted language, styles, tropes, and themes. Sluggish change may have come about in certain circles, for example, among mantics, when acolytes of trend-setting, probably charismatic, slightly innovative auteurs such as Isaiah of Jerusalem and Jeremiah, also—for all practical purposes—of Jerusalem, accepted the newish rhetoric of their masters as models to be imitated. Thereafter, they would not deign to consider oracles authentic if they lacked whatever had come to be considered the conventional, au courant "prophetic sound."

A hypothesis based on the idea that pre-exilic Hebrew literature was in orientation whatever could be considered the antithesis of postmodern explains the repetitive sameness of prophetic oracles against the nations as well as repetitions within the book of Isaiah. It accounts also for the recurrence of trite-sounding phrases in hymnic psalms and, especially, in psalms of individual complaint; and even, in part, for the use of permutated and partially rewritten proverbs in the book of Proverbs.[29] Commonplace themes would be expressed in shared language; similar plots would use

28 Adele Berlin (1985: 31–126) discusses the stocks of linguistic materials—phonologic, morphological, syntactical, lexical, and semantic—available to Israelite poets and, using psycholinguistic insights, describes many subconscious ways in which these could be combined in the creation of texts. Additional insights on this topic are to be found scattered in Y. Avishur 1984.

29 See Schultz 1999: 56–61, 330–34, 339–40; Culley 1967: 102–111; Snell 1993: 5–10, 83–85; Fox 2009: 487–93; and Heim 2013: 5–6, 615–17, 624–28. The case of allusions to specific Torah laws in narratives or other texts outside the Pentateuch is problematic. It is analyzed from the perspective of legal history in social context by B. S. Jackson 2015: 75–81. The problem of using a number of objective criteria for critically evaluating claims that Exodus texts contain citations and translations from Egyptian texts and that they allude to Egyptian images, motifs, and themes has been tackled recently by B. C. Sparks (2015: 269–76).

similar language.[30] The dictates of literary orthodoxy enforced primarily by public opinion, taste, and sensibilities were obeyed.[31]

According to this explanation, what contemporary scholars denominate as conscious allusions, citations, and echoes originated when workers in words drew from a large but limited pool of language and literary resources encountered in the marketplace, Wisdom school, or Temple. I think it likely that, in many cases, the ancient creators of texts were unaware of the written texts to which they ostensibly alluded or from which they allegedly cited even though such texts apparently existed and could be cited verbatim by some learned people (Jer 26: 4–19).[32]

* * *

Essays in this volume are expansions of research presented at the Fall meetings of the National Association of Professors of Hebrew (NAPH) between 2012 and 2014. Most were written in 2015. The sessions in which they were delivered and discussed, often vociferously and at length, were entitled "Subtle Citation, Allusion, and Translation in the Hebrew Bible: Evidence, Evaluation, and Implications." The motivation for convening these sessions was the perception that terminological solipsism accompanied by a lack of mindful attention to research methodology were having a deleterious effect on research into the historical development and evolution of ancient Israelite literature as known to us from biblical texts.

Participants were invited to describe: (1) how they define and describe the sources of literary emergences when based on obvious citations and

---

30 Lindey 1952: 25, 38–40.

31 To be sure, biblical literature contains many examples of explicit literary allusions as in cases where characters in one story refer to or allude to another story or to something that happened to a character in a different story: Gen 27:36 alludes to Gen 25:19-26; Josh 22:9-34 alludes to Num 25:1-18 and Josh 7:1-26; Josh 14:6-15 alludes to Num 13-14; 2 Sam 11:14-27 alludes to Jud 9:50-55. See Galen Marquis 1999: x–xxiv.

32 If so, in Israel there may have been very few "full-knowing readers"—a useful coinage by Joseph Pucci (1998: xi)—that is, very competent readers (or listeners) who, meeting authors' expectations, could catch their literary winks and understand their allusions. This would have been because the authors themselves were not full-knowing. Contemporary scholars, in contrast, working with lexicons, concordances, computers, and access to more than a century of published critical research may very well be full-knowing readers, but hardly what an ancient author might have imagined. See the rather entertaining remarks about "parallel hunters" collected by Lindey 1952: 51–53.

allusions; (2) how they determine the sources of true emergences in biblical texts even when not obvious; (3) how they establish criteria that enable distinguishing between real and spurious claims about citations and allusions; and (4) how they recognize "translations" of non-Israelite texts within biblical literature that, had they remained unrecognized, might have been credited to biblical authors.[33] All participants in this volume address the first point, but with differing emphases. Some address the second and third points because their research concentrates mainly on connections—apparent, real, imagined, or alleged—between various literary elements of biblical texts in a range of genres composed or edited in different historical periods. Others also address the fourth point because their research focuses on biblical texts in the broader context of ancient Near Eastern literature.

In additional to the four "how's" listed above, participants were requested to illustrate how they apply their *modus operandi* to texts in order to answer the implicit or explicit questions precipitating their research. The objective of this request was to enable readers of this book to match the descriptions of a method with its application (or vice versa), to observe their congruence, and, thereby, to enable interested readers to replicate or modify the method when working on other texts. Its ultimate aim was to make the individual articles—even when they disagree about definitions, questions, procedures, and conclusions—and this book as a whole not only informative but also useful.

Some papers presented in sessions precipitated discussions on how to help scholars avoid pitfalls and pratfalls. They addressed how the notion of conventional language and phraseology in a living speech community explains some resemblances between texts, and how stock themes and/or genres suffice to explain many similarities between compositions. Others evaluated arguments based on the rarity of similar linguistic forms as an indicator of connectedness between texts. I refer to arguments such as "expression X, or the hitpael of root Y, or even the root Z occurs only twice or thrice or four times in the whole Bible, or in Psalms, or even in Northwest Semitic; therefore, text A must be based on or allude to text B."[34] This *must* in scholarly rhetoric—sometimes softened and replaced by

---

33 This formulation of my request was developed for this essay. The actual requests concerning these topics were informal and phrased differently.

34 Rare words, whether defined on the basis of their root consonants, orthography, or morphology, regularly appear in statistically measurable patterns in any defined body of literature, sometimes as *dis legomena* and as *tris legomena*. The term "rare" itself bespeaks of statistics, not literary significance. More

probably—is intended to imply a necessary conclusion based on data whose interpretation and implications are thought so self-evident that nothing more need be said.

Two problems with such arguments are the degree of authority assigned to *must*, and the lack of specific analytical details concerning what is held to be self-evident. A third problem is the tendency in such arguments to downplay contextual and structural dissimilarities between the allegedly related texts, when such exist, that might clutter the clear vision.[35] A fourth problem with the "must" argument lies in its implication that what is claimed is beyond doubt. Doubting readers are thereby confronted by a written assertion calling their own intuitions, knowledge, and critical skills into question.[36] Wielders of the "must" argument, or the closely related "doubtless" or "no doubt" arguments deploy agonistic rhetoric to score debate points, not to make their points.

Some papers in the NAPH sessions attended, at least in part, to the vocabulary that biblicists use in a technical way to describe the phenomena on which the sessions focused. In a recent publication, Russell Meeks comments, with justified impatience, that contemporary research on these topics is plagued by unclear terminology, the consequence of different scholars using the same words to refer to different ideas.[37] The situation is akin to that described by Lewis Carol in *Through the Looking Glass*. There, Humpty-Dumpty disputes with Alice over the meaning of the word *glory*: "When *I* use a word," Humpty Dumpty said in rather a scornful tone, "it means just what I choose it to mean" (emphasis in original).

The reason for this semantic blurriness in biblical studies is that the terms and their definitions are borrowed eclectically by biblicists from

---

often than not, their infrequent appearance in the defined body of literature, be it the Bible, works of Shakespeare, travel brochures, or automobile repair manuals, is linked with the subject matter and genre of the texts within which they are embedded. See Cohen 1978: 4–7, but note that he writes only about *hapax legomena*, and Greenspahn 1984: 27–29.

35 To be sure, in the case of actual allusions to an earlier text, the differences between the first and second text may contain the key to understanding the second text as a commentary on or exposition of the first. Much depends on the adjective used before the word *allusion* in such studies.

36 This is akin to rejections and dismissals of ideas expressed in language akin to "I am not convinced or I remain unconvinced by X's argument" without clarifying what exactly is lacking in the argument of X that might clinch the argument in his/her favor.

37 Meeks 2014: 280–82; see also Miller 2011: 285–90.

scholars specializing in general or comparative literature. Both of these are large, prestigious fields in the humanities, but they themselves are rent by competing sets of terminology and beset by terminological vagueness.

The terminology problem was addressed almost twenty years ago by Benjamin Sommer in his book, *A Prophet Reads Scripture: Allusion in Isaiah 40-66*. Sommer noted it in passing, isolated some of its sources, and suggested how to resolve it, at least for his own project.[38] But, since Sommer's reasonable suggestions in a publication about Second Isaiah have had relatively little observable effect on colleagues (many of whom, uninterested in Second Isaiah, had no reason to open his book and discover his analyses), Meeks' article in a widely read journal is a timely kick in the pants for the field as a whole.[39]

Meeks proposes to remedy the situation by prescribing simple definitions for a few key terms. If adopted broadly, they can enhance clarity and efficiency in communications between biblical scholars undertaking to recognize, describe, and analyze subtle citations and allusions. Clarity is important because terminology influences the ways scholars imagine, perceive, and understand the dynamic processes giving rise to the texts with which they engage. If not adopted, then the terms will remain jargon.

These are Meeks' recommendations:[40]

Re: *Intertextuality* and, by inference, the related *intertexts*. These terms refer to two or more texts studied *synchronically* on the assumption that they are relevant to/for each other. Although the assumption of chronological flatness may or may not be true, comparisons of intertexts by exceptionally creative readers often generate interesting insights and interpretations;

---

38 Sommer 1998: 6–10 specifically, but 6–31 for a general overview and most productive definitions.

39 To be sure, there are exceptions, e.g., Miller 2011: 294, 301–03; Crouch 2014: 26–31, 51–54, that appeared too late for Meeks to consider. Meeks' article appeared after most manuscripts submitted for this book had been edited. A decade before Sommer, Devorah Dimant (1988: 400–19) tackled the problem of defining terms for Qumran studies where links between biblical texts and the later compositions are assumed and listed by scholars. Dimant noted that the types of links had not yet been categorized or described thoroughly. Her programmatic study undertook to fill the lack by describing different types of links and providing analytical categories within which they could be studied. Unfortunately, it never caught the eye of biblicists interested in implicit citations and allusions outside of the Qumran texts.

40 Meeks 2014: 289–90.

but reading texts this way does not generate statements bearing diachronic validity.[41]

Re: *Inner-biblical allusion* or *inner-biblical exegesis.* These terms refer to the relationship between texts or elements of different texts when studied to

41 In a recent article, John Barton (2013: 3–7) explores whether *intertextuality*, as used nowadays refers to a method of studying texts by reading them against each other or to a theory about the relationships between texts. He points out, that biblicists who use *intertextuality* to describe their method often read "to get religious truth" from the texts, believing that "it [that is, the method] may improve the quality of the religious 'information' that may be extracted"(7). Thus, the ill-defined term allows for subjective conclusions to be presented as based on intertextual—whose meaning is determined by the person making the argument—analysis (see Barton, 2013: 12–15). It is akin, so far as I can discern, to what Brevard Childs referred to as "canonical reading" and to what Michael D. Matlock (2015: 121–31) refers to as "reading deeply." Geoffrey D. Miller discusses scholars who refer to their work as based on an intertextual approach but fail to disclose their methodology. He explains that this most likely "is a reflection of the author's reluctance to expose him or herself to the harsh critiques levied against those who have articulated principles of intertextual readings" (2011: 290–91; citation from 291). Louis C. Jonker's discussion of *inner-biblical exegesis* reveals that although it originally referred to a diachronic approach, it came to be used with a synchronic sense also (2013: 279–83). Many senses of *inner-biblical exegesis* as used in bibliology were transferred to *intertextuality*.
    Intertextuality, coined by Julia Kristeva in 1966, originally referred to every-thing in culture viewed from a structuralist perspective. She was interested in a broad range of semiotic, cultural inter-connections involving an exten-sive three-dimensional network of literary products, linguistic systems, and antecedent cultures and the dialogic interactions between them (see Elkad-Lehman and Greensfeld 2011: 260). This is something much more complex than literary connections alone, a point rarely mentioned in biblical studies using the term. In contemporary bibliology, following trends among students of gen-eral literature, the word itself devolved from a technical term to a buzzword and Kristeva's original idea has become simplified and generalized. Kristeva herself, aware of the breakdown of her term's semantics, stopped using the term around 1984, preferring instead "transposition." I suspect that its contin-ued use in biblical studies is explicable because it is perceived as a chic, sophis-ticated, polysyllabic word whose meaning is thought to be transparent and therefore self-evident. See the critical observations of W. Irwin, a philosopher of literature and no fan of post-structuralism (2004: 229–30, 237–40). Meeks (2014: 89–90) defines it anew for biblicists. Most recently *reverberation* has been used in the title of an edited collection of studies, *Reverberations of the Exodus in Scripture*, as a term referring to the appropriation of old narratives for reuse and theological (re)interpretation in younger stories, all within the Bible (R. Fox 2014: xiv). It is used there as a synonym for *intertext*, e.g., 72.

determine the directionality of influence and authorial intentionality in appropriating something from an earlier text. The objective of such studies is to generate statements claiming historical validity through a study of the emergences discerned in the younger of the two parallel texts.[42]

The distinction between synchronic and diachronic approaches in this area of research is of major consequence. Each has its own set of questions, and when questions overlap, each has different criteria for determining what constitutes an acceptable answer. Even though essentially synchronic studies occasionally kowtow to historical concerns by means of occasional citations and references, they are very much focused on the aesthetic judgments and subjective ingenuity of their authors.[43] Readers can take them or leave them. *De gustibus non est diputandem.* Each study is unique.[44]

Diachronic studies, in contrast, are focused on methodologically controlled observations claiming to be objective and, what is more important, replicable. Readers being asked to accept their conclusions must critically evaluate the data and validate the justifications provided to support interpreting the relationship between designated texts on diachronic grounds. The articles in this volume are all concerned with diachronic matters.

* * *

To be sure, the situation of biblicists today differs greatly from that of Eliot and scholars of his and later generations when they set out to track

42 A most useful introduction to this method illustrated by a plethora of examples is Fishbane, 1985.

43 Redfield 2015: 121–24, 147–50. Authors of good handbooks illustrating literary approaches to narratives in the Bible distinguish clearly between historical approaches and the particular philosophy underlying the approach of their book, e.g., Berlin 1985: 111–34; Gunn and Fewell 1993: 3–12. Studies written by biblicists tend to be descriptive in their approach to narrative poetics and are interested primarily in gaining new insights into the art of the ancient writers of the narratives; those authored by scholars of general literature tend to impose the authority of their discipline on the biblical texts that they study as if they are contemporary *belle lettres*. I can speak only of a tendency since disciplinary borders are transgressed regularly. See the trenchant, if somewhat overwritten, analysis of some recent literary approaches (from the perspective of cultural criticism) by James Redfield (2015).

44 Interesting close readings are found in the books mentioned in the preceding note, in Sternberg 1985, in Zakovitch 1991: 15–98; 2012, and his programmatic studies (1993; 1995), in Dell and Kynes 2013, and in Wolpe 2014, an extended

citations and allusions in the canonical works of Western civilization. They started out with canons that included the Greek and Roman classics and the Bible and collections of European folklore and the learned lists of the best in English, French, German, Italian, and Spanish literature in the original or in translation. And they researched. For example, James Joyce delighted in exercising literary one-upmanship by citing partially, alluding to minor or obscure sources, and in using rare or dialect words that he collected in the course of his travels. The discursive world of the authors whose works were studied by Eliot and his generation through the 1950s was largely known.

The situation of contemporary biblicists is different. The discursive world of authors whose works are found in the Bible is not known completely. Even to state that it is known incompletely exaggerates, I believe, both the quantity and quality of our knowledge.

Continuing research into the ancient Near East that began in the nineteenth century, a few score of contemporary scholars have heavily invested their intellectual capital to discover the discursive world of Israelite authors, to describe it, and to illustrate where and how it left traces in biblical literature.[45] They are providing the data that define its

---

literary analysis of the David stories. The Hebrew journal *Megadim* publishes many articles following synchronic literary approaches, mainly structuralist in orientation. Although the underlying method has links to general literary theory of the 1970s and earlier, publications in *Megadim* are viewed by their authors and readers as representing a distinctively innovative, Jewish Orthodox approach to the literary study of the Bible (see Fischer 2015: 37, and compare John Barton's observation cited above in note 41).

45   The best example of ancient writers who drew historical conclusions on the basis of what they considered lexical clues and textual allusions is provided by the historical titles that they appended to some psalms. On the assumption that David wrote these psalms, one such writer/historian, curious as to the circumstances under which they had been written, worked back from the content of each psalm to the David narratives in Samuel. He connected key words in the psalms to the same words in Samuel looking for clusters of parallels. On the basis of these parallels, he identified the particular psalm composed "when he fled from Absalom, his son" (Ps 3), "concerning Cush the Benjaminite" (Ps 7), "when he changed his demeanor before Abimelech" [Achish = Abimelech—zz] (Ps 34), "when Nathan the prophet came unto him after he had gone into Bathsheba" (Ps 51), etc. See Slomovic 1979, especially 365–77. Slomovic refers to this method, based on apparent allusions in thematically appropriate contexts, as "connective midrash" (352–55) and finds it also in unique LXX psalm titles unattested in the MT as well as in Chronicles.

porous borders. Thereby, they contribute to the intellectual history, not of all ancient Israel, but of some of its literate groups.

With this nod to echoes of texts past, to the background of this book, and to the clever remark of Emily Dickinson and the pithy observations of T. S. Eliot, I turn to the present.

* * *

Articles in this volume are gathered into four sections based on their emphases and choice of case studies. The first section, *Clarifying Matters of Theory and Method* contains studies by Joseph Ryan Kelly and David Carr. These scholars provide a sophisticated overview of contemporary thought about allusions and textual dependence in general literature. Their studies introduce articles in the following sections by clarifying terminology and by describing some "rules for the game" that enable researchers to distinguish between relevant and irrelevant data and to assess the significance of those that are relevant. Issues raised by these two studies reverberate in different ways throughout this book.

The second section, *Multi-Lingual Scribes and Their Archives*, contains a single study by Ada Taggar-Cohen. She surveys Hittite scribal archives over a few continuous centuries in order to provide a glimpse of scribes composing and copying texts, translating them from one language into another, and recasting or reformulating them for use in different contexts. Taggar-Cohen's research indicates that what has to be inferred from texts in the Bible on the basis of anthropological parallels, is actually attested in autographs and copies from the Hittite capital of Hattusha. Her descriptions provide grit and a sense of imaginable historical texture to the studies on the formation and history of Israelite literature that follow hers.

Section three, *Inner Biblical Allusions and Citations*, presents studies by Marc Brettler, Jeffery Leonard, Joel Baden, and Marvin Sweeney. The articles of Brettler and Leonard describe methods by which ostensible allusions in Psalms to events described in the Pentateuch may be evaluated as real or only apparent and they explore how some psalms can be exploited critically to trace (and date relatively) the historical development of Torah narratives. Baden addresses D's allusions to other sources in the Pentateuch, their significance in D, and raises the question of whether or not D's use may be understood as indicating that the source texts were "authorized" in some way. But, beyond the literary analyses, Baden's study remains focused on the ancient authors and their imagined audiences. Sweeney explores how prophetic texts originating in different historical periods and addressing different situations could be drawn into textual juxtaposition and coordinated theologically. This happened, he explains, through a reading process in which ancient editors used citations and allusions that smoothed differences between the original meaning of the older texts and newer comprehensions of their significance. Sweeney's exegetical research reveals the dynamics of ancient synchronic eisegesis in the diachronic shaping of an extant text.

Articles in the fourth and final section, *Extra Biblical Allusions, Citations, and Translations*, explore in detail allusions, citations, and translations that crossed cultural and linguistic borders. Edward Greenstein evaluates what may and may not be said about the many cases of alleged Mesopotamian influence on Job using linguistic criteria in combination with a methodologically sophisticated understanding of how textual dependence may be determined. David Wright, incorporating insights from recent criticism of his earlier research, reanalyzes arguments that the Covenant Code, including both its apodictic and casuistic components, was strongly influenced by the Laws of Hammurabi. Peter Machinist studies an idiom for "to slander", one passage each from First Isaiah and Second Isaiah, and Ps 29 in their ancient Near Eastern cultural and linguistic contexts. He illustrates how reading these texts with prompts from curiosity but with a worked out, sophisticated methodology, can tease important, valid information bearing on literary continuity, influence, and allusion from very small units in biblical texts. In part, he does this by reflecting on his own conclusions and subjecting them to close, critical scrutiny. Finally, Michael Fox describes the methodology by which he is able to determine that proverbs in Prov 22:17-23:11 were not influenced by the Egyptian Instructions of Amenemope, but translated into Hebrew directly from a scroll that contained a translation, most likely into Aramaic, of the Egyptian text.

The chapters in this book do not lend themselves to casual skimming. They are best read slowly and appreciated with or without a single malt splashed with water in a tulip-shaped or, perhaps, a lily-shaped glass.

BIBLIOGRAPHY

Avishur, Y. 1984. *Stylistic Studies of Word-Pairs in Biblical and Ancient Semitic Literatures*. Neukirchen-Vluyn: Neukirchener.

Bannet, D. Z. 1979. *Basic Principles in the History of Arabic Literature* (Hebrew). Jerusalem: Hebrew University.

Barthes, R. 1981. "Theory of the Text." In *Untying the Text: A Post-Structural Reader*, edited by R. Young, 31–47. London: Routledge.

Barton, J. 2013. "Déja Lu: Intertextuality, Method or Theory?" In *Reading Job Intertextually*, edited by K. Dell and W. Kynes, 1–6. New York/London: Bloomsbury.

Beetham, C. A. 2008. *Echoes of Scripture in the Letter of Paul to the Colossians*. Leiden: Brill.

Berlin, A. 1985. *The Dynamics of Biblical Parallelism*. Bloomington, IN: Indiana University Press.

Carr, D. M. 2005. *Writing on the Tablet of the Heart: Origins of Scripture and Literature*. Oxford: Oxford University Press.

Clayton, P. 2006. "Conceptual Foundations of Emergence Theory." In *The Re-Emergence of Emergence: The Emergenist Hypothesis from Science to Religion*, edited by P. Clayton and P. Davies, 1–31. Oxford: Oxford University Press.

Cohen, H. R. 1978. *Biblical Hapex Legomena in the Light of Akkadian and Ugaritic*. Missoula, MT: Scholars Press.

Corbett, E. P. J., and R. J. Connors. 1999. *Style and Statement*. Oxford: Oxford University Press.

Crouch, C. L. 2014. *Israel and the Assyrians: Deuteronomy, the Succession Treaty of Esarhaddon, and the Nature of Subversion*. Atlanta, GA: SBL Press.

Culley, R. C. 1967. *Oral Formulaic Language in the Biblical Psalms*. Toronto: University of Toronto Press.

Dana, J. 2014. "Moshe Ibn Ezra and His Ars Poetica: Imitation and Innovations According to Kitab al-Muhadara val-Mudhakara." *Hebrew Studies* 55: 89–116.

Davies, P. C. W. 2006. "Preface." In P. Clayton and P. Davies, *The Re-Emergence of Emergence: The Emergenist Hypothesis from Science to Religion*, ix–xiv. Oxford: Oxford University Press.

Dell, K., and W. Kynes. 2013. "Introduction." In *Reading Job Intertextually*, edited by K. Dell and W. Kynes, xvi–xxiii. New York/London: Bloomsbury.

Dimant, D. 1988. "Use and Interpretation of Mikra in the Apocrypha and Pseudepigrapha." In *Mikra: Text, Translation, Reading and Interpretation of the Hebrew Bible in Ancient Judaism and Early Christianity*, edited by M. J. Mulder, 379–419. Assen/Maastricht: Van Gorcum and Philadelphia, PA: Fortress.

Eliot, T. S. 1930. *The Wasteland*, fourth printing. New York: Liveright.

Eliot, T. S. 1950. *The Sacred Wood: Essays on Poetry and Criticism*, seventh edition. London: Methuen.

Elkad-Lehman, I., and H. Greesfeld. 2011. "Intertextuality as an Interpretative Method in Qualitative Research." *Narrative Inquiry* 2: 258–75.

Farr, J. 2004. *The Gardens of Emily Dickinson*. Cambridge, MA: Harvard University Press.

Fischer, E. 2015. "New Gleanings from an Old Book." *Jewish Review of Books* 6(2): 36–38 = http://jewishreviewofbooks.com/articles/1649/new-gleanings-from-an-old-book/ (May 21, 2015).

Fishbane, M. 1985. *Biblical Interpretation in Ancient Israel*. Oxford: Clarendon Press.

Fox, M. V. 2009. *Proverbs 10-31*. New Haven, CT: Yale University Press.

Fox, R. M. 2014. *Reverberations of the Exodus in Scripture*. Eugene, OR: Pickwick.

Frus, P., and Williams, C. 2010. *Beyond Adaptation: Essays on Radical Transformations of Original Works*. Jefferson, NC: McFarland & Co.

Greenspahn, F. E. 1984. *Hapax Legomena in Biblical Hebrew: A Study of the Phenomenon and Its Treatment Since Antiquity with Special Reference to Verbal Forms*. Chico, CA: Scholars Press.

Gunn, D. M. and D. N. Fewell. 1993. *Narrative in the Hebrew Bible*. New York: Oxford University Press.

Heim, K. M. 2013. *Poetic Imagination in Proverbs: Variant Repetitions and the Nature of Poetry*. Winona Lake, IN: Eisenbrauns.

Heit, J. 2013. *Liturgical Liasons: The Textual Body, Irony, and Betrayal in John Dunne and Emily Dickinson*. Eugene, OR: Pickwick Publications.

Irwin, W. 2004. "Against Intertextuality." *Philosophy and Literature* 2: 229–42.

Jackson, B. S. 2015. "Ruth, The Pentateuch and the Nature of Biblical Law in Coversation with Jean-Louis Ska." In *The Post-Priestly Pentateuch. New Perspectives on its Redactional Development and Theological Profiles*, edited by K. Schmid and F. Giuntoli, 75–111. Tübingen: Mohr Siebeck.

Jonker, L. C. 2013. "Introduction." *Hebrew Bible and Ancient Israel* 2: 275–86.

Johnson, T. H. 1958. *The Letters of Emily Dickinson*, Vol. III. Cambridge, MA: Belknap Press of Harvard University.

Leppihalme, R. 1997. *Cultural Bumps: An Empirical Approach to the Translation of Allusions*. Clevedon, UK: Multilingual Matters Ltd.

Lindey, A. 1952. *Plagiarism and Originality*. New York: Harper and Brothers.

Marquis, G. 1999. "Explicit Literary Allusions in Biblical Historiography (The Pentateuch and Former Prophets)" [Hebrew with English summary]. Ph.D. diss., Hebrew University.

Matlock, M. D. 2015. "Please Try This at Home: Steps for Reading Scripture Deeply." In *Reading Scripture Deeply: Millennials Take a Fresh Look at the Bible*, edited by R. S. Hess and E. R. Richards, 121–31. Charleston, SC: International Reference Library for Biblical Research.

Miller, G. D. 2011. "Intertextuality in Old Testament Research." *Currents in Biblical Research* 9: 283–309.

Meeks, R. 2014. "Intertextuality, Inner-Biblical Exegesis, and Inner-Biblical Allusion: The Ethics of a Methodology." *Biblica* 85: 280–91.

Pucci, J. 1998. *The Full Knowing Reader: Allusion and the Power of the Reader in the Western Literary Tradition*. New Haven: Yale University Press.

Redfield, J. A. 2015. "Behind Auerbach's 'Background': Five Ways to Read What Biblical Narratives Don't Say." *AJS Review* 39: 121–50.

Safire, W. 1991. "About Language; Poetic Allusion Watch." *New York Times Magazine* December 1: http://www.nytimes.com/1991/12/01/magazine/about-language.

Sandmel, S. 1962. "Parallelomania." *Journal of Biblical Literature* 81: 1–13.

Schultz, R. L. 1999. *The Search for Quotation: Verbal Parallels in the Prophets*. Sheffield: Sheffield Academic Press.

Slomovic, E. 1979. "Toward an Understanding of the Formation of Historical Titles in the Book of Psalms." *Zeitschrift für die Alttestamentliche Wissenschaft* 91: 350–80.

Snell, D. C. 1993. *Twice Told Proverbs and the Composition of the Book of Proverbs*. Winona Lake, IN: Eisenbrauns.

Sommer, B. D. 1998. *A Prophet Reads Scripture: Allusion in Isaiah 40-66*. Stanford, CA: Stanford University Press.

St. Onge, K. R. 1988. *The Melancholy Anatomy of Plagiarism*. Lanham/New York: University Press of America.

Sparks, B.C. 2015. "Egyptian Texts Relating to the Exodus: Discussions of Exodus Parallels in the Egyptology Literature." In *Israel's Exodus in Transdisciplinary Perspective: Text, Archaeology, Culture, and Geoscience*, edited by T. E. Levy, T. Schneider, and W. H. Propp, 259–76. Switzerland: Springer.

Sternberg, M. 1985. *The Poetics of Biblical Narrative: Ideological Literature and the Drama of Reading*. Bloomington, IN: Indiana University Press.

Walton, J. H. 2011. *Genesis 1 As Ancient Cosmology*. Winona Lake, IN: Eisenbrauns.

Wolpe, D. 2014. *David: The Divided Heart*. New Haven: Yale University Press.

Yogev, J. and S. Yona. 2015. "Opening Alliteration in Biblical and Ugaritic Poetry." *Zeitschrift für die Alttestamentliche Wissenschaft* 127: 108–13.

Zakovitch, Y. 1991. *"And You shall Tell Your Son..." The Concept of the Exodus in the Bible*. Jerusalem: Magnes.

Zakovitch, Y. 1993. "Through the Looking Glass: Reflections / Inversions of Genesis Stories in the Bible." *Biblical Interpretation* 1: 139–52.

Zakovitch, Y. 1995. *Through the Looking Glass: Reflection Stories in the Bible* (Hebrew). Tel Aviv: Hakibbutz Hameuchad.

Zakovitch, Y. 2012. *Jacob: Unexpected Patriarch*. New Haven: Yale University Press.

Zevit, Z. 1986. "Psalms at the Poetic Precipice." *Hebrew Annual Review* 10: 351–66.

Chapter 2

Identifying Literary Allusions:
Theory and the Criterion of Shared language

JOSEPH RYAN KELLY[*]

INTRODUCTION

We might for our purposes define parallelomania as that extravagance among scholars which first overdoes the supposed similarity in passages and then proceeds to describe source and derivation as if implying literary connection flowing in an inevitable or predetermined direction.... It seems to me that we are at a junction when biblical scholarship should recognize parallelomania for the disease that it is. It is time to draw away from the extravagance which has always been a latent danger. (Sandmel 1962: 1, 13)

Without a basic model of literary production, I would argue, the philologist's collecting of comparative and contrastive materials (loans, debts, parallels, etc.) suffers from what I may disrespectfully name "comparisonitis"— collecting for the sake of collecting. (Conte 1986: 23)

It should be possible for an interpreter to dismiss some similarities between texts as historically insignificant, lacking literary filiation. Connections may be coincidental, similarly focused but independently derived, products of stock language, or evidence of a shared cultural repertoire. But occasionally an interpretive psychosis or an inflamed comparative methodology sets in, and scholars who succumb develop a certain lack of restraint when analyzing parallels and making comparisons. According

---

[*] Joseph Ryan Kelly teaches history and humane letters at Tempe Preparatory Academy in Tempe, Arizona.

to Samuel Sandmel, parallelomania exaggerates the conclusions that
rational interpreters would draw regarding the sources and derivations of
alleged parallels. It is interesting that Sandmel portrays this extravagance
as a *psychological* disease. Romantic literary critics believed a psychological
relationship linked discrete texts with the literary stream of tradition, and
we have seen this view rearticulated in contemporary poetics in Harold
Bloom's *Anxiety of Influence: A Theory of Poetry*.

One could argue that Sandmel's disease is merely the critic experienc-
ing and extending the anxiety of the poet, as Bloom does:

> Every poem is a misinterpretation of a parent poem. A poem is not an over-
> coming of anxiety, but is that anxiety. Poets' misinterpretations or poems
> are more drastic than critics' misinterpretations or criticism, but this is only
> a difference in degree and not at all in kind. There are no interpretations
> but only misinterpretations, and so all criticism is prose poetry. (Bloom
> 1997: 94–95)

However interesting this line of investigation, the question I intend to discuss concerns mechanics more than it concerns mentality.

What role should shared language play as a criterion for identifying
literary allusions? Scholars generally recognize that a work of literature,
when it contains language similar or identical to an earlier work of literature, indicates the possible patterning of the posterior text on the anterior
text. Scholars rely primarily—in some cases exclusively—on shared language when identifying literary allusions in biblical texts. Armin Lange
and Matthias Weigold's book, *Biblical Quotations and Allusions in Second
Temple Literature* (2011), exemplifies an approach to identifying allusions
that relies almost exclusively on key-word association. The authors aim to
provide an extensive catalog of quotations of and allusions to the Hebrew
Bible in "literature which was written between the years 520 BCE. and
70 CE," excepting works redacted during that time, the works of Philo of
Alexandria, and those portions of the New Testament written before 70 CE
(Lange and Weigold 2011: 36). Because previously published material was
not as comprehensive as the catalog they desired to create, and because
they could not ensure the completeness and accuracy of this previously
published material, they developed a method for constructing their own
catalog with the aid of the software program Accordance. For each verse of
the Hebrew Bible they performed a search for shared words. The criteria
varied based on language and genre, but they required anywhere from two
to six shared words while permitting one word ignored from the anterior

text and one word added in the posterior text. Their research resulted in extensive lists of "quotations and allusions."

Because they rely so narrowly on shared vocabulary, some of the relationships they identify are far-fetched. For example, they identify an allusion to Gen 1:6-9, where God creates a firmament separating the waters above the firmament from the waters below the firmament, with the Psalmist's words, "Praise him, you highest heavens, and you waters above the heavens!" (Ps 148:4 NRSV); and they identify an allusion to Gen 1:26-27, where God creates humanity (ʾādām) in the divine image, in the words of Qohelet: "See, this alone I found, that God made human beings (ʾādām) straightforward, but they have devised many schemes" (Eccl 7:29 NRSV). While not all scholars interested in allusion rely as exclusively or mechanically on shared vocabulary, *Biblical Quotations and Allusions* underscores its primary significance for biblical scholarship (Kelly 2013b: 413–15). Aware of a tendency toward excessiveness when it comes to identifying literary allusions, it is worth considering if the significance that some biblical scholars attach to shared language helps to ease or exacerbate this lack of restraint.

LITERARY ALLUSION AND THEORY

In contrast to the psychological diagnosis of Sandmel, Gian Biagio Conte imagines scholars stricken with a *physical* malady—comparisonitis. Afflicted as we are with an inflamed inclination to collect comparative and contrastive materials, Conte considers literary theory the best prescription for reducing our excessive tendencies.

Generally speaking, biblical studies has not devoted significant attention to theoretical literature on literary allusion. There are many reasons for this neglect, and a couple of them are worth mentioning. First, biblical studies tends to be an insular field of study. Despite acknowledging the value of cross-disciplinary scholarship, it is an ideal that our field more often aspires to than one it achieves. Even when a scholar makes a significant achievement applying the insights of a certain discipline, as Benjamin Sommer did with literary theory in his book *A Prophet Reads Scripture: Allusion in Isaiah 40-66* (1998), little drives biblical studies to guarantee that future work in the field will continue drawing upon that discipline to critique and fortify practices within our field.

Second, in biblical studies there are available a variety of alternative vocabulary that allow indirect discussion about the phenomenon of allusion. Many prefer to use the term "intertextuality", and their theoretical discussions about intertextuality are typically restricted to arguing for the merits of what they consider a diachronic as opposed to a synchronic approach (Miller 2010: 283–309; McKay 2013: 84–106).[1] Others use the language of "inner-biblical exegesis and interpretation" or "echoes" where one might otherwise speak of allusion, and these alternatives are associated with their own unique theoretical discourses.[2] Such alternatives make theoretical literature on literary allusion seem unnecessary, if not irrelevant.

Despite the tendency to neglect it, there is a pressing need for scholars in biblical studies to engage literary theory because it challenges basic instincts about the figure of literary allusion that operate in the field. What are these basic instincts? Scholars in biblical studies generally recognize and privilege three attributes of literary allusion: an identifiable form, a hermeneutically active and intentional author, and a hermeneutically passive and receptive reader. Lange and Weigold provide this kind of definition when they write: "Allusions are employments of anterior texts in which the anterior text is still linguistically recognizable in the posterior text but not morphologically identical with it" (Lange and Weigold 2011: 26). Lange and Weigold's emphasis on linguistic similarity highlights the form of a literary allusion. The posterior text resembles the linguistic structure of the anterior text. Though obscured by the nominalization "employments," the author is hermeneutically active in this definition as the agent who employs anterior texts. By contrast, the reader is a hermeneutically passive figure who recognizes that a literary allusion exists. Richard Hays's understanding of literary allusion similarly recognizes these formal, authorial, and readerly attributes. Regarding its form, he situates allusion on a spectrum between explicit quotations and subliminal echoes (Hays 1989: 23). He claims the allusion, though presumably implicit, is still more obvious than the echo, and this is likely due to the allusion's greater degree of formal correspondence with the anterior text. Furthermore, Hays argues, "[t]he concept of allusion depends both on the notion of authorial intention and on the assumption that the reader will share with the author the requisite 'portable library' to recognize the source of the allusion" (1989:

---

1 See my evaluation of this practice in Kelly 2014.
2 Bernard Levinson (2008) makes the canon the dominant theoretical concern for those engaged in the study of inner-biblical interpretation and exegesis. Richard Hays (1989: 1–33) does not critically evaluate his understanding of allusion before developing an alternative category, the figure of echo.

29). This understanding of literary allusion, like the one before it, presents the author as a hermeneutical agent who intends and the reader as a hermeneutically passive figure who recognizes the allusion.

Work in literary theory has proven inadequate the understanding of literary allusion that emphasizes an identifiable form and attributes hermeneutical agency solely to the author, not the reader. Conte compares allusion to the trope of classical rhetoric, arguing that "the gap between the letter and the sense in figuration is the same as the gap produced between the immediate, surface meaning of the word or phrase in the text and the thought evoked by the allusion.... In both allusion and the trope, the poetic dimension is created by the simultaneous presence of two different realities whose competition with one another produces a single more complex reality" (Conte 1986: 23–24). Conte emphasizes the rhetorical function of the literary allusion without specifying any necessary formal characteristics. Similarly, Ziva Ben-Porat defines literary allusion as "a device for the simultaneous activation of two texts [which] results in the formation of intertextual patterns whose nature cannot be predetermined" (Ben-Porat 1976: 107–8). Both Conte and Ben-Porat speak primarily of the way in which a literary allusion functions by virtue of two fields of signification. A primarily functional understanding of the concept requires that matters of form occupy a secondary status.

Regarding the roles of authors and readers, Conte and Ben-Porat disagree. Conte believes the trope-like qualities of the allusion render it "substantially motivated" by the intentionalities of the author, thus rendering the semiotic capacity of the allusion fully determined by the author (Conte 1986: 50). Consequently, Conte's reader is a hermeneutically passive figure. Ben-Porat, however, argues that authors are incapable of predetermining the intertextual patterns formed by a literary allusion. More recently, Joseph Pucci argues in *The Full-Knowing Reader: Allusion and the Power of the Reader in the Western Literary Tradition* that the allusion is "a discrete literary phenomenon that partakes of the intentionalites of both reader and author, a phenomenon that arises in the collusion of literary works, desires, and intents—not despite them" (1998: 30). He attributes to the intentionality of the author "the potential for meaning" and to the intentionality of the reader "the actualization of that potential" (1998: 40). Despite the desire of some critics to continue talking about (i.e., constructing) an "intention-bearing authorial voice," literary theory has come to recognize the inadequacy of thinking solely in terms of a hermeneutically active and intentional author that requires a hermeneutically passive and receptive reader (Hinds 1998: 49–50).

SHARED LANGUAGE

The theory of literary allusion as developed by literary critics counters basic assumptions that characterize the understanding of this figure in biblical studies. In particular, biblical studies tends to place greater emphasis on literary form than on rhetorical function. The primary characteristic of a literary allusion according to literary theory—the way it *functions* by virtue of two fields of signification—has implications for understanding the role of shared language—a *formal* category—as a criterion for identifying literary allusions.

AN INSUFFICIENT CRITERION

The exclusive or near-exclusive use of shared language as a criterion for identifying literary allusions creates a problem with the theoretical understanding of this figure. When an allusion patterns itself on the text it evokes, this shared language represents a formal feature of the allusion. But identification based on formal features does not recognize if and how the allusion functions by virtue of two fields of signification. According to Ben-Porat, the formal aspects involved in the process of recognizing and interpreting a literary allusion are minor: "Identification of veiled referents and realization of by-products do partake in the actualization of a literary allusion; but they constitute only a small part of the process" (Ben-Porat 1976: 109). She also implies that the form of the marker, by which she means "the element or pattern belonging to another independent text," can take a variety of forms: "In terms of the end product, the formation of intertextual patterns, the marker—*regardless of the form it takes*—is used for the activation of independent elements from the evoked text" (Ben-Porat 1976: 108-9). According to Ben-Porat, one should not define literary allusion exclusively on the basis of its form since form is a minor aspect of the larger concept, and her theory suggests that a variety of forms could contribute to the function of a literary allusion.

Using a heuristic outline developed by Ben-Porat, it is possible to articulate more precisely the problem of relying primarily or exclusively on a formal feature like shared language (Ben-Porat 1976: 109-11). Her outline traces the four stages a reader experiences in determining the presence of and in interpreting a literary allusion. I illustrate these four stages with an allusion in the book of Jonah to a verse in the book of Exodus.[3] A chart appears below to facilitate the comparison of the two passages.

In the first stage, readers recognize a marker that refers to an independent text. This marker may or may not correspond verbally to the marked material in the evoked text; verbal correspondence, where it occurs, can vary by degree. Readers recognize in Jonah 4:2 a frequently recycled theological expression potentially referring to an independent text. The elements in this expression often shift around or disappear, and new elements can also appear. In this case, the allusion reverses the terminology of and truncates the marked text, Exodus 34:6.

Second, readers identify the evoked text. This second stage distinguishes itself from the first stage when a text contains an obvious marker but its referent is not immediately obvious. Generally speaking, the allusion in Jonah 4:2 may initially evoke for broadly informed readers numerous iterations of this theological expression throughout the Hebrew Bible (Kelly 2013a: 805 n1, 807). Scholars have long debated whether Jonah is directly alluding to Exodus 34:6 or whether his words allude more directly to Joel 2:13-14, which would itself then be a direct allusion to Exodus 34:6. The need to determine the trajectory of influence in a case like this represents one way of realizing this second stage.

In the third stage, readers modify their understanding of the marker in the alluding text based on their interpretation of the marked in the evoked text. The interaction between the two texts generates a new understanding of the marker, an understanding not achieved when the marker is interpreted exclusively within the frame of reference of the alluding text. For Ben-Porat, once readers complete this third stage they have confirmed the presence of an allusion. Jonah's articulation of this theological expression omits a characteristic from the evoked text, an omission made significant by the fact that this characteristic—faithfulness (אמת)—functions as Jonah's patronym. By omitting this characteristic, the character of Jonah does not merely accuse YHWH of being (too) gracious, he accuses YHWH of not being faithful (Kelly 2013a: 822–25). It would not be possible to understand Jonah's words in the latter sense without recognizing the allusion to the text in Exodus where the characteristic of faithfulness actually appears.

The fourth stage represents an unnecessary though common feature of literary allusions. In it, readers' focus shifts from the marker and the marked to their corresponding texts as related wholes. The reader

---

3 For a fuller discussion of this allusion, see Kelly 2013a: 805–26.

incorporates features beyond the marker or the marked when considering the significance of the interplay between alluding and evoked texts. While Jonah's words attribute to YHWH characteristics of grace and compassion, the identification of this language as an allusion and the broader contexts of these texts elevate the discussion by probing the potential universal dimensions of YHWH's covenantal character (Dozeman 1989: 218–23).

These four stages provide a way of recognizing the role shared language plays in identifying allusions. The reader who identifies shared language can only have completed the first two stages: recognizing a marker and identifying the evoked text. Successful identification of an allusion, however, turns on the third stage: readers must modify their understanding of the marker based on their interpretation of the marked in the evoked text. Only once an allusive function of the marker is detected can readers claim to have identified an allusion. Benjamin Sommer suggests that readers who do not transition from the second to the third stage identify an echo, a formal literary figure with less interpretive significance than a literary allusion.[4] Readers who identify shared language, no matter how extensive, cannot complete this third stage without additional considerations. This raises an important observation: the identification of literary allusions is a cumulative judgment on the part of a reader (Sommer 1996: 485–86; 1998: 35).

What happens when shared language functions as the sole criterion for identifying literary allusions, when such identification is not the result of a cumulative judgment? In an article proposing how interpreters can confidently identify literary allusions using shared language, Jeffery Leonard (2008: 241–65) enumerates eight principles as methodological guidelines. Leonard tests his principles on Psalm 78, a psalm recounting the historical traditions of Israel which we encounter also in the Pentateuch. Because each one of these eight principles involves the presence of shared language, the focus rests on matters primarily related to literary form:

> (1) Shared language is the single most important factor in establishing a textual connection. (2) Shared language is more important than nonshared language. (3) Shared language that is rare or distinctive suggests a stronger connection than does language that is widely used. (4) Shared phrases

---

4 According to Sommer's proposal for categorizing a literary echo, the marked in the evoked text does not impact interpretation. This differs from allusion which "consists not only in the echoing of an earlier text but in the utilization of the marked material for some rhetorical or strategic end" (Sommer 1998: 15, see also 15–17, 30–31).

suggest a stronger connection than do individual shared terms. (5) The accumulation of shared language suggests a stronger connection than does a single shared term or phrase. (6) Shared language in similar contexts suggests a stronger connection than does shared language alone. (7) Shared language need not be accompanied by shared ideology to establish a connection. (8) Shared language need not be accompanied by shared form to establish a connection. (Leonard 2008: 246)

The seventh principle uniquely departs from the emphasis on form to discuss the role of ideology, but it only denies that shared ideology is necessary—a valid point in its own right. It does not ask how ideological similarities or differences factor into the process of determining the presence of an allusive function within the literary relationship. Why should readers understand the language of Psalm 78 within a (proto-)Pentateuchal frame of reference, or vice versa? This question remains unanswered. Leonard's allusions, as identified by these eight principles, merely establish that the Pentateuch (or its documentary sources) functioned as a literary source for the formation of, or was itself formed from, Psalm 78. This is not a discussion of literary allusion but of source criticism! Without additional guidelines that establish a rhetorical function within the literary relationship—a cumulative approach—source criticism and literary allusion become theoretically and practically indistinct disciplines.[5]

A NONESSENTIAL CRITERION

Given the progressive nature of Ben-Porat's four stages, it makes sense to focus initially on formal criteria that help to establish literary borrowing or patterning, like shared language, before transitioning to questions of allusive functioning (Ben-Porat 1976: 109). The criterion based on shared language proposed by biblical scholars usually prefers relatively extensive shared language. Already, we have seen Lange and Weigold creating a verbal threshold below which they do not consider shared language

---

5 When Leonard (2008: 256) goes on to discuss how to determine the direction of influence, he enumerates six principles, two of which do factor in the rhetorical function of the literary relationship: "(4) Does one text assume the other? ... (6) Are there rhetorical patterns in the texts that suggest that one text has used the other in an exegetically significant way?" But Leonard already claims to have identified the allusion before asking these questions, and as guidelines they do not test for an element essential to Leonard's understanding of allusion.

allusive. In Michael Fishbane's discussion of "aggadic exegesis," a category Benjamin Sommer observes is more appropriately recognized as allusion, Fishbane proposes "the identification of aggadic exegesis ... is proportionally increased to the extent that multiple and sustained lexical linkages between two texts can be recognized" (Fishbane 1988: 285).[6] Citing Fishbane's proposal, Jeffery Leonard praises the principle of shared language for providing "the most objective and verifiable criteria for identifying allusion" (Leonard 2008: 246–68, quote from 247). Richard Hays's criterion of "volume" is also relevant to this discussion: "The volume of an echo is determined primarily by the degree of explicit repetition of words or syntactical patterns" (Hays 1989: 30).

While shared language may function as an initial indication of a literary allusion, there is no reason to require a certain threshold of shared language. In cases like the use of Exodus 34:6 in Jonah 4:2, extensive shared language makes the identification of literary borrowing easy to recognize, and the allusion is readily apparent when Jonah's words are understood within a broader frame of reference (Kelly 2013a: 805–8).

Exodus 34:6-7—"YHWH, YHWH, a deity who is compassionate and gracious, slow to anger and exceedingly kind and faithful, guarding kindness to the thousandth generation, forgiving iniquity, and transgression, and sin, but who will not surely acquit, visiting the iniquity of the fathers on the sons and on the grandsons to the third and fourth generations."	Jonah 4:2—"And Jonah prayed to YHWH and he said, 'Indeed, YHWH! Was this not my word while I was still in my country? Therefore, I initially fled toward Tarshish, for I knew that you are a deity who is gracious and compassionate, slow to anger and exceedingly kind, and who relents from disaster.'"
יהוה יהוה <u>אל רחום וחנון ארך אפים ורב־חסד</u> ואמת נצר חסד לאלפים נשא עון ופשע וחטאה ונקה לא ינקה פקד עון אבות על־בנים ועל־בני בנים על־שלשים ועל־רבעים	ויתפלל אל־יהוה ויאמר אנה יהוה הלוא־זה דברי עד־היותי על־אדמתי על־כן קדמתי לברח תרשישה כי ידעתי כי אתה <u>אל־חנון ורחום ארך אפים ורב־חסד</u> ונחם על־הרעה

But the reference to Exodus 34:6 would not necessarily be more allusive if Jonah 4:2 provided a fuller reference by incorporating the noun "faithfulness" (אמת) from Exodus 34:6. Nor would it be less allusive if, in addition to omitting "faithfulness" (אמת), Jonah 4:2 also omitted "and exceedingly kind" (ורב־חסד)?[7] Either way, interpreters who read Jonah 4:2

---

6 For Sommer's assessment of Fishbane's category of "aggadic exegesis," see 1998: 23.

7 For example, Neh 9:31 (cf., 9:17). See also the elements typically found in allusions to Exod 34 6(-7) that are omitted in Num 14:18 and Nah 1:3 (Kelly 2013a: 807).

within a broader frame of reference (Exodus 34) will begin to modify their understanding of the language and its signifying potential. The marker of an allusion may involve a single word, a name perhaps (e.g., the names "Enoch" or "Lamach" in Genesis 5 alluding to the genealogy in Genesis 4). Given the cumulative nature of identifying allusions and their functional significance, the theory of allusion does not require a certain length or degree of verbal precision in its markers (Ben-Porat 1976: 118–22; Perri 1978: 297–99).

Scholars who study ancient Near Eastern literature, where literary allusions tend toward brevity and subtlety, are the most vocal in resisting substantial shared language as a criterion. For example, Jeffrey H. Tigay writes:

> As a safeguard, this demand for complexity or pattern seems so reasonable that few would want to challenge it. Although there is a danger that the principle might cause us to overlook some real parallels, on the whole, when applied judiciously, it seems a handy criterion for ruling out the spurious. *It is when it is applied too rigidly, when it is given the status of inviolable law, that the principle threatens to exceed its usefulness.* (Tigay 1993: 251, emphasis added)

Christopher B. Hays is more assertive in resisting the need for substantial shared language when he discusses the relevance of Richard Hays's criterion of "volume" for literary borrowing in ancient Near Eastern literature: "It is predominantly the quieter echoes of the ancient Near East that remain to be noticed, *and other criteria might outweigh sheer volume* .... One should not despair or set the bar unduly high for 'commensurate terms'" (Hays 2008: 37, emphasis added).

Taking his cue from Tigay's work, Charles Halton identifies three such "quiet" allusions that require minimal shared language between the allusive and evoked text (Halton 2009: 50–61). For example, he identifies a Neo-Assyrian oracle that alludes to *Adapa and the South Wind*.

Prophecy 1.1 from *Assyrian Prophecies*	*Adapa and the South Wind*
"what wind (is there) which has risen against you, (and) whose wing I have not clipped?"	"Adapa broke the wing of the south wind"
ayyû šāru ša īdibakkani aqappušu lā aksupūni	Adapa ša šūti kappaša išbir

Halton admits "the allusion to *Adapa* in this oracle seems quite tangential. In fact, apart from the semantic parallel between breaking the wind's wing there is hardly any similarity" (Halton 2009: 53). He enumerates four points of weakness for identifying this literary allusion on the assumption that shared language is important for identification. The word for wind in each text is different; "wing," the only common word shared between the texts, occurs in a different form in each; the verbs that express the subjugation of the wind in each text are different; and the oracle omits the name *Adapa* (Halton 2009: 53). Halton goes on, however, to demonstrate that these differences are significant. The prophecy uses a more general term for wind than *Adapa,* thus expanding the scope of Ištar's royal protection. Furthermore, the prophecy uses a less intense verb to express the subjugation of the wind, one that does not imply utter destruction. As Halton observes: "A prophecy that at first seems more like a bright-eyed platitude is actually a sensible word of encouragement. The king will not lack opponents, but Ištar will ensure their eventual subjugation" (Halton 2009: 54). In the absence of substantial shared language, Halton must appeal to other criteria to establish the validity of this literary allusion. In so doing, he demonstrates Christopher Hays's insight that other criteria can outweigh sheer volume and justifies Tigay's caution against turning shared language into an inviolable law when identifying allusion.

NON-REFERENTIAL SHARED LANGUAGE

One additional cautionary matter concerning shared language deserves careful attention. It does not follow that shared language necessarily indicates reference or literary borrowing between two texts. Paul R. Noble writes:

> [Resemblances between two texts] could be purely coincidental; or, each text might have independently drawn upon the same stream of traditions (written or unwritten); or, the second, later text may be alluding to yet a third text, which independently treats themes similar to those in the first text. (Noble 2002: 220)

Noble is unpersuaded by attempts to establish a literary relationship on the basis of shared language between the narrative of Judah and Tamar in Genesis 38 and the Succession Narrative in 2 Samuel 11 through 1 Kings 2. Without denying these texts resemble one another in certain ways, Noble accuses scholars of being selective, focusing on striking correspondences, and ignoring otherwise significant incongruities (Noble 2002: 225). On the bases that some have linked Genesis 38 to the succession narrative, Noble proposes that one could make similar arguments for linking Genesis 38 to the stories of Samson and of Lot, links which, on similar grounds, he argues are equally tenuous.

It is important for those interested in literary allusion to recognize non-referential shared language and distinguish it from referentially significant occurrences of shared language. Noble listed three non-referential alternatives to explain the presence of shared language—coincidence, independent traditions, and a third, distinct source. In Sommer's book on allusion in Isaiah 40-66, he places non-referential shared language at the forefront of the methodological discussion (Sommer 1998: 32–35). He distills his concerns into this principle: "we cannot view an older text as a source for a passage in Deutero-Isaiah if both utilize stock vocabulary, exemplify a literary form such as lament, or treat a subject that calls for certain words" (Sommer 1998: 33, see also 218 n5–7). He catalogs eight items—vocabulary clusters or motifs—that belong to traditions in Deutero-Isaiah common to contemporary Mesopotamian literature. In the absence of other allusive indicators, he does not consider the presence of these items in Deutero-Isaiah formal referential markers, even if they closely resemble language in Jeremiah (e.g., Isa 41:8, 10//Jer 1:8) (Sommer 1998: 33–34).

John Choi also raises concerns about "stock or common vocabulary," particularly in "psalms and poetic material" (Choi 2010: 29–30). He writes:

> When faced with similar lexical content, we cannot automatically assume that the similarity signifies anything other than the fact that there may not have been any other way to say something, or conversely, the fact that there is only one way of saying something. (Choi 2010: 30)

Sommer attributes the pervasiveness of non-referential shared language in the Bible to the "highly traditional" character of biblical literature (Sommer 1998: 32).

Scholars frequently identify in Ecclesiastes 9:7-9 an allusion to Siduri's advice to Gilgamesh in an Old Babylonian recension of the Gilgamesh epic, but the language in the Ecclesiastes passage is an excellent example of non-referential shared language.[8] While the vocabulary and structure between the two texts resemble one another, this vocabulary is not uncommon in skeptical ancient Near Eastern wisdom traditions. The same elements shared between Ecclesiastes and Gilgamesh are also present in the Instruction of Ptahhotep, and some of these elements are also present in

---

8   For a defense of the dependency between these two texts, see van der Toorn 2001: 87–98 and Samet 2015.

the Song from the Tomb of King Intef (not to mention others texts belonging to the Egyptian Harpers' Songs collection) and the Poem of Early Rulers (Kelly 2010: 117–34). Each of these ancient Near Eastern texts share other common language and/or motifs with Ecclesiastes. Roland Murphy is certainly correct that these similarities across the ancient world "cancel each other out, as far as dependence is concerned" and that they "witness to certain relatively common ideas of the ancient world" (Murphy 1992: xlv).

Recognizing that shared language is a non-essential criterion and that shared language does not always indicate literary borrowing since non-referential shared language exists, it is appropriate to highlight *how* shared language can prove advantageous in identifying literary allusions. Much depends on the nature and volume of the shared language.

UNIQUE LEXICAL CONGRUITY

When verbal correspondence concerns unique lexical congruity, there are fewer explanations that would preclude literary borrowing. Consequently, unique lexical congruity represents a stronger form of reference than correspondences based on commonplace vocabulary.[9] However, modern interpreters must remember that what appears unique from a contemporary perspective does not necessarily reflect language that was actually considered unique to ancient authors or audiences. The boundaries of canon or the accidents of history may arbitrarily narrow our field of vision and impoverish our cultural repertoire. What appears unique to us might have been more commonplace to ancient audiences and less likely to have triggered allusive patterning for ancient readers.

> Recurrent use of rare, but not unique, expressions may support an argument for literary interrelationship, but should not be viewed as decisive evidence since our knowledge of the language of the biblical authors is limited to a closed corpus of texts, and what appears to be rare within the framework of those texts, may have had wider actual usage. (Edenburg 1998: 72).[10]

9 Hays (1989: 30) employs "volume" as an aural metaphor for this criterion. Cynthia Edenburg (1998: 72) refers to this as "unique recurrence of peculiar formations." Leonard (2008: 251) expresses the principle in this way: "Shared language that is rare or distinctive suggests a stronger connection than does language that is widely used." See also Tooman 2011: 27–28.

10 I essentially agree with Edenburg, though I believe this caution must still apply to unique expressions.

That said, it is valuable to observe from a contemporary vantage point the recurrence of otherwise unique language and make cautious and modest judgments about the likelihood of literary borrowing.

When verbal correspondence concerns distinctive lexical congruity, similar prospects and problems arise. Compared to the recurrence of commonplace vocabulary, language that is distinctive of a particular corpus, though not unique to it, suggests fewer explanations that would preclude literary borrowing. And yet, what appears distinctive to modern interpreters may have been commonplace to ancient audiences. Moreover, the claim that language is distinctive of a particular text can involve a subjective judgment on the part of the modern interpreter. Would all ancient audiences agree with William Tooman (2011: 28) that ‏ראשית‎ + ‏ב‎ - is distinctive of Genesis 1:1 over against its other occurrences (Jer 26:1; 27:1; 28:1; 49:34; Hos 9:10), or does this represent a bias of those who inherit the canonical Hebrew Bible alongside traditions that assign significant weight to the first chapter of Genesis? Again, it is valuable to make observations about distinctive language from a contemporary vantage point, but interpreters must employ what David Carr refers to as "methodological modesty"—the gap that exists between "ontology and epistemology"—when issuing such judgments (Carr 2011: 4).

VOLUME OF SHARED LANGUAGES

As the volume of shared lexical material between two texts increases, the explanations that preclude literary borrowing decrease. Consequently, a larger volume of shared material represents a stronger form of reference than correspondences based on minimal shared vocabulary. Volume can be measured in different ways, from the accumulation of shared vocabulary terms to the recurrence of phrases and clauses.[11]

It is important to consider the relevance of volume alongside one of Leonard's other methodological guidelines: "Shared language is more important than nonshared language" (Leonard 2008: 249–51). Leonard considers shared language determinative in cases involving a seemingly

---

11 Leonard expresses the latter criterion first, followed by the former criterion. "The accumulation of shared language suggests a stronger connection than does a single shared term or phrase." "Shared phrases suggest a stronger connection than do individual shared terms" (Leonard 2008: 253–55, 252–53). On the former criterion, see also Tooman 2011: 28–29.

significant volume of shared material. He attributes minimal significance to the nonshared elements in such cases. Regarding Psalm 78, he argues that this text directly depends on the plague narratives in Exodus, despite the presence of distinct language, a distinct sequence, and material in Exodus disregarded in the Psalm. Leonard is correct that an allusion need not slavishly and comprehensibly reproduce the evoked text. But he over-extends his argument by precluding any role these nonshared elements might play in disqualifying the alleged allusion (Leonard 2008: 250). On the relationship between Psalm 78 and the Pentateuch, the absence of Sinai in a Psalm otherwise concerned with divine commandments and the covenant suggests the Psalmist is not literarily dependent on the Pentateuch as a source text (Choi 2010: 117–21). While arguments from silence can be problematic, the question of relevance justifies this line of investigation. Choi writes: "... the absence of an element that appears to be highly relevant to the discussion at hand likely indicates something is amiss" (Choi 2010: 34, see 33–34). Choi also considers the plague list in Psalm 78 problematic because it lists only seven plagues—water to blood, flies, frogs, locusts, hail, pestilence, killing the firstborn—and they appear in an alternative order to the plague narratives in Exodus.[12] In Exodus, the frogs precede the flies and the locusts, hail, and pestilence occurs in reverse order (with an additional intervening plague, boils). Choi's argument demonstrates how nonshared language can serve an important role in discouraging the identification of literary dependency.

CONCLUSIONS

To whatever interpretive psychoses or inflamed comparative methodologies scholars may succumb, greater attention to literary theory restores sanity or otherwise reduces our swollen tendencies. By applying literary theory to biblical studies' quest to identify literary allusions, the inadequacies of our assumptions are revealed and alternative areas of emphasis come into focus.

Literary allusions are not primarily formal features within the text that involve a hermeneutically active and intentional author combined with a hermeneutically passive and receptive reader. The primary characteristic

---

12 Even if one focuses on the order of the seven plagues that source critics assign to an earlier form of the text, as Leonard argues, the order of the plagues do not match each other (Choi 2010: 124–27 compare to Leonard 2008: 250–51).

of the figure of allusion is the way in which it functions by virtue of two fields of signification, and this characteristic requires attention to the hermeneutical intentionalities of both authors and readers.

This understanding of allusion has implications for how biblical studies generally applies the criterion of shared language when identifying allusions. Shared language must not be considered sufficient when attempting to identify the presence of an allusion, nor should it be considered a necessary criterion. Scholars should also be careful to distinguish between referential and non-referential occasions of shared language, not assuming that all shared language inevitably indicates textual filiation. When applied judiciously, shared language is a useful preliminary indicator of an allusion. Unique lexical congruity represents a stronger form of reference than correspondences based on commonplace vocabulary, but we must keep in mind that the boundaries of canon or the accidents of history may arbitrarily narrow our field of vision and impoverish our cultural repertoire. What appears unique to contemporary readers was not necessarily unique in the ancient world. Additionally, a larger volume of shared material represents a stronger form of reference than correspondences based on minimal shared vocabulary, but we must also keep in mind that non-shared elements, otherwise hermeneutically relevant, might compel us to disqualify an alleged allusion, even in the presence of a relatively large volume of shared language.

REFERENCES

Bloom, Harold. 1997. *The Anxiety of Influence: A Theory of Poetry*, 2nd ed. New York: Oxford University Press.

Carr, David M. 2011. *The Formation of the Hebrew Bible: A New Reconstruction.* New York: Oxford University Press.

Choi, John H. 2010. *Traditions at Odds: The Reception of the Pentateuch in Biblical and Second Temple Period Literature.* Library of Hebrew Bible/Old Testament Studies, 518. New York: T&T Clark.

Conte, Gian Biagio. 1986. *The Rhetoric of Imitation: Genre and Poetic Memory in Virgil and Other Latin Poets.* Translated by Charles Segal. Cornell Studies in Classical Philology, 44. Ithaca, NY: Cornell University Press.

Dozeman, Thomas B. 1989. "Inner-Biblical Interpretation of Yahweh's Gracious and Compassionate Character." *Journal of Biblical Literature* 108.2: 207–23.

Edenburg, Cynthia. 1998. "How (Not) to Murder a King: Variations on a Theme in 1 Sam 24; 26." *Scandinavian Journal of the Old Testament: An International Journal of Nordic Theology* 12.1: 64–85.

Fishbane, Michael. 1988. *Biblical Interpretation in Ancient Israel.* Oxford: Clarendon Press.

Halton, Charles. 2009. "Allusions to the Stream of Tradition in Neo-Assyrian Oracles." *Ancient Near Eastern Studies* 46: 50–61.

Hays, Christopher B. 2008. "Echoes of the Ancient Near East? Intertextuality and the Comparative Study of the Old Testament." In *The Word Leaps the Gap: Essays on Scripture and Theology in Honor of Richard B. Hays*, edited by J. Ross Wagner, C. Kavin Rowe, and A. Katherine Grieb, 20–43. Grand Rapids: Eerdmans.

Hays, Richard B. 1989. *Echoes of Scripture in the Letters of Paul*. New Haven: Yale University Press.

Hinds, Stephen. 1998. *Allusion and Intertext: Dynamics of Appropriation in Roman Poetry*. Roman literature and its contexts. Cambridge: Cambridge University Press.

Kelly, Joseph Ryan. 2010. "Sources of Contention and the Emerging Reality Concerning Qohelet's *Carpe Diem* Advice." *Antiguo Oriente* 8: 117–34.

Kelly, Joseph Ryan. 2013a. "Joel, Jonah, and the YHWH Creed: Determining the Trajectory of the Literary Influence." *Journal of Biblical Literature* 132.4: 805–26.

Kelly, Joseph Ryan. 2013b. Review of *Biblical Quotations and Allusions in Second Temple Jewish Literature* by Armin Lange and Matthias Weigold. *Bulletin for Biblical Research* 23.2: 413–15.

Kelly, Joseph Ryan. 2014. "Intertextuality and Allusion in the Study of the Hebrew Bible." PhD diss., The Southern Baptist Theological Seminary.

Lange, Armin, and Matthias Weigold. 2011. *Biblical Quotations and Allusions in Second Temple Jewish Literature*. Journal of Ancient Judaism Supplements, 5. Göttingen: Vandenhoeck & Ruprecht.

Leonard, Jeffery M. 2008. "Identifying Inner-Biblical Allusions: Psalm 78 as a Test Case." *Journal of Biblical Literature* 127.2: 241–65.

Levinson, Bernard M. 2008. *Legal Revision and Religious Renewal in Ancient Israel*. Cambridge: Cambridge University Press.

McKay, Niall. 2013. "Status Update: The Many Faces of Intertextuality in New Testament Study." *Religion & Theology* 20: 84–106.

Miller, Geoffrey D. 2010. "Intertextuality in Old Testament Research." *Catholic Biblical Review* 9.3: 283–309.

Murphy, R. E. 1992. *Ecclesiastes*. Word Biblical Commentary, 23A. Waco, TX: Word Books.

Noble, Paul R. 2002. "Esau, Tamar, and Joseph: Criteria for Identifying Inner-Biblical Allusions." *Vetus Testamentum* 52.2: 219–52.

Perri, Carmela. 1978. "On Alluding." *Poetics* 7: 289–307.

Ben-Porat, Ziva. 1976. "The Poetics of Literary Allusion." *PTL: A Journal for Descriptive Poetics and Theory of Literature* 1: 105–28.

Pucci, Joseph M. 1998. *The Full-Knowing Reader: Allusion and the Power of the Reader in the Western Literary Tradition*. New Haven: Yale University Press.

Samet, Nili. 2015. "The Gilgamesh Epic and the Book of Qohelet: A New Look." *Biblica* 96.3: 375–90.

Sandmel, Samuel. 1962. "Parallelomania." *Journal of Biblical Literature* 81.1: 1–13.

Sommer, Benjamin D. 1996. "Exegesis, Allusion and Intertextuality in the Hebrew Bible: A Response to Lyle Eslinger." *Vetus Testamentum* 46.4: 479–89.

Sommer, Benjamin D. 1998. *A Prophet Reads Scripture: Allusion in Isaiah 40-66*. Conversations: Jews and Other Differences. Stanford: Stanford University Press.

Tigay, Jeffrey H. 1993. "On Evaluating Claims of Literary Borrowing." In *The Tablet and The Scroll: Near Eastern Studies in Honor of William W. Hallo*, edited by Mark E. Cohen, Daniel C. Snell, and David B. Weisberg, 250–55. Bethesda, MD: CDL Press.

Tooman, William A. 2011. *Gog of Magog: Reuse of Scripture and Compositional Technique in Ezekiel 38-39*. Forschungen Zum Alten Testament, 2. Reihe 52. Tübingen: Mohr Siebeck.

Van der Toorn, Karl. 2001. "Echoes of Gilgamesh in the Book of Qohelet? A Reassessment of the Intellectual Sources of Qohelet." In *Veenhof Anniversary Volume: Studies Presented to Klaas R. Veenhof on the Occasion of His Sixty-Fifth Birthday*, edited by W. H. van Soldt, 87–98. Uitgaven van het Nederlands Historisch-Archaeologisch Instituut te Istanbul, 89. Leiden: Nederlands Instituut voor het Nabije Oosten.

Chapter 3

Method in Determining the Dependence of Biblical on Non-Biblical Texts

DAVID M. CARR[*]

I am happy to contribute to a volume devoted to a very timely topic, namely, focused reflection on how one establishes dependence of biblical texts on known non-biblical texts. There is no shortage of proposals for dependence of biblical texts on non-biblical ones. But it is not so common for biblical scholars to reflect on criteria and method in making such proposals.

CRITERIA FOR ESTABLISHING INTERTEXTUAL DEPENDENCE OF BIBLICAL TEXTS ON NON-BIBLICAL TEXTS

A starting point for such reflection, I believe, is some work that has already been done by biblical scholars to reflect on criteria and method for determining dependence of biblical texts on each other, places where what I will term a "receptor text" draws in an identifiable way on what I will term the "source text." Here I am thinking particularly of the oft-cited criteria for intertextual "echoes" developed by Richard Hays in his 1989 book on *Echoes of Scripture in the Letters of Paul* (building on John Hollander's 1981 *The Figure of Echo*) and refined for Hebrew Bible study in an excellent 2008 essay by Christopher B. Hays in a Festschrift for Richard B. Hays (R. Hays

---

[*] David M. Carr is Professor of Old Testament/Hebrew Bible at Union Theological Seminary, New York.

1989; C. Hays 2008).[1] Of course, Michael Fishbane (1985), Benjamin Sommer (1996; 1998) and others also have very important discussions, but Richard Hays developed the most varied and often-cited list of criteria, and as such provides a good starting point.[2]

I emphasize the term "often-cited" here, because Hays' list of criteria often seem to function much like criteria for just wars often do. People may argue for various criteria that would qualify, say, the fight against Hitler as a just war, but then the same individuals often forget such criteria in the rough and tumble of figuring out whether an attack by the United States on Grenada or Iran makes sense. Similarly, people often cite Hays' criteria in a methodological introduction to a work before discarding most of them in the process of making their arguments. That said, I think Hays' criteria are worth concrete attention at the outset of this discussion.[3]

Richard Hays proposes seven criteria. The first, "availability", is rephrased by Christopher Hays as asking "was the proposed source of the echo available to the author and/or his original readers?" (C. Hays 2008: 34). As Christopher Hays has noted, this is a particularly important question to raise about dependence of biblical texts on non-biblical ones. For example, we can ask when and how the author of Proverbs 22-24 might have had access to the Instruction of Amenemope. We could draw on evidence for Israelite dependence on Egyptian scribal traditions through reference to Judean use of Egyptian hieratic numeral notations (Sanders 2009: 128–29, 218), and we might even note the possibility that David's scribe was referred to by the Egyptian word for scribe (Cody 1965; Williams 1975: 236; Mettinger 1971: 45–51).

---

1   On pp. 18–19 of *Echoes of Scripture*, Richard Hays explains his choice of Hollander's word "echo" over other terms, such as "allusion" preferred by other literary critics, saying that Hollander's echo-focused approach "exemplifies a style of interpretation that focuses neither on the poet's psyche nor on the historical presuppositions of poetic allusions but on their rhetorical and semantic effects."

2   The "other important discussions" mentioned here include methodological comments in Fishbane's classic work (1985), starting with his introductory remarks on pp. 9–14, but then strewn across the introductory sections of most of its chapters. Benjamin Sommer's important work (1998) adds significant additional methodological and terminological provisos, as does his defense of Fishbane's work (1996: 486–89) .

3   For the purposes of this article, Christopher B. Hays's adaptations of Richard Hays's criteria are particularly pertinent and will be referenced in the following.

Conversely, one reason many scholars have been less inclined to consider Greek literature as possible source texts for the Bible is the presupposition, vigorously contested by some, that Greek literature was not widely available to authors of Hebrew biblical texts, particularly during earlier periods of the Bible's composition.[4] So also, there is much room for debate, I believe, about whether the Babylonian exile, when Judeans were living in relatively isolated communities in Babylon, is the most likely time for encounter with Mesopotamian literary traditions, as some suppose. Or might the late pre-exilic period of Neo-Assyrian domination have been a more likely time when some Judean youths might have been exposed to the Assyrian educational system and Mesopotamian literature, much as youths in some other Assyrian-dominated areas were?[5]

The third criterion, "recurrence or clustering," is related to this question of availability (I address his second criterion in the following paragraph). This third criterion asks: "[H]ow often elsewhere does the author cite or allude to the same text" (C. Hays 2008: 36). For example, the more one can build a case that different parts of Deuteronomy allude to the Neo-Assyrian treaty tradition, the more one can conclude that the treaty tradition was available to the author of those parts of Deuteronomy. And this, in turn, can bolster arguments for the likelihood that Neo-Assyrian treaty traditions influenced Deuteronomic laws and/or terminology even when the evidence is slight and subtle. The same also could be true for the Amenemope tradition. Although scholars have focused most on potential echoes of Amenemope in Prov 22:17-23:11, some have found echoes of Amenemope elsewhere in the Bible as well.[6] Insofar as these proposals are compelling, they build a case that Amenemope, though a relatively obscure Egyptian instruction, was available to some Judean authors, and furthermore that such authors were inclined to adapt parts of it in writing Judean wisdom.

Richard Hays' second criterion (Hays, C.B., 2008: 34) is one of volume: "How 'loud' is the echo; that is how explicit and overt is it?" For Richard Hays, this meant looking in Paul's letters for verbatim repetition

---

4   John Van Seters (e.g., 1983) is just one major example, among others, of scholars who vigorously contest the idea that Greek literature was not available to biblical authors.

5   I have made an argument to this effect (Carr 2011a: 305–306) drawing on others' work, such as Parpola 1972: 21–34; Lamprichs 1995: 256–57; and Hurowitz 2008: 75.

6   See, for example Bryce 1979: 71–74, on the possibility of a borrowing from Amenemope in Prov 15:16.

of words and syntactical patterns found in the Greek versions of the Old Testament. Other scholars, such as Michael Fishbane, for example, have likewise focused on verbal overlap, in his case searching for "multiple and sustained lexical linkages between two texts" (Fishbane 1985: 285). As Christopher Hays (2008: 35, 37) noted, it often is far more difficult to identify such specific lexical linkages between biblical and non-biblical texts, especially because most non-biblical texts are written in languages other than Hebrew, some of which are distant from Hebrew linguistically.[7] This is not just a technical issue of Hebrew scribes needing to translate a given non-biblical text into Hebrew. Rather, my own non-systematic survey of possible cases of cross-linguistic borrowing in the Ancient Near East suggests that ancient authors gave themselves even more freedom to adapt traditions across language barriers than they did in adapting traditions in their own language.

Often they drew on foreign traditions from memory (Carr 2005; 2011: 13–65, 105–110). Thus, when using foreign texts, they typically accessed them in their own memory, recalling their *content* (as translated in their mind) rather than reproducing them in a word-for-word translation. Consequently, when an Israelite author drew on a text written in a foreign language, such as Amenemope (which is written in Egyptian), the output in Hebrew would be a vague set of topical parallels, aside, perhaps from an occasional specific borrowing, as in the case of the reference to 30 sayings in Prov 22:30. This stands in contrast to inner-language borrowing. In these cases, a Hebrew author could, when writing a new literary text, draw on Hebrew proverbs, psalms, and the like that he had memorized verbatim. In such cases, the new composition would overlap the memorized one lexically, albeit with occasional exchanges of semantically equivalent words/phrases (memory variannts).

And this does not account for the diverse ways that biblical authors might have been exposed to non-biblical texts, a question that returns us to the issue of availability. Not only would such authors often have needed to have competence in the other language such as Aramaic and Akkadian, but they may, in some cases, have been exposed to these foreign language texts purely orally, as opposed to being able to read and memorize them. This possibility of oral exposure (to foreign texts) has been raised in particular in recent work by William Morrow. He explores modes by which

---

7 See, for example, C. Hays 2008: 35, 37. In this article, note 11 includes a useful reference to Heinrich Plett's discussion of "transcoding" in relation to language cross-over in textual dependence (1991: 11).

Judean scribes might have been exposed to Neo-Assyrian treaty traditions (in Akkadian or Aramaic) through recitation of such traditions (Morrow 2005; 2009b; 2009a).

All this is not to suggest that Hebrew biblical scholars therefore should ignore questions of volume in evaluation of cases where a biblical text may be dependent on a non-biblical text or tradition. After all, there is very little to support *any* case for genetic dependence aside from places where a receptor text echoes themes, topic, and even specific words and phrases of a possible source text. That said, however, we must recognize that the search for such echoes in the Hebrew Bible can be complicated by the linguistic gap, a gap that in turn probably prompted a greater degree of creativity in adaptation of non-biblical, non-Hebrew source texts than was characteristic of adaptations of Hebrew texts.

Finally, considerations of availability dictate one final tweak to the criterion of volume when considering non-biblical texts. It is not enough that a potential non-biblical source text thematically or topically parallels a biblical receptor text. The volume of these potential echoes of the non-biblical text should surpass that of potential inner-biblical source texts. After all, if a biblical text has a closer parallel within Hebrew literature, we are generally on firmer ground in believing that a potential Hebrew source text was available to our Hebrew author than in hypothesizing multilingual dependence of that author on a distant scribal tradition. Perhaps in some cases, we might be so sure of dating that we could rule out certain potential biblical source texts because we know them to post-date our receptor text. That said, as a specialist in history of Israelite literature, I think we rarely have such surety in dating biblical texts.

Hays's criteria 4, 5 and 7 share a similar focus on how fitting the alleged adaptation of non-biblical tradition is in the ideology and historical situation of the receptor text. Criterion 4 asks: "how well does the alleged echo fit into the line of argument of the passage in question?" (C. Hays 2008: 38). Criterion 5 asks whether an ancient author in fact could have intended the alleged meaning of the proposed adaptation (C. Hays 2008: 41). And criterion 7 asks: "does the proposed intertextual reading illuminate the surrounding discourse and make some larger sense of the author's argument as a whole?" (C. Hays 2008: 44). These three criteria stress different dimensions of "fit" of a given hypothesis of literary dependence (of a biblical text on another text) with both the broader context of the receptor biblical text and what we know of that text's author. The emphasis on "fit" (to use a word from criterion 4) does not mean that the proposed source text—whether biblical or non-biblical—must conform in message with the biblical text that uses it. On the contrary, especially from the Neo-Assyrian period onward, Judean scribes seem to have been inclined to invert, mock and otherwise reject foreign source texts when they appropriated them. Again, the apparent use of Assyrian treaty traditions in Deuteronomy serves as a prime example, where Judean authors, perhaps in the immediate wake of Assyrian domination, configured Deuteronomy as a vassal treaty of Israel with Yahweh in place of the Assyrian tradition of vassal loyalty to the Assyrian king. It appears that Judean scribes over time became increasingly hostile toward foreign influence. This led them to be increasingly inclined to adapt foreign textual traditions in slanted and inversive ways, rather than merely echoing them as some sort of ancient authority. This then represents an important difference in the stance toward source traditions between, say, the appropriation of Amenemope in Proverbs 22-23 and the inversion of Assyrian treaty traditions in Deuteronomy. Indeed, this might lead us, using Hays's criteria, to look first in Deuteronomy and Deuteronomistic tradition for ways that tradition inverts or undermines Assyrian and perhaps other foreign traditions. But Peter Machinist has made substantial arguments that yet earlier, potentially eighth century material from the prophet Isaiah, especially seen in Isaiah 10:8-15, may invert Neo-Assyrian royal propaganda cataloguing royal victories and mocking the trust of other nations in the power of their own monarchs (Machinist, 1983). This (potential) inversion of Neo-Assyrian foreign traditions in eighth (or possibly seventh) century layers of Isaiah probably represents the beginning in biblical tradition of polemical inversive use of non-biblical texts. Before the Neo-Assyrian onslaught (and subsequent experiences with the Neo-Babylonian and other empires), it is likely that earlier biblical texts, such as Proverbs or parts of it, had less complicated, inversive connections to non-biblical traditions.[8]

One criterion that does not seem to be highlighted in Hays's or Fishbane's discussions, but that can be particularly helpful, is that of a place where particularly odd features of a biblical text can be explained as blind motifs resulting from the appropriation in that biblical text of elements from a non-biblical precursor. A "blind motif" is an element or theme from a borrowed tradition appearing in a later text that does not fit well in the new context. The word "blind" in the expression refers to the lack of fit of the borrowed element in its new context. For example, the argument for prosecuting treasonous professional dreamers in Deut 13:2 seems odd,

---

8 I discuss this at more length in my book on the *Formation of the Hebrew Bible* (2011a: 399–400 among other loci).

given the general lack of reference to such *professional* dreamers elsewhere in Deuteronomy and the rest of the Hebrew Bible. Nevertheless, a reference to professional dreamers makes sense in the original source text, the Esarhaddon Succession Treaty (EST), where it is an echo of the EST provision 10 calling similarly for punishment of treasonous dreamer/prophet/ecstatic (Morrow 2009b: 229). Similarly, the sequence of curses seen in Deut 28:27-35 has no particular rhyme or reason in itself, but it conforms well with the sequence of gods invoked as destroyers in EST 39-42 (Kübel 2004; Morrow 2009: 230). Finally, I have already noted the mention of 30 sayings in Prov 22:20, an apparent echo of Amenemope's heading, even though the following text of Proverbs cannot be clearly divided into 30 sections. In cases like these, the foreignness of the non-biblical tradition can be a *help* in recognizing adaptation. Even though biblical authors may have felt free to adapt such traditions across linguistic lines and even invert them, the traditions were sometimes foreign enough that their adapted features still stand out. Finding such *blind motifs*, such places where the source text blends incompletely into the receptor text, can help us recognize free adaptation of non-biblical texts.

APPLICATION OF THE CRITERIA FOR ESTABLISHING DEPENDENCE—SEVERAL CASES

This list of criteria sounds clear enough in theory, but one soon finds places where a proposal of dependence of a biblical text on a non-biblical one involves questions of dating of the biblical text in question. If the proposed intertextual dependence holds, then the biblical text should be dated one way. But if one dates the biblical text in another way, it is unlikely that it is dependent on the proposed non-biblical tradition.

A major example of this would be the potential relationship between the speech of Siduri in the *Old Babylonian* form of the Gilgamesh epic and core themes of the book of Qohelet. Siduri speaks to a grieving Gilgamesh after Enkidu's death and urges him to enjoy life day and night, fill his belly, enjoy clean clothes and a washed head, and his wife's embrace in the face of the universal human destiny of death. This parallels both Qohelet's critique of all values in the face of mortality and Qohelet's exhortation to enjoy virtually the same list of daily pleasures mentioned in Siduri's speech—food, washed clothes, oiled head, wife's embrace (Qoh 9:7-9; cf. similar lists 2:24-26; 5:18-19; 8:15; 11:7-10). In my view, the "volume" of this potential echo of Old Babylonian Gilgamesh in Qohelet is impressive, surpassing both any biblical parallels and any of the Hellenistic Greek parallels that I and others have proposed as the background of Qohelet's message (Hengel 1974: 115–28; Carr 1991: 143–44). Nevertheless, if one dates Qohelet to the Persian or Hellenistic periods on linguistic or other grounds, it is difficult to know how the *Old Babylonian* form of Gilgamesh with Siduri's speech would have been available to Qohelet's author. Gilgamesh was common enough in first millennium Mesopotamian education, but Judean scribes in the Neo-Assyrian, Babylonian, Persian or Hellenistic periods would have encountered it, if at all, in its later Standard Babylonian form *lacking* Siduri's speech. On the other hand, if one doubts that linguistic and/or other criteria decisively date Qohelet as a whole to the Hellenistic period, then one can consider the possible dependence of core Qohelet on the message of Siduri's speech as evidence that some form of Qohelet dates toward the very beginnings of Judean scribalism, during a time when some form of the Old Babylonian Gilgamesh might have survived in parts of the Levant. Thus, the case of potential dependence of Qohelet on *Old Babylonian* Gilgamesh either supports an early dating of part of the book or is destroyed by late dating of the book on other grounds.

Twenty-five years ago I agreed with the consensus on late dating of Qohelet and rejected the proposed dependence on Siduri's speech (Carr 1991: 143–44). In my more recent history of Israelite literature I expressed doubts about the consensus perspective on late Qohelet, based partly on the potential echo of Siduri's speech in Qohelet's core message.[9] The point here is that the argument could go either way depending on how one weighs the evidence.

I conclude with more consideration of two more cases, the potential relationship between multiple biblical texts and the Deir Alla Plaster Inscription and then Psalm 72 and Ashurbanipal's coronation hymn.

The Deir Alla case can be discussed briefly. Combination A of the Deir Alla Inscription overlaps with the Balaam narratives on the one hand and with biblical literary prophecy on the other. It not only mentions Balaam son of Beor, but parallels Numbers, even verbally, in describing a visit to him by divine beings, their giving a message to him, and his arising the next morning to go on his way. That said, the *content* of the revelation given to Balaam in the two texts is quite different. In Numbers 22-24, God (אלהים) initially tells him not to go with the Moabites (Num 22:9-13) before eventually instructing him to go ahead and accompany them (Num 22:20-21).

---

9 Carr 2011a: 448–55, with a focus on possible genetic dependence on the Siduri speech (448–49), with particular dependence on Loretz 1964: 117–20, 132–34.

The Deir Alla inscription, in contrast, describes how Balaam was visited by the divine council at night, whereupon El pronounced a death sentence on the city and the divine council announced the beginning of a drought that would devastate the city. Such a judgment theophany has no parallel in the Numbers 22-24 Balaam story, but it does provide an evocative non-biblical parallel to literary judgment prophecy of the sort found in Amos, Hosea, and other biblical prophets.

Furthermore, this parallel in Deir Alla is particularly important, since there are signs that the Deir Alla inscription is a wall replica of a columnular scroll and may even have been labelled as the *scroll* of Balaam, son of Beor. As such, it represents a crucial example in scroll culture of a literary judgment prophecy that stands as a far closer generic parallel to biblical judgment prophecies than the more annalistic royal recordings of prophecies found at Mari and Neo-Assyrian archives. Nevertheless, the nature of the parallels between the Balaam inscription and biblical materials are such that I think it hard to argue for specific *dependence* of either Numbers 22-24 or biblical literary prophecy on the literary tradition seen in the Deir Alla inscription. To do so would misconstrue the significance of the inscription. The inscription is precious evidence for the existence of literary scribalism in the pre-Neo-Assyrian Levant, including literary judgment prophecy. But it does not, in my view, stand as a probable specific precursor to either Numbers 22-24 or various biblical prophetic texts. At the most, it probably witnesses to a stream of tradition on which both Numbers 22-24 and the Deir Alla inscription are dependent.

Finally, I consider here the case of the proposed dependence of Psalm 72 on Asshurbanipal's coronation hymn. The most extensive arguments for this dependence, particularly those of Arneth (2000; 2002), propose that an early form of Psalm 72, without the proclamations of universal kingship in verses 8-11, 15, and 17, was modelled on the internally-focused portions of Ashurbanipal's coronation hymn, often referred to as SAA III,11. In particular, Arneth stresses the structural parallels that he sees between the core of Ashurbanipal's hymn, which starts with a frame and then features two sections, each of which states a way that the king will bring prosperity and then concretizes that description with two or three specific promises. Though the content of these middle sections (SAA III 11, 8-13 and Ps 72:3-7) is fairly different, Arneth stresses the numerical-structural parallels between these sections (wish followed by two [or three] concretizations and a final wish) that he thinks establish a special relationship between the older core of Psalm 72 and the Ashurbanipal hymn (Arneth 2000: 71-73; Arneth 2002: 157-61). I myself, and others before me, such as Bernd

Janowski, are skeptical about these arguments (Janowski 2002: 106–107). Instead, psalm 72 appears to be part of a broader set of royal traditions, attested both in Israel and beyond, linking the king with the provision of justice and prosperity in the land (Paul 1972; Kraus 1978: 657–59 [ET Vol. 2, 77–79]; Hossfeld and Zenger 2005 [Original 2000]: 210–13; Janowski 2002: 114–20). I do not see specific links of Psalm 72 to the Neo-Assyrian royal tradition, and therefore I am not persuaded by Arneth's and others' claims on the basis of such dependence for a Neo-Assyrian or later date for Psalm 72. If anything, I see the non-inversive adaptation of broader ancient royal traditions in Psalm 72 and several other royal psalms as an argument for dating them in some form to the pre-Neo-Assyrian period.[10] But such suppositions must remain, in my judgment, quite tentative.

ONE FINAL METHODOLOGICAL PITFALL: LOOKING FOR THE CLOSEST NON-BIBLICAL ANALOGY TO A BIBLICAL TEXT

This discussion of Arneth's work on Psalm 72 raises one final point about weaknesses in the way that some cases of potential dependence on non-biblical texts are discussed.[11] Biblical scholars sometimes seem to work as if their task was the following: to find the closest analogy to a given biblical text in the wider world of ancient texts and let that analogy inform our dating and interpretation of the given biblical text. That is what seems to have occurred in proposing a Neo-Assyrian or later dating of Psalm 72 because Ashurbanipal's hymn is taken to be the closest known correlate to Psalm 72.

It may be true that Ashurbanipal's coronation hymn happens to be closer in many respects to Psalm 72 than any other *known* non-biblical text. But that still does not prove that Psalm 72 is dependent on Ashurbanipal's coronation hymn. Our preserved evidence from the Near East is profoundly lopsided and gapped. Cuneiform literary texts, for example, are far more widely preserved thanks to the fact that they were written on clay tablets, which survive the test of time well, even surviving fires yet harder and more permanent than before. Much less frequently, some very

---

10 For some more argumentation, see my book on the formation of the Hebrew Bible (2011: 393–94), as part of a broader case for earlier monarchal Judean appropriation of neighboring royal traditions (386–402).

11 This paragraph overlaps in basic content with points already made in my 2010 IOSOT lecture (2011b).

ancient Egyptian scrolls were preserved in the extremely dry climate of the Egyptian desert. In contrast, extended copies of ancient Hebrew, Aramaic, and other Northwest Semitic literary texts were not preserved from the pre-Hellenistic period, at least partly because such texts were generally written on organic materials (papyrus and parchment) that were highly perishable, and the climate of the Israelite highlands and of many other cultures using scrolls was too humid for such scrolls to be preserved over thousands of years.

The comparatively broad preservation of cuneiform literature (versus the lack of preservation of much literature from Egypt and especially Syro-Canaan written on scrolls) means that we will likely see an ever increasing number of proposals of dependence of biblical texts on cuneiform parallels. The more that the libraries of Neo-Assyrian kings are published and analyzed, the more tempting it is to find potential examples of biblical texts that are dependent on Neo-Assyrian (or other cuneiform) exemplars. In cases, such as the potential links between parts of Deuteronomy and Esarhaddon's treaty, these arguments are relatively persuasive (because of blind motifs and other elements). But in others, such as Psalm 72 and Ashurbanipal's hymn, the proposed links are far too tenuous to support arguments for a strong relationship.

We must be careful as biblical scholars not to work with the gappy, partially preserved corpus of diverse Near Eastern literatures as if this motley body of diverse texts formed a semi-canon that interprets itself. It is insufficient to find the closest non-biblical analogy to a biblical text. Instead, that analogy must be close and supported by other criteria such as blind motifs. Moreover, especially because the Neo-Assyrian material is well attested, we must be particularly careful how to treat it. Insofar as the relative weight of Neo-Assyrian literary evidence leads to a greater number of proposed cases of biblical dependence on cuneiform, especially Neo-Assyrian analogues, it would be tempting to have all such proposals reinforce each other on the basis of Hays's third criterion, "recurrence or clustering." In other words, the clustering of proposals of dependence of biblical materials on Neo-Assyrian analogues, may say more about the relatively good attestation of cuneiform literary materials than it does about the particularly intense dependence of biblical material on the Mesopotamian tradition (largely written on clay tablets).

CONCLUSION

Given all those cautions, I end by stressing that I do find some cases for biblical dependence on Neo-Assyrian materials very compelling, as I do cases for dependence on other cuneiform and on Egyptian, Greek, and other materials. In the end, no list of criteria, no methodological process will solve the problem of determining literary dependence without using *judgment* on how to apply and weigh a given set of criteria. Nevertheless, having more discussions like the ones included in this volume will hopefully help us be better informed as we make such critical judgments.

REFERENCES

Arneth, M. 2000. *'Sonne der Gerechtigkeit': Studien zur Solarisierung der Jahwe-Religion im Lichte von Psalm 72*. BZAR 1. Wiesbaden: Harrassowitz.

Arneth, M. 2002. "Psalm 72 in seinen altorientalischen Kontexten." In *'Mein Sohn bist du' (Ps 2,7): Studien zu den Königspsalmen*, edited by E. Otto and E. Zenger, 135–72. Stuttgart: Verlag Katholisches Bibelwerk.

Bryce, G. E. 1979. *A Legacy of Wisdom: the Egyptian Contribution to the Wisdom of Israel*. Lewisburg, PA: Bucknell University Press.

Carr, D. M. 1991. *From D to Q: A Study of Early Jewish Interpretations of Solomon's Dream at Gibeon*. SBLMS, 44. Atlanta: Scholars Press.

Carr, D.M. 2005. *Writing on the Tablet of the Heart: Origins of Scripture and Literature*. New York/Oxford: Oxford University Press.

Carr, D.M. 2011a. *The Formation of the Hebrew Bible: A New Reconstruction*. New York/ Oxford: Oxford University Press.

Carr, D.M. 2011b. "The Many Uses of Intertextuality in Old Testament Studies: Actual and Potential." In *Congress Volume IOSOT: Helsinki 2010*, edited by M. Nissinen, 519–49. Leiden: Brill.

Cody, A. 1965. "Le titre égyptien et le nom propre du Scribe de David." *Revue Biblique* 72: 381–93.

Fishbane, M. 1985. *Biblical Interpretation in Ancient Israel*. Oxford: Clarendon.

Hays, C. B. 2008. "Echoes of the Ancient Near East? Intertextuality and the Comparative Study of the Old Testament." In *The Word Leaps the Gap: Essays on Scripture and Theology in Honor of Richard B. Hays*, edited by J. R. Wagner, C. K. Rowe and A. K. Grieb, 20–43. Grand Rapids: Eerdmans.

Hays, R. 1989. *Echoes of Scripture in the Letters of Paul*. New Haven: Yale University Press.

Hengel, M. 1974. *Judaism and Hellenism: Studies in Their Encounter in Palestine During the Early Hellenistic Period*, translated by John Bowden. Philadelphia: Fortress.

Hollander, John. 1981. *The Figure of Echo: A Mode of Allusion in Milton and After*. Berkeley: University of California Press.

Hossfeld, F.-L., and Zenger, E. 2005 [Original 2000]. *Psalms 2: A Commentary on Psalms 51-100*, translated by L. M. Maloney. Hermeneia. Minneapolis: Augsburg Fortress.

Hurowitz, V. A. 2008. "Tales of Two Sages—Towards an Image of the 'Wise Man' in Akkadian Writings." in *Scribes, Sages, and Seers: The Sage in the Eastern Mediterranean World*, edited by L. Perdue, 64–94. Göttingen: Vandenhoeck & Ruprecht.

Janowski, B. 2002. "Die Frucht der Gerechtigkeit: Psalm 72 und die judäische Königsideologie." In *'Mein Sohn bist du' (Ps 2,7): Studien zu den Königspsalmen*, edited by E. Otto and E. Zenger, 94–134. Stuttgart: Verlag Katholisches Bibelwerk.

Kraus, H.-J. 1978. *Psalmen II*, 5th edition. BKAT 15/2. Neukirchen-Vluyn: Neukirchener Verlag.

Kübel, P. 2004. "Zum Aufbau von Dtn 28." *Biblische Notizen* 122: 5–7.

Lamprichs, R. 1995. *Die Westexpansion des neuassyrischen Reiches: eine Strukturanalyse.* Alter Orient und Altes Testament, 239. Kevelaer: Verlag Butzon Neukirchen-Vluyn.

Loretz, O. 1964. *Qohelet und der alte Orient: Untersuchungen zu Stil und theologischer Thematik des Buches Qohelet.* Freiburg: Herder.

Machinist, P. 1983. "Assyria and Its Image in the First Isaiah." *Journal of the American Oriental Society* 103: 719–37.

Machinist, P. 2003. "Mesopotamian Imperialism and Israelite Religion: A Case Study from the Second Isaiah." In *Symbiosis, Symbolism and the Power of the Past: Canaan, Ancient Israel, and Their Neighbors from the Late Bronze Age Through Roman Palestina*, edited by W. G. Dever and S. Gitin, 237–64. Winona Lake, IN: Eisenbrauns.

Mettinger, T. 1971. *Solomonic State Officials: A Study of the Civil Government Officials of the Israelite Monarchy.* Coniectanea biblica–Old Testament Series. Lund: Gleerup.

Morrow, W. S. 2005. "Cuneiform Literacy and Deuteronomic Composition." *Bibliotheca Orientalis* 62: 204–13.

Morrow, W. S. 2009a. "Barriers to Akkadian Literacy during the Late Iron Age." Paper presented at the 2009 SBL Annual Meeting, New Orleans, LA.

Morrow, W. S. 2009b. "The Paradox of Deuteronomy 13: A Post-Colonial Reading." In *»Gerechtigkeit und Recht zu üben«(Gen 18,19): Studien zur altorientalischen und biblischen Rechtsgeschichte, zur Religionsgeschichte Israels und zur Religionssoziologie (FS Otto)*, edited by R. Achenbach and M. Arneth, 227–39. Wiesbaden: Harrassowitz.

Parpola, S. 1972. "A Letter from Šamaš-šumu-ukin to Esarhaddon." *Iraq* 34, 21–34.

Paul, S. 1972. "Psalm 72:5—A Traditional Blessing for the Long Life of the King." *Journal of Near Eastern Studies* 31: 351–55.

Plett, H. F. 1991. "Intertextualities." In *Intertextuality*, edited by H. F. Plett, 3–29. Berlin: De Gruyter.

Sanders, S. L. 2009. *The Invention of Hebrew.* Traditions. Urbana: University of Illinois Press.

Sommer, B. 1996. "Exegesis, Allusion and Intertextuality: A Response to Lyle Eslinger." *Vetus Testamentum* 46: 479–489.

Sommer, B. 1998. *A Prophet Reads Scripture: Allusion in Isaiah 40-66.* Contraversions. Stanford: Stanford University Press.

Van Seters, J. 1983. *In Search Of History: Historiography in the Ancient World and the Origins of Biblical History.* New Haven: Yale University Press.

Williams, R. 1975. "A People Come Out of Egypt." In *Congress Volume: Edinburgh, 1974*, edited by G. W. Anderson, 231–52. Vetus Testamentum Supplements, 28. Leiden: Brill.

Chapter 4

Subtle Citation, Allusion, and Translation: Evidence in Hittite Texts and Some Biblical Implications

ADA TAGGAR-COHEN*

The corpus of Hittite texts in ancient Near Eastern archival documents is unique in that its continuous survival is due to it having been owned and controlled by the same ruling dynasty for some five centuries. Changes and developments observed by scholars within this corpus of documents were implemented by scribes working within a stable scribal tradition, mainly in the Hittite capital of Ḫattuša, today's Boğazköy in central Anatolia (Weeden, 2011b: 1–2; 2011a). Despite the difference in time, language and writing materials, insights gathered from examining their work helps in understanding how scribes in ancient Israel and Judah may have proceeded when engaged in editing older texts and creating new ones.

It is widely acknowledged that ancient Near Eastern civilizations shared a cultural background that included oral and written literary texts, spanning many genres: cultic instructions, mythology, prayers, and historiography. How those parts of this cultural heritage that developed in second millennium central Anatolia passed to first millennium Israel is still not known well. It is, however, gradually becoming clear that one route of transfer was via the Neo-Hittite kingdoms that flourished in the southeast Anatolia and northern Syria after the demise of the Hittite empire. This view gains strength from archaeological evidence indicating the integration of Luwian and Semitic societies in those areas and is reinforced by

---

* Ada Taggar-Cohen is Professor in the School of Theology at Doshisha University, Kyoto, Japan.

recent archaeological excavations that uncovered data indicative of commercial contacts between Anatolia and Israel (and the Levant in general).[1]

In this survey, I first describe evidence of Hittite scribal activity with regard to translation and copied and re-copied records as part of the process of preserving and transferring of knowledge. I explain writing methods and current knowledge of scribal education and work, focusing on the fact that the system of writing used by the Hittites originated in Mesopotamia. This clarifies that Mesopotamian lore was acquired together with writing skills and was adapted for Hittite tastes and sensibilities. Second, I touch on the relationship between the translated Hittite corpus and texts from other cultures. Certain points of language usage are examined in order to understand the methods employed by scribes when translating, copying, and editing. Finally, I explore how insights from this survey may be applied to better our understanding of textual management in ancient Israel.

CULTURAL BACKGROUND

The Hittites originated from regions outside Anatolia, but adopted Anatolian cultural traditions, especially in the cultic sphere, from its indigenous peoples.[2] These cultic traditions often appear in the Hittite texts

---

1 For an overview of the state of research on the relations between the Hittites and ancient Israel see Singer 2006: 723–56; see also a follow-up by Amir Gilan (2013: 39–52). Crucial for understanding the cultural contacts were the Neo-Hittite Kingdoms that have yielded some interesting material written in Hieroglyphic Luwian as well as Semitic languages, especially Phoenician. For an overview of the Neo-Hittite kingdoms and their relations with Ancient Israel, see Bryce 2012: esp. 64–75; Weeden 2013: 1–20; Hawkins 2011: 35–54; and a recent attempt at historical reconstruction by Galil 2014: 74–104. Two interesting recent archaeological findings in Israel come from Tel Rehov and Hazor excavations—both from the 11th–10th centuries BCE. The one from Tel Rehov shows the economic relations between South Anatolia and Tel Rehov by the discovery of beehives with Anatolian bees; for a recent treatment of this issue see Simon 2014: 715–38. The findings from Hazor, to be formally published soon, include impressions of Anatolian hieroglyphs on the handles of a cooking pot dated to the mid-10th century BCE; see report by Ben-Ami 2012: 79, 132. Important evidence on scribal activity during the second half of the second millennium are the tablets from the city of Emar in north Syria for which see Cohen 2009.

2 For detailed descriptions of the suppositions regarding the origins of the Hittites and that period in Hittite history see Bryce 2005; a concise historical description can be found in Collins 2007: 21–90.

in their original languages, such as Ḫattic, Palaic, and later, after certain Hurrian traditions had been absorbed during the 14th century BCE, also in Hurrian. During the Hittite empire period, Luwian, written in both cuneiform and Anatolian hieroglyphs, was also used extensively. The languages of these various cultures embedded in Hittite texts are the core materials used for understanding the transfer of written cultural knowledge and for the examination of subtle citation and translation.

Hittite texts were inscribed on clay tablets using a system of writing based on the Sumero-Akkadian cuneiform script of the Old Babylonian period in North Syria during the first half of the second millennium.[3] Their cuneiform script has close connections with the Alalah script from north Syria of the 18th–17th centuries BCE (Hout 2012: 147–70). The Hittites adapted this script to the phonetic needs of their own language and employed it when incorporating portions in Ḫattian, Palaic, and later also in the Ḫurrian and Luwian languages, into their own Hittite texts.

The writing system that the Hittites adopted for their own Indo-European language was originally used for a Semitic language. The script was adapted as a syllabic writing system for the Hittite language, maintaining Sumerian and Akkadian ideograms for writing professional titles, verbs, adjectives, prepositions, as well as determinatives, but following Hittite syntax. In fact, we cannot always be sure of how a Sumerogram or an Akkadogram in a Hittite text was pronounced by the Hittites. They may have read it in Sumerian or Akkadian. Occasionally, when duplicate copies of the same texts are available, we can sometimes learn the Hittite word behind an ideogram.

THE HITTITE WRITING SYSTEM AND SCRIBAL PROFESSION

The Hittite writing system employed ideograms with syllabic signs as complements, for example: ŠEŠ in Sumerian means "brother": with an Akkadian

---

3 We also know that they used wooden boards for writing, from the scribal title [LÚ]DUB.SAR.GIŠ ("scribe of the wooden tablets"). The assumption is that wax was applied to the boards to be written on, thus making re-use possible. Weeden (2011b: 236) suggests that writing on wooden boards should be regarded as a "different functional sphere of use," rather than seeing the clay tablet as original and the wooden tablet being used for making copies. Weeden 2011b: 236 n. 1052: KUB 10.45 iii 12ff: "The scribes on wood have a wooden writing board (concerning) how the king performs offerings on a daily basis." Scholars debate whether they wrote on these boards in cuneiform script or hieroglyphic script. See Waal 2012 for more on the writing in Anatolia.

particle *-YA* (first person possessive) it means "my brother"; written ŠEŠ-(plus) complement *-na-tar* it stands for the Hittite word *negnatar*, a noun meaning "brotherhood." *A-BU* in Akkadian is "father," *A-BU-KA* is "your (sg.) father" in Akkadian, and can appear written as such in the Hittite texts. However, it can also be written syllabically in Hittite as *at-ta-aš-miš* (*attaš* "father" + *miš* "my"). LUGAL in Sumerian is "king"; in a Hittite text LUGAL-*uš* is the nominal form of the Hittite word for king *ḫaššu-*, which also appears written syllabically: *ḫa-aš-šu-uš*.[4] The fact that the writing system originally included the two languages Sumerian and Akkadian, presupposes that the writers had knowledge of these two languages.

Scholars assume that although most Hittite scribes have learnt the logograms (Sumerograms or Akkadograms), they did not really know the Sumerian language well, and were not highly proficient in Akkadian either. Some learned scribes or "scholars" had a good command of Sumerian, especially in the early stages of Hittite writing (Old Kingdom), but later their knowledge would be mostly of Akkadian. Native Akkadian scribes are known to have resided in Ḫattuša, such as the scribe with the Akkadian name Anu-šar-ilāni whose son had a Hittite name Ḫanikuili.[5] While the word for scribe was usually DUB.SAR, Ḫanikuili designated his father as DUB.SAR BAL, in Akkadian *targumannu*, which we can take to mean "translator scribe."[6] Indeed, there must have been some professional scribes who knew Akkadian well and were able to translate from Hittite to Akkadian and vice versa. These Hittite scribes were taught both Sumerian and Akkadian, as testified by the curriculum found in Ḫattuša archives and libraries (Hout 2008; Hout 2009a: 71–96; Hout 2015).

In a recent paper Jeanette Fincke (2012: 85–102) has studied "school curricula" for the cities of Ḫattuša, Emar, and Ugarit. In these three places, school education was basically Mesopotamian, going back to genres known from the Old Babylonian school curriculum. Thus Mesopotamian proverbs, letters, historical texts, divination texts and the like were found among

---

4 According to Hittitological conventions for transcribing texts, Sumerograms are written in regular capital letters (ŠEŠ); Akkadograms are written in italicized capital letters (*A-BU*); Hittite (as well as Ḫattian, Hurrian and Luwian) are written in small italicized letters. For more on idiographic or syllabic writing see Busse 2013, as well as Hout 2011.

5 For the foreign scribes in Ḫattuša see Beckman 1983: 97–114. For an overview of the scribal profession in Ḫatti see Bryce 2002: 56–72; Hout 2009b; Klinger 1998; Weeden 2011b: 81–131.

6 As suggested by Beckman (1983: 103–6), it is possible to trace the family roots of Ḫanikuili from about the middle of the 15th century down to the late 13th century. For more on the Hittite scribes' profession and families see Gordin 2010.

the students' tablets. Of these three cities Ḫattuša had the largest variety of texts.[7]

On another and more important level, Hittite texts from Ḫattuša during the Old Kingdom (17th–16th centuries BCE) attest to a system in which the same texts were written both in Hittite and in Akkadian on separate tablets. Hittitologists agree that the texts must have been written in Hittite first and then translated into Akkadian since they were clearly Hittite compositions, and thus directed at Hittite-speaking audiences. These texts must have been translated into Akkadian due to the prestige of that language as the source for Hittite writing. The practice of translating into Akkadian would disappear sometime after king Telipinu, around 1500 BCE.[8]

A few words are required regarding Hurrian and Luwian, the other two languages current in Hittite tablets.[9] For Hurrian we were fortunate to recover a Hittite-Hurrian bilingual tablet which shows that the scribe had a good command of both languages (CTH 789[10]). Unfortunately, not enough Hurrian texts are available as yet and scholars are still struggling to establish its complete grammar and vocabulary. In contrast, Luwian, an Indo-European language, was employed by the Hittite ruling elite, when engraving building inscriptions, boundary markers, perhaps as a form

---

7 Each of these cities had its curricular emphasis: in Ḫattuša, for example, medical texts, found in large numbers, are almost not found in Emar and Ugarit (Fincke 2012: 98). In Ḫattuša an actual school area (as for example in Emar) has not been located in the city, nor have any copies of students' tablets been found (Weeden 2011b: 15). Veldhuis (2014) recently presented a detailed overview of lexical lists in the ANE. In historical perspective he terms the period of the second half of the second millennium "the international period," when the regions west of Mesopotamia—basically the periphery for cuneiform writing including Ḫattuša, Emar and Ugarit, Alalakh, Nuzi, Ekalte, Canaan, El Amarna, and Elam—show how different places "display various ways in which the Mesopotamian intellectual tradition was received and handled" (2014: 311). As for the Ḫattuša lexical texts, he writes that they "are characterized by a number of features that indicate their learned character, supplying specialized and often arcane knowledge of a writing system that was closely connected to royalty and royal power" (2014: 271). For the concept of scribal schools in Ḫatti see Weeden 2011c.

8 For this date see Hout 2012: 164–65.

9 On the Ḫurrians and their cultural influence in the ANE see Wilhelm 1989.

10 CTH is the abbreviation for Emmanuel Laroche's *Catalogue des Textes Hittites* (1971). It has been uploaded and extended on the website "Hittite Portal Mainz" where all Hittite textual editions and commentaries to known and published texts are listed—see: http://www.hethport.uni-wuerzburg.de/HPM/index.html under Konkordanz.

of propaganda during the New Kingdom (Hout 2007: 238). Hittite scribes would also employ elements of the Luwian in Hittite records (written in cuneiform) using either "genuine Luwian or [a] 'Hittitized' form in Hittite context" (Hout 2007: 227). Luwian words in most cases appear marked with two wedges, from the time of Muršili II (end of the 14th century BCE).[11]

This mixture of languages is reflected in Hittite royal titles from the Old Kingdom (1650–1400 BCE). Initially, the origin of the titles for King and Queen (*L/tabarna* and *Tawananna* respectively), were thought to be Hattic, but recent convincing explanations show the origin of *L/tabarna* to be Luwian (Melchert 2003: 18–19). The title for the crown prince *tuḫ(u)kanti-* and the word for the throne *ḫalmaššuitt-* are nevertheless Hattic.[12]

It is therefore evident that at least some, if not all Hittite scribes during various periods of the kingdom's existence, were able to work with several languages and different systems of writings (cuneiform, hieroglyphic). These abilities allowed them to absorb and transform data from many cultures, rendering them useful to serve their monarch's needs.

EVIDENCE REGARDING THE TRANSLATION, REWRITING, AND COPYING OF TEXTS

The lexical lists found in Ḫattuša, which were a kind of dictionary (CTH 300–306), are similar to those found in other cities of the Ancient Near East that employed the use of cuneiform. An entry in a lexical list in Ḫattuša is as follows: the same Sumerian word appears several times in the left column; the Akkadian equivalent for each word is given in the middle column, while the equivalents in Hittite reflecting the Hittite "edition" of the text, are in the right column; for example:

gú	nap-ḫa-ru	ta-ru-up-pí-eš-šar	"all"
gú-si	nap-ḫa-ru	ta-ru-up-pí-eš-šar-pát	"every single one"
gú	ki-el-la-du	ḫu-u-ma-an	"all"
gú-si	ki-el-la-du	ḫu-u-ma-an-pát	"every"

11 The wedges made for the benefit of the reader indicated that the following word was non-Hittite. They show the "intensely multi-lingual scribal environment, and awareness of the differences between separate languages" (Weeden 2011b: 1 with footnote 3).

12 Beckman (2002: 15–21) has shown how the titles of the Hittite king, written Sumerographically LUGAL.GAL LUGAL KUR ḪATTI UR.SAG ("Great king, king of the land of Ḫatti, Hero") and the ᵈUTU-ŠI, ("his/my majesty"; lit. "his/my sun") have their roots in Mesopotamian conventions.

Here two words in Sumerian are equivalent to two words in Akkadian but there are four forms in Hittite that can be translated into English in three different ways.[13]

Texts translated from Akkadian into Hittite are generally taken to be part of Babylonian literary tradition. These texts include hymns and prayers, epics, mythology and legends, and some rituals or omen texts. Some texts found in Ḫattuša were in both Akkadian and Hittite translation, or in a Hittite version which can be traced to an Akkadian origin. As noted by Singer (2002: 3), "all the foreign hymns (to the Sun-god, the Storm-god, and Ishtar) discovered at Boğazköy seem to have had strictly educational functions, such as scribal training and scholarly interest, and did not serve any 'practical' cultic purposes." Still, those texts translated into Hittite left their mark on the structure of original Hittite prayers that would later be created under the influence of these earlier prayers and hymns. A hymn to the Storm-god in Hittite only (CTH 313) is an example of this influence as is an Akkadian prayer to Ištar (CTH 312), where the scribe indicated on the tablet that he had "a better copy in which the verses were separated correctly."[14]

There are also texts written in Akkadian originating from Ḫattuša itself, such as the famous Hittite international treaties, of which copies in Akkadian were made by Hittite scribes (CTH 41, 46, 49 and more), since Akkadian was the *lingua franca* of the region. Akkadian versions of the treaties, as well as copies of royal letters, are clearly texts which were in common use, in contrast to the prayers.[15]

We find Hittite prayers that were composed using the same *topoi* as Akkadian ones. Especially well known is the hymn to the Sun-god, which, as Daniel Schwemer describes it, "is clearly influenced by Babylonian Šamaš Hymns; probably whole chunks of text were taken over from a Hittite translation of a Sumero-Akkadian Šamaš hymn, rephrased and combined with motifs and phraseology of the Hittite tradition."[16] On the basis of this

---

13 For this and more examples see Campbell 2011: 165–67.

14 For this translation see Archi 2007: 185. On this prayer Reiner and Güterbock wrote that: "The discovery of an exact duplicate to the late Neo-Babylonian copy of the hymn in the Boğazköy archives [....] indicates a date around the middle of the second millennium" (1967: 256).

15 Still, one must be cautious not to see Hittite literature as a version of Babylonian or Hurrian literature as Güterbock cautioned as long ago as 1964 and as critically presented by Singer in 1995, who opted for the definition "original Hittite literature." For an overview of Hittite literature see Hout 2002; Beckman 2009.

16 Schwemer 2015: 349. On the god Šamaš and its adoption in Hittite culture see Beckman 2012.

hymn format we find three similar Hittite hymns which are clearly not copies but rather free compositions made by Hittite scribes (these are CTH 372–374).

A particularly celebrated and fortunate find coming from Ḫattuša are the tablets of the epic of Gilgamesh, found in three languages: Middle Babylonian copies in Akkadian, which were edited by A. R. George (2003), and versions in Hittite and in Hurrian (CTH 341) translated and compared by Gary Beckman (2003). All the tablets are broken and in some cases very fragmentary, but it is obvious that the Hittite translation is a free one and that it seems to represent a different version of the Babylonian tale. Based on the fact that the text is titled a "song" in its colophon, as is common in Hurrian tablets, it may have been translated from a Hurrian version of the tale, or was a simplified free translation made by Hittite scribes who chose the interesting and relevant parts of the epic that spoke to a Hittite audience.

Some examples: The Hittite Gilgamesh is not born, but created by the gods; the cedar forest is located in Anatolia; the name of Utnapishtim is Ullu (Beckman 2003: 53–57). One important part missing from the Ḫattuša epic of Gilgamesh is the story of the flood. It is possible that the version of the Babylonian epic, which reached the Hittites, had not yet incorporated the part about the flood. Two fragments of the epic of Atraḫasis were also found in Ḫattuša in both Akkadian and Hittite (CTH 347).

The Hittites also knew the very old story of Sargon, titled *šar tamḫari* ("King of Battle"), as well as the story of his son Naram-Sin. Both stories were probably known in Anatolia as early as the Old Assyrian period ca. 1900–1700 BCE (CTH 310, 311). The texts relating the stories of both kings were found in Ḫattuša in Akkadian and in Hittite.[17] Here again we find that the Hittite scribes adapted these stories and gave these two ancient Mesopotamian kings a new image, which fitted Hittite perceptions of royalty. In the annals of Ḫattušili I (ca. 1650 BCE), a reference is made to Sargon's crossing of the Euphrates:

> No one had crossed the Euphrates, but I, the great king Tabarna (a title of the Hittite monarch) crossed it on foot, while my army crossed it after me on foot. Sargon had also crossed it. He defeated the army of Ḫaḫḫa, but he did nothing to Ḫaḫḫa and did not burn it down.... But I, the Great King Tabarna, destroyed Ḫaḫḫa and burned it down. I displayed its smoke to the Sun-god in Heaven and to the Storm-god. (translation by Beckman 2001: 91)

---

17 Both texts from Ḫattuša are Old Hittite stories copied in the New Hittite era (Haas 2006: 68, 72).

Ḫattušili portrays himself as greater than the greatest ancient king—not only did he cross the river to defeat his enemy but he also obliterated it. Sargon and Ḫattušili I are separated by some 600 years. The historical sources for such a figure must have been the historical accounts kept in Akkadian and Hittite.

An interesting example of translation comes from an original Babylonian text of proverbs written in Akkadian from Ugarit (RS. 22.439). Titled by scholars as "The Dialog between Šupe-ameli and his Father," it was found in Hittite translation in Ḫattuša (KUB 12.70+KUB 4.3). A sample of the Ugarit Akkadian text reads as follows:

> Do not buy an ox at the time of grass growing (i.e., spring)
> Do not take in marriage a young woman at the festival time
> (since) that ox is good (only) in the month of spring
> (and) that young woman is dressed with appropriate female clothing
> (but) during the (year?) she will not anoint with borrowed good oil.
> (Dietrich 1991: 52–3)

The Hittite translation found in Ḫattuša, when translated into English, reads as follows:

> Do not buy an ox in the spring / and a young woman
> Do not take (as a wife) in the festival / (since) a poor quality
> Ox is good only in spring / and an evil (looking?)
> Young woman is festively adorned / and is dressed in a desired robe
> But is anointed with borrowed oil.[18]

There are at least two subtle differences between the texts: the Hittite version adds an explanation that the ox is of poor quality, which the original Akkadian does not specify. The case of the woman is interpreted differently. In the Akkadian text she uses oil which later she will not be able to afford, while in the Hittite version the very use of borrowed oil during festival time is held against her. Whether these are the result of differing cultural perspectives or an error in translation is hard to judge.

18   Keydana 1991: 71 n. 13. My English translation for the following transliteration:
ḫa-me-iš-ḫi-za GUD-un li-e wa-aš-ti / kar-ša-an-ten-ma-za
gal-liš-tar-wa-ni li-e da-at-ti / mar-ša-an-za
GUD-uš ḫa-me-iš-ḫi-pát SIG$_5$-ri / i-da-lu-uš-ma-za
kar-ša-an-za gal-liš-tar-wa-ni-li u-nu-wa-ta-r[i]
nu-za ú-e-kán-ta-an TÚG-an wa-aš-ši-ia-[zi]
ku-uš-ša-ni-an-ma-za IÀ-an iš-ki-ia-[zi]

Among other genres of translated texts found in Ḫattuša libraries are Akkadian-Hittite bilingual omen texts and mythological songs of Hurrian origin in Hittite translation including one bilingual Hurrian-Hittite song.[19]

REFERENCES TO AND CITATIONS FROM OLD TEXTS IN THE ARCHIVES OF ḪATTUŠA

The Hittites referred back to the history of their own kingdom regularly in an attempt to explain the present by learning from the past. Because their documents were kept for several centuries in the same libraries and archives, they were able to visit them, read about previous events and refer back to them.

In his second plague prayer to the Storm-god of Ḫatti (CTH 378), King Muršili II writes that he sought the reason for the terrible plague that gripped Ḫatti during the reigns of his father and brother, as well as his own, by oracular means. He finally found what he was looking for in two tablets preserved in Ḫattuša's archives:

[I found] two old tablets: one tablet dealt with [the ritual of the Mala River]. Earlier kings performed the ritual of the Mala River, but because [people have been dying] in Ḫatti since the days of my father, we never performed [the ritual] of the Mala River.

The second tablet dealt with the town of Kuruštamma: How the Storm-god of Ḫatti carried the men of Kuruštamma to Egyptian territory and how the Storm-god of Ḫatti made a treaty between them and the men of Ḫatti, so that they were put under oath by the Storm-god of Ḫatti. Since the men of Ḫatti and the men of Egypt were bound by the oath of the Storm-god of Ḫatti, and the men of Ḫatti proceeded to get the upper hand, the men of Ḫatti thereby suddenly transgressed the oath of the gods. My father sent infantry and chariotry, and they attacked the borderland of Egypt, the land of Amqa. And again he sent, and again they attacked. When the men of

---

19 The bilingual texts show the Hittite language in the right column and the Akkadian or Hurrian in the left column. For more detailed descriptions of these texts see Güterbock 1988, Campbell 2011: 172–3, Archi 2007, and Gilan 2010: 58–9. For the Hurrian-Hittite bilingual "song of release" see especially Archi 2007. Another interesting but very fragmentary text is CTH 342 a myth of Canaanite origin on the deities El Ba'al and Ashera originating in ancient Amorite tradition of North Syria; see Hoffner (1990), 69–70 (text 23: "Elkunirsa and Ashertu").

Egypt became afraid, they came and asked my father outright for his son for kingship. But when my father gave them his son, as they led him off, they murdered him. My father was appalled and he went to Egyptian territory, attacked the Egyptians, and destroyed the Egyptian infantry and chariotry. (translation by Singer 2002:58).

Hittitologists have studied the recopied texts closely, focusing on the issue of accuracy, that is to say looking for mistakes in copying, sloppy reading of the original, and tendentious alterations. Some such changes are to be expected and considered normal scribal practice even in texts copied to preserve knowledge. Amazingly enough, the Hittite scribes, in general, copied tablets quite faithfully, although some changes and revisions were introduced. Small changes can be found in the use of ideograms for syllabic writing or vice versa,[20] or the occasional change of a word or two in a text. On the whole it can be said that the scribes were basically faithful to the original text; only rarely was a text altered considerably resulting in a different version of the same text.[21]

CONCLUDING REMARKS ABOUT HITTITE SCRIBES AND TEXTS, ISRAELITE SCRIBES, AND BIBLICAL TEXTS

The preceding survey shows that when the Hittites translated texts they sometimes, but not always, conformed them to Hittite tastes and sensibilities as in the cases of the Gilgamesh stories and those about Sargon. In each of these two cases, it is important to emphasize that the Hittite scribes—a polyglot group—depended not on one, but on several versions of the same text in the original language, that is, Sumero-Akkadian or Hurrian texts, or on translations of the same texts, and also on several versions of Hittite translations that were considered independent texts.

It is evident from this review, that the Hittite scribes, working with sources from their archives that originated in different times and places, took liberties with them, thus creating new comprehensible and coherent texts. They rephrased their sources, when appropriate, and functioned as senior editors. In other cases described above, where scribes understood

---

20 In general Hittitologists have noted a tendency for scribes to alter syllabic writing in old texts for ideographic writing during the late Hittite period (mainly 13th century BCE). This criterion often helps in dating texts.

21 Taracha (2011) suggested some editorial strategies used by scribes while copying the genre of ritual texts.

their role to be that of copyists, preserving and disseminating ancient knowledge, they functioned as copyists by reproducing exactly what they saw. And just like ancient copyists in other scribal traditions, Hittite scribes occasionally substituted words, or switched signs and ideograms, and committed tolerable (and usually explicable) writing transgressions not intended to alter the meaning of the texts being copied. Scribes functioning as translators, not as copyists, operated differently. Often bi- or multilingual and probably able to read texts in different writing systems, they translated both literally and paraphrastically, depending on the genre, and took license to tweak the source texts, rendering them suitable for their audience.

All this information about attested Hittite scribal practices, and archives has important implications for inferring something about largely unattested Israelite scribal practices and traditions of the first millennium BCE. In the closing paragraphs of this survey, I consider data that draw the two scribal traditions into a relationship that may be described as one of tenuous, interrupted continuity.

The scribal tradition of the second millennium was shared by the people living in Canaan, who also had archives of their own, as proved by finds in places such as Hazor and by the Amarna letters.[22] It is not farfetched to assume that this tradition continued into the first millennium, and that the Hebrew scribal tradition did not emerge *ex nihilo*. To some extent, Israelite scribes in the service of palaces and temples continued earlier traditions, adapting them to specific needs and tastes, as did the Hittite scribes.

In an article published more than 20 years ago, Moshe Greenberg (1994) described similar themes in Hittite royal prayers and biblical psalms. He wrote that in both cultures this genre was a product of "schooled authors," but cautioned that he was "not at this juncture postulating genetic connections."[23] Greenberg highlights interesting correlations between the corpus of Hittite prayers and biblical psalms. He points out that in the Hittite case, a significant part of the liturgy consists of royal prayers written and

---

22 These letters from ca.1400 BCE testify to the use of the Akkadian language by the scribes of Jerusalem as part of the Levant occupied by the Egyptians. At the same time this collection of letters included also the correspondence in Hittite language with the king of Arzawa, a land on the western border of the Hittite empire to be conquered by the Hittites in the 13th century BCE (see Moran 1992). For the entire corpus of cuneiform clay tablets found in Israel see Horowitz and Oshima 2006.

23 In none of these cases do I suggest "genetic" connections as will be concluded in the following.

polished by professional scribes for the king and queen. In the psalter, he suggests, the psalms attributed to David suppose "that polished literary prayers were composed by court priest-scribes for recitation by and for the king [...]. The idea of a king able to compose prayers on his own is not plausible" (Greenberg 1994: 25). Greenberg's second point is that both the Hittite prayers and the psalms share a number of themes relating to sacrifice, divine intercession, inherited guilt, and the use of a "pleading, argument" theme (Greenberg 1994: 18), which is one of the most characteristic themes of Hittite prayers (Singer 2005). His third point is that there are a number of "expressions evocative" of Psalms in the Hittite prayer of Kantuzzili (CTH 373) including the following: "negative confession = Ps 26:4-5; my protector since I was born = Ps 71:5-4; human life is short = Ps 144:4; you are my father and mother = Ps 27:9-10 my condition is an offence to others = Ps 38:12; 69:9; to whom I did good repaid with evil = Ps 38:21" (Greenberg 1994: 24–25). These "expressions" cannot be Hebrew translations from the Hittite or allusions to Hittite texts. They may, however, have originated in the Hittite tradition from which, in different translations, they became part of the liturgical vocabulary used in the region.[24]

An interesting biblical narrative in the book of Amos suggests how such liturgical traditions may have moved from Anatolia, south in the Levant, ending up in the Hebrew Bible. Amos 7:7-17 contains a prophecy by Amos concerning the Northern Kingdom of Israel and its king Jeroboam II, delivered at the sanctuary of Bethel. It then goes on to narrate the extremely negative reaction of the main priest of the temple, Amaziah.

Amaziah termed the prophecy an act of קשר "conspiracy" or "rebellion" against the king, and alerted the latter, saying: "Amos is conspiring against you within the House of Israel. The country cannot endure the things he is saying" (7:10, JPS translation).[25] He then ordered the prophet to flee from the place after he had informed the king about him. His words to Amos are as follows: "O you seer, go flee away into the land of Judah, and **there eat bread**, and also prophesy there," חזה לך ברח לך אל ארץ יהודה ואכל שם לחם ושם תנבא

---

24 See recently Carr 2012: 529: "I suggest that we biblical scholars sometimes act almost as if the *existing corpus* of *preserved* non-biblical images and texts was a proto-canon, complete in itself as a source for potential analogies to biblical texts, rather than treating it as the highly gapped set of records that happened to be found at isolated places and times from various cultures surrounding Israel."

25 The term קשר is directly connected with attempts of assassinating a king in the Bible such as 1 Sam 22:13; 2 Sam 15:6; 1 Kgs 15:27 (passim).

(Amos 7:12). I mark the phrase "there eat bread, ואכל שם לחם" in bold because it is unique in biblical Hebrew, already noted as such by Meir Weiss (1992: 233). As Weiss indicated, scholars in the past interpreted this phrase with the meaning "run away, so that in Judah you will be able to *earn a living* by prophesying." However, in other passages in the Bible "eat bread" means simply to *live*.[26] In Amos' case it reflects the idea that fleeing will save his life because should he remain in Israel he would surely be executed as a foreign agitator.[27]

The same phrase occurs in Hittite in cases where a king punishes members of his own family whom he regarded as hostile to his sovereignty. In these cases the king expels his kin from the capital to a rural area. There, he provides them with resources enabling them "to eat bread and drink water." An especially intriguing example is King Muršili II's expulsion of the Tawananna queen dowager. In a prayer to the gods the king declares that he did not execute the queen dowager, but only expelled her from the palace deposing her from her high priestly post:

> [...] she killed [my wife ...] she bereaved(?) me [...]. Was it a capital crime for me if she was not executed? I consulted the gods, my lords, and it was determined for me by oracle to execute her. To dethrone her was also determined for me by oracle. But even then I did not execute her; I only deposed her from the office of *siwanzanna*-priestess. Since it was determined for me by oracle to dethrone her, I dethroned her and I gave her a house. Nothing is lacking that she desires. She has food and drink (lit. **bread and water**) and everything stands at her disposal. She lacks nothing. She is **alive**. She sees the Sun-god of Heaven with her eyes and **eats the bread of life**. (CTH 71 ii, 5–10; translation by Singer 2002: 77–78)[28]

This phrase, occurring in Hittite and biblical texts, is an idiom for life and living. In both cultures, it is employed in similar socio-political contexts. It may not be possible to prove connections between them with confidence until more archives are discovered, but we already know enough to infer that the Hittite expression entered Hebrew through as yet unknown channels associated with scribal traditions.

Summing up the evidence of the well-established scribal activity of the Hittite kingdom that lasted for more than five centuries, showing constant

---

26　See for example 1Sam 2:36.
27　Nowhere in the Bible is expelling a person for betrayal termed with the phrase of being able to eat bread; the consequence of disloyalty is basically death for the culprit.
28　For this special prayer see Hoffner 1983.

contacts with Mesopotamian and North Syrian cultures and their respective languages, leads us to regard it as part of the tradition that somehow transferred literary knowledge to the ancient Israelites. This short survey highlights the variety of texts and versions of the same texts available to those scribes and scholars. Their ability to copy as well as rewrite and compose new texts based on earlier forms or genres (prayers or treaties, rituals as well as legal texts) should be a constant factor in discussions on how Israelite texts were composed. The vast number of translated texts and versions of original texts that circulated in the second as well as the first millennium should be considered part of the Israelite heritage, and interpretations of biblical texts should take into account the scribal work and environment of these cultures as the background for Israelite compositions.

BIBLIOGRAPHY

Archi, Alfonso. 2007. "Transmission of Recitative Literature by the Hittites." *Altorientalische Forschungen* 34: 185–203.

Ben-Ami, Doron. 2012. "The Early Iron Age II (Strata X–IX)." In *Hazor VI—The 1990-2009 Excavations: The Iron Age*. Edited by Amnon Ben-Tor, Doron Ben-Ami and Déborah Sandhous, 52–153. Jerusalem: Israel Exploration Society, Institute of Archaeology, The Hebrew University of Jerusalem.

Beckman, Gary. 1983. "Mesopotamians and Mesopotamian Learning at Hattusa." *Journal of Cuneiform Studies* 35: 97–114.

Beckman, Gary. 2001. "Sargon and Naram-Sin in Hatti: Reflections of Mesopotamian Antiquity among the Hittites." In *Die Gegenwart des Altertums: Formen und Funktionen des Altertumsbezugs in den Hochkulturen der Alten Welt*, edited by Dieter Kuhn and Helga Stahl, 85–91. Heidelberg: Edition Forum.

Beckman, Gary. 2002. "'My Sun-God': Reflections of Mesopotamian conceptions of Kingship Among the Hittites." In *Ideologies as Intercultural Phenomena: Proceedings of the Third Annual Symposium of the Assyrian and Babylonian Intellectual Heritage Project held in Chicago USA, October 27-31, 2000*, edited by A. Panaino and G. Pettinato, 15–21. Melammu Symposia 3; Milano: -Universitá di Bologna; Roma: IsIAO.

Beckman, Gary. 2003. "Gilgamesh in Hatti." In *Hittite Studies in Honor of Harry A. Hoffner Jr. on the Occasion of his 65th Birthday*, edited by G. Beckman, R. Beal and G. McMahon, 37–57. Winona Lake, IN: Eisenbrauns.

Beckman, Gary. 2009. "Hittite Literature." In *From an Antique Land: An Introduction to Ancient Near Eastern Literature*, edited by Carl S. Ehrlich, 215–54. Lanham, MD: Rowman & Littlefield Publishers.

Beckman, Gary. 2012. "Samas Among the Hittites." In *Theory and Practice of Knowledge Transfer: Studies in School Education in the Ancient Near East and Beyond: Papers Read at a Symposium in Leiden, 17-19 December 2008*, edited by W. S. van Egmond and W. H.

van Soldt, 129–35. Uitgaven van het Nederlands Instituut voor het Nabije Oosten te Leiden, 121. Leiden: Netherland Instituut voor Nabije Oosten.

Bryce, Trevor. 2002. *Life and Society in the Hittite World*. Oxford: Oxford University Press.

Bryce, Trevor. 2005. *The Hittite Kingdom*. Oxford: Oxford University Press.

Bryce, Trevor. 2012. *The World of the Neo-Hittite Kingdoms: A Political and Military History*. Oxford: Oxford University Press.

Busse, Anja. 2013. "Hittite scribal habits: Sumerograms and Phonetic complements in Hittite Cuneiform." In *Scribes as Agents of Language Change*, edited by Esther-Miriam Wagner, Ben Outhwaite, Bettina Beinhoff, 85–96. Studies in Language Change, 10. Berlin: Walter De Gruyter.

Campbell, Dennis R. M. 2011. "Translation Among the Hittites." In *Complicating the History of Western Translation: The Ancient Mediterranean in Perspective*, edited by Siobhán McElduff and Enrica Sciarrino, 161–75. Manchester: St. Jerome Publishing / London: Routledge, 2014.

Carr, David, M. 2012. "The Many Uses of Intertextuality in Biblical Studies: Actual and Potential." In *Congress Volume Helsinki 2010*, edited by Martti Nissinen, 505–35. Vetus Testamentum Supplements, 148. Leiden: Brill.

Cohen, Yoram. 2009. *The Scribes and Scholars of the City of Emar in the Late Bronze Age*. Harvard Semitic Studies, 59. Winona Lake, IN: Eisenbrauns.

Collins, Billie Jean. 2007. *The Hittites and their World*, Archaeology and Biblical Studies, 7. Atlanta: Society of Biblical Literature.

Dietrich, Manfred. 1991. "Der Dialog Zwischen Šupe-ameli und seinem 'Vater': Die Tradition babylonischer Weisheitssprüche im Westen." *Ugarit-Forschungen* 23: 52–53.

Fincke, Jaenette. 2012. "The School Curriculum from Ḫattuša and Ugarit: A Comparison." In *Theory and Practice of Knowledge Transfer: Studies in School Education in the Ancient Near East and Beyond: Papers Read at a Symposium in Leiden, 17–19 December 2008*, edited by W.S. van Egmond and W. H. van Soldt, 85–102. Leiden: Nederlands instituut voor het Nabije Oosten.

Galil, Gershon. 2014. "A Concise History of Palistin/Patin/Unqi/'mq in the 11th–9th Centuries BC." *Semitica* 56: 74–104.

George, A.R. 2003. *The Babylonian Gelgamesh Epic: Introduction, Critical Edition and Cuneiform Texts*. Oxford: Oxford University Press.

Gilan, Amir. 2010. "Epic and History in Hittite Anatolia." In *Epic and History*, edited by David Konstan and Kurt A. Raaflaub, 51–65. Malden, MA: Wiley-Blackwell.

Gilan, Amir. 2013. "Hittites in Canaan? The Archaeological Evidence." *Biblische Notiezen* 156: 39–52.

Gordin, Shai. 2010. "*Scriptoria* in Late Empire Period Hattusa: The Case of the É GIŠ. KIN.TI." In *Pax Hethitica: Studies on the Hittites and their Neighbours in Honour of Itamar Singer*, edited by Yoram Cohen, Amir Gilan, and Jared L. Miller, 158–177. Studien zu den Boğazköy-Texten, 51. Wiesbaden: Harrassowitz.

Greenberg, Moshe. 1994. "Hittite Royal Prayers and Biblical Petitionary Psalms." In *Neue Wege der Psalmenforschung Für Walter Beyerlin*, edited by Klaus Seybold and Erich Zenger, 15–27. Freiburg-Basel-Wien: Herder.

Güterbock, Hans. G. 1964. "A View of Hittite Literature." *Journal of the American Oriental Society* 84: 107–15.

Güterbock, Hans. G. 1988. "Bilingual Moon Omens from Bugazküy." In *A Scientific Humanist: Studies in Memory of Abraham Sachs*, edited by E. Leichty, M. de Ellis and P. Gerardi, 161–74. Philadelphia: University of Pennsylvania Museum.

Haas, Volkert. 2006. *Die hethitische Literatur: Texte, Stilistik, Motive*. Berlin: Walter de Gruyter.

Hawkins, David. 2011. "The Inscriptions of the Aleppo Temple." *Anatolian Studies* 61: 35–54.

Hoffner, Harry, A. Jr. 1983. "A Prayer of Muršili II about his Stepmother." *Journal of the American Oriental Society* 103: 187–92.

Hoffner, Harry, A. Jr. 1990. *Hittite Myths*, 2nd edition, edited by Gary M. Beckman. SBL Writings from the Ancient World, 2. Atlanta: Scholars Press.

Horowitz, Wayne and Oshima, Takayoshi. 2006. *Cuneiform in Canaan: Cuneiform Sources from the Land of Israel in Ancient Times*. Israel Exploration Society; Jerusalem: Hebrew University of Jerusalem.

Hout, Theo, P. J. van den. 2002. "Another View of Hittite Literature." In *Anatolia Antica: Studi in memoria di Fiorella Imparati* (= Eothen11), edited by St. de Martino and F. Pecchioli Daddi, 857–78. Firenze: LoGisma.

Hout, Theo, P. J. van den. 2007. "Institutions, Vernaculars, Publics: The Case of Second Millennium Anatolia." In *Margins of Writing, Origins of Cultures*, edited by Seth Sanders, 221–62; Second printing with postscripts and minor corrections. Chicago: Oriental Institute.

Hout, Theo, P. J. van den. 2008. "A Classified Past: Classification of Knowledge in the Hittite Empire." In *Proceedings of the 51st Rencontre Assyriologique Internationale held at the Oriental Institute of the University of Chicago July 18-22, 2005*, edited by R. D.Biggs, J. Myers, and M. Roth, 211–19. Chicago: The Oriental Institute.

Hout, Theo, P. J. van den. 2009a. "Reflections on the Origins and Development of the Hittite Tablet Collections in Ḫattuša and their Consequences for the Rise of Hittite Literacy." In *Central-North Anatolia in the Hittite Period: New Perspectives in Light of Recent Research*, edited by F. Pecchioli-Daddi, G. Torri, and C. Corti, 71–96. Studia Asiana, 5. Rome: Herder.

Hout, Theo, P. J. van den. 2009b. "Schriber bei den Hethiter." *Reallexikon der Assyriologie* 12: 273–80.

Hout, Theo, P. J. van den. 2011. "The Written Legacy of the Hittites." In *Insights into Hittite History and Archaeology*, edited by H. Genz and D. P. Mielke, 47–84. Colloquia Antiqua, 2. Leuven/Paris/Walpole, MA: Peeters.

Hout, Theo, P. J. van den. 2012. "The Ductus of the Alalaḫ VII Texts and the Origin of Hittite Cuneiform." In *Paleography and Scribal Practices in Syro-Palestine and Anatolia in the Late Bronze Age. Papers Read at a Symposium in Leiden, 17-18 December 2009*, edited by E. Devecchi, 147–70. Publications de l'Institut historique et archéologique néerlandais de Stamboul, 119. Leiden: Nederlands Instituut voor het Nabije Oosten.

Hout, Theo, P. J. van den. 2015. "In Royal Circles: The Nature of Hittite Scholarship." *Journal of Ancient Near Eastern History* 2: 203–27.

Keydana, Götz. 1991. "Der Dialog zwischen Šupe-ameli und seinem Vater: Die hethitische Version." *Ugarit-Forschungen* 23: 68–74.

Klinger, Jörg. 1998. "Wer lehrte die Hethiter das Schreiben?" In *III. Uluslararasi Hititoloji Kongresi Bildirileri, Corum 16–22 Eylül 1996*, edited by S. Alp and A. Süel, 365–75. Ankara: Uyum Ajans.

Laroche, Emmanuel. 1971. *Catalogue des Textes Hittites*. Etudes et Commentaires, 75. Paris: Klincksieck.

Melchert, H. Craig. 2003. *The Luwians*. Handbook of Oriental Studies, 68. Leiden: Brill.

Moran, William L. 1992. *The Amarna Letters*. Baltimore: Johns Hopkins University Press.

Reiner, Erica and Hans G. Güterbock. 1967. "The Great Prayer to Istar and its two Versions from Bogazköy." *Journal of Cuneiform Studies* 21: 255–56.

Schwemer, Daniel. 2015. "Hittite Prayers to the Sun-God for Appeasing an Angry Personal God: A Critical Edition of CTH 372–74." In *Mon dieu qu'ai-je fait? Les digir-sà-dab-ba et la piété privée en Mésopotamie*, edited by M. Jaques, 349–393. Orbis Biblicus et Orientalis 273. Fribourg: Academic Press; Göttingen: Vandenhoeck and Ruprecht.

Simon, Zsolt. 2014. "Remarks on the Anatolian Background of Tel Rehov Bees and the Historical Geography of the Luwian States in the 10th C. BC." In *Studies in Economic and Social History of the Ancient Near East in Memory of Péter Vargyas*, edited by Z. Csabi, 715–38. Ancient Near Eastern and Mediterranean Studies, 2. Budapest: The University of Pécs.

Singer, Itamar. 1995. "Some Thoughts on Translated and Original Hittite Literature." *Israel Oriental Studies* 15: 123–28.

Singer, Itamar. 2002. *Hittite Prayers*, edited by H. A. Hoffner Jr. Society of Biblical Literature Writings of the Ancient World, 11. Atlanta: Society of Biblical Literature.

Singer, Itamar. 2005. "Sin and Punishment in Hittite Prayers." In *"An Experienced Scribe who Neglects Nothing": Ancient Near Eastern Studies in Honor of Jacob Klein*, edited by Yitschak Sefati, Pinhas Artzi, Chaim Cohen, Barry L. Eichler, and Victor A. Hurowitz, 557–67. Bethesda, MD: CDL Press.

Singer, Itamar. 2006. "The Hittites and the Bible Revisited." In *'I Will Speak the Riddles of Ancient Times' Archaeological and Historical Studies in Honor of Amihai Mazar on the Occasion of His Sixtieth Birthday*, edited by Pierre de Miroschedji and Aren M. Maeir, 723–56. Winona Lake, IN: Eisenbrauns.

Taracha, Pioter. 2011. "Hittite Rituals as Literary Texts: What do we Know about their Original Editions?" In *Hethitische Literatur: Überlieferungsprozesse Textstrukturen, Ausdrucksformen und Nachwirken; Akten des Symposiums vom 18. Bis 20. Februar 2010 in Bonn*, edited by Manfred Hutter and Sylvia Hutter-Braunsar, 275–83. Alter Orient und Altes Testament, 391. Münster: Ugarit-Verlag.

Veldhuis, Niek. 2014. *History of the Cuneiform Lexical Tradition*. Guides to the Mesopotamian Textual Record, 6. Güttingen: Hubert & Co.

Wilhelm, Gernot. 1989. *The Hurrians*, translated by Jennifer Barnes. Warminster: Aris and Philips.

Waal, Willemeijn. 2012. "Writing in Anatolia: The Origins of the Anatolian Hieroglyphs and the Introductions of the Cuneiform Script." *Altorientalische Forschungen* 39: 287–315.

Weeden, Mark. 2011a. "Adapting to New Contexts: Cuneiform in Anatolia." In *The Oxford Handbook of Cuneiform Culture*, edited by Karen Radner and Eleanor Robson, 597–617. Oxford: Oxford University Press.

Weeden, Mark. 2011b. *Hittite Logograms and Hittite Scholarship*. Studien zu den Boğazköy-Texten, 54. Wiesbaden: Harrassowitz Verlag.

Weeden, Mark. 2011c. "Hittite Scribal Schools Outside of Ḫattuša?" *Altorientalische Forschungen* 38: 116–34.

Weeden, Mark. 2013. "After the Hittites: The Kingdoms of Karkamish and Palistin in Northern Syria." *Bulletin of the Institute of Classical Studies* 56: 1–20.

Weiss, Meir. 1992. *The Book of Amos*, volume 1. Jerusalem: Magness Press. [Hebrew]

Chapter 5

Identifying Torah Sources in the Historical Psalms[†]

MARC ZVI BRETTLER[*]

This article is meant to be suggestive, rather than comprehensive. It focuses on method, and does not attempt to clarify each and every case where a psalm may be using a source that is extant in the Torah.

As others have noted, the term intertextuality has many meanings. This article explores author-centered rather than reader-centered intertextuality. I will use the term "allusion" throughout to describe this phenomenon, as advocated more than fifteen years ago by Benjamin Sommer (1998: 8). I also understand "literary borrowing" as a subcase of allusion. I will also use Carr's term "influence" (2012: 516) as the opposite of "allude." In other words, an earlier text influences a latter one, and the later one may borrow from, or allude to, that earlier text.

THE TORAH AND OTHER LITERATURE IN THE
SECOND TEMPLE PERIOD

My focus is on books four and five of the Psalter (Psalms 90-150), which is a post-exilic collection, with most of the psalms in them being either

[†] I would like to thank Mr. Jamie Bryson for his assistance with this article, and Dr. Jeffery Leonard for sharing with me several of his unpublished papers on allusions in the Psalms.

[*] Marc Z. Brettler is Bernice and Morton Lerner Professor in Judaic Studies at Duke University, Durham, North Carolina.

exilic or post-exilic.[1] Thus, given that it is likely that the Torah came into being in the exilic or early post-exilic period, many of these Psalms could have known the Torah, and therefore could allude to it. But opportunity to allude does not prove allusion.[2] It is not prudent to claim that each and every psalmist knew the Torah—and only the Torah—as we more or less have it, by which I mean the Torah with the same contents it would later assume in MT, though not as a fixed text.[3]

Even once the Torah was created, it was not accepted overnight, displacing all other *torot*—it did not for all become "The Torah."[4] Furthermore, the Dead Sea texts of the sort that Sidnie White Crawford has explored, often called "rewritten scripture," may have influenced individual psalmists.[5] These texts contain parts of what is in the MT Torah, but often in a different form; namely, they are shorter than what appears in the MT Torah or, in places, they contain material absent from MT Torah. The term "rewritten scripture"—and what texts it might include—is contested in scholarship, but most scholars agree that rewritten scripture had the same status for some that the proto-MT Torah had for others.[6] The Temple Scroll in particular was likely a very influential example of rewritten scripture, especially if, as many scholars have argued, it is not a sectarian document.[7] It is thus with good reason that Levinson named his recent book on this

---

1 Many of the Psalms of books IV–V have been dated to the post-exilic period using the methods of linguistic dating; see Qimron (1978). For more on the method, see Hurvitz (1972), and for a collection of late biblical Hebrew words see Hurvitz (2014). For a critique of Hurvitz' methods for linguistic dating, see Young and Rezetko (2008), and also their more recent volume on historical linguistics (Rezetko and Young: 2014). For a recent defense of the method, see Hornkohl (2014). The method of Hurvitz is useful for proving that particular psalms are late, but more problematic for claiming that they are early.

2 See recent discussion about the use of תורה in Ezra/Nehemiah, Chronicles, and other late biblical texts in Schaper (2011: 31). The view that the Chronicler had the Torah more or less as we have it is the standard view, see Japhet (1993: 16); and Hanson (1986: 93).

3 See discussion in Tov (2012: 180–190).

4 See my forthcoming article in BZAW 486, "Those Who Pray Together Stay Together: The Role of Late Psalms in Creating Identity."

5 See Crawford (2008). These texts are now collected in Feldman and Goldman (2014). Also see general discussions about the genre in Zahn (2000).

6 See the literature in the previous note.

7 Molly Zahn suggests there are four key texts in the Rewritten Scripture category; these are *Jubilees*, the *Temple Scroll*, *Genesis Apocryphon*, and the five manuscripts of *4QReworked Pentateuch* (4Q158, 4Q364–367) (Zahn 2010: 325).

scroll *A More Perfect Torah* (2013). Jubilees, as another noteworthy example, likely belongs in this same category. As VanderKam suggests, "There is strong reason for believing that Jubilees was considered authoritative at Qumran" (2000: 437).[8] Even if VanderKam is mistaken, or we wish to debate the use of such a vague word as "authoritative," Jubilees is very well attested among the Dead Sea Scrolls, and, furthermore, later sources may allude to it. We should wonder if some Jewish groups, like the later Abyssinian Church, considered it to be part of the Torah (VanderKam 2000: 437). Thus, we must remember that "our" Torah, in one of its many text-forms, is not the only text that our psalmists may have used when they referred to traditions from creation up to the conquest. J. Shaver (1989) makes this point about Chronicles and the Torah. Although I dispute his method and evidence, I do agree in part with his conclusions. To paraphrase, changing "the Chronicler" to "the Psalmists": "the psalmists were not limited to pentateuchal material" (Shaver 1989: 128).

In addition, the creation of the Torah should not be confused with its broad dissemination. Seth Schwartz made this point a decade ago about rabbinic literature (2001), and Talya Fishman made a similar claim for later material in her book, whose title is self-explanatory, *Becoming the People of the Talmud* (2011). At an earlier time, Jews *became* the people of the Torah, but this development did not happen to all Jews immediately after the Torah was promulgated, whenever that process may have occurred. This is the major claim of Michael Satlow's provocative book, *How the Bible Became Holy* (2014). The word "became/becoming," shared in the titles of these last two books, highlights that this was a (long) process.[9]

Many of the psalms contained in books four and five contain traditions that are not found in, and differ from, current Torah traditions. If the Torah was fully and exclusively authoritative—however we might define that slippery term[11]—then there would have been more concord between the Torah and the psalms' "historical traditions." In addition, several of these late psalms, especially but not exclusively Psalm 119, so overemphasize the Torah and its importance that they likely functioned within

---

8 Jubilees is better represented there than Genesis; only more copies of Psalms, Deuteronomy, Isaiah, and Exodus are found among the biblical texts. The book of Jubilees is also mentioned as an authority in the *Damascus Document* (CD 16:3-4) alongside the "Law of Moses" (VanderKam 2000).

9 A similar position emerges from Noll (2011). He answers the question negatively. I agree with many, but not all of his conclusions.

10 For a discussion of this term and its problems see Brown-deVost (2015).

a polemical atmosphere, where not all in Israel agreed on the Torah as a single authoritative text.[11]

METHODOLOGICAL CONSIDERATIONS

Properly identifying allusions in the Psalms is important for two reasons. How various psalms reuse and reinterpret the Torah or Torah traditions, if that indeed is the case, is important for the exegete of the Psalms—but this can only be done once we know what these psalmists were familiar with, as well as the direction of the allusions. The second reason relates to the Torah and its development. To use the term "empirical evidence," employed by Tigay (1985) and reused by Carr (2011: 37) and others, some psalms do not know the Torah as a complete redacted or compiled book, and thus the Psalms may be able to provide empirical evidence for how the Torah developed.[12] This issue has already been explored by Thomas Römer (2011). He concludes: "Nonetheless, I think it has been demonstrated that allusions to 'history' in the Psalms indeed belong to current pentateuchal research" (Römer 2011: 488). I agree with this broad conclusion, though we differ in many specifics since I remain committed to a traditional form of the documentary hypothesis.

"Historical psalms" are not a form-critical *Gattung* (Römer 2011: 477, esp. n. 34). In isolating them, I use my definition of "history" from *The Creation of History in Ancient Israel*, that is, "a narrative that presents a past" (Brettler 1995: 10–12). Thus a psalm that contains such a presentation of the past (outside of the superscriptions, which I believe, following the consensus, to be secondary) is a historical psalm. It does not matter what percentage of the psalm is comprised of such depictions—in other words, I include Psalm 95, which focuses on Meribah and Massah in only four of eleven verses, alongside Psalm 136, which is very history-heavy. In

---

11 It is likely that Torah in Psalm 119 refers to *the* Torah; see Hossfeld and Zenger (2002: 183). Even if this is not certain, this psalm is best explained by understanding it within a polemical context. Psalm 111 needs to be considered in this context as well (see Brettler 2009: 62–73); this psalm is a riddle, enhancing the status of the Torah. A polemic around the place of the Torah also explains verses such as Ps 147:19-20.

12 I do not share the skepticism about empirical evidence voiced by Sanders in "What if There Aren't Any Empirical Models for Pentateuchal Criticism?" (forthcoming).

addition, with scholars such as Richard Clifford,[13] I think creation is part of history; psalms that recall creation narrate a past, and some psalms make no distinction as they present both creation and events that transpired specifically in Israel's past.

IDENTIFYING ALLUSION

I largely rely on Leonard's criteria for discovering allusions, and on Carr's criteria for determining the direction of borrowing.[14] Also, with Leonard and others, I believe that finding allusion "is an art, not a science," to quote Sommer (1998: 35).[15] The treatment of intertextuality and allusion

13 Clifford argues that cosmogony and history are different only in the matter of perspective; the cosmogonies found in the Psalms (often intertwined with histories, e.g. Ps 77:17-21) function the same way as other national stories, such as the exodus, even though the actors are superhuman. He suggests the use of the terms "history" and "suprahistory" to describe the difference between accounts of the human world vs. the heavenly world (Clifford 1992: 57-69).

14 Leonard uses the following criteria to identify allusion: 1. Shared language is the single most important factor in establishing a textual connection; 2. Shared language is more important than non-shared language; 3. Shared language that is rare or distinctive suggests a stronger connection than does language that is widely used; 4. Shared phrases suggest a stronger connection than do individual shared terms; 5. The accumulation of shared language suggests a stronger connection than does a single shared term or phrase; 6. Shared language in similar contexts suggests a stronger connection than does shared language alone; 7. Shared language need not be accompanied by shared ideology to establish a connection; and 8. Shared language need not be accompanied by shared form to establish a connection (Leonard 2008).

Carr's method determines that a text is dependent on another text if it 1. verbally parallels that text and yet includes *substantial* pluses vis-à-vis that text, 2. appears to enrich its parallel (fairly fully preserved) with fragments from various locations in the Bible (less completely preserved), 3. includes a plus that fills what could have been perceived as an apparent gap in its parallel, 4. includes expansive material in character speeches, particularly theophanic speech, 5. has an element that appears to be an adaptation of an element in the other text to shifting circumstances/ideas, and 6. combines linguistic phenomena from disparate strata of the Pentateuch (Carr 2001: 110-11).

15 Sommer's sentiment is echoed in Leonard's claim that his criteria should be used as "guidelines" that "do not hold true in every situation" (Leonard 2008: 246); Carr also notes, "such criteria are only rough guides requiring judicious use" (2001: 126), and speaks of "the art in our discipline" (2001: 130). In contrast, at least two studies have tried to apply mathematical models to this issue.

in Schmitz, *Modern Literary Theory and Ancient Texts: An Introduction* (2007), highlights the problems of the overused and differently used term "intertextuality," but does not add anything new to Leonard's criteria, which I still feel should be the basic starting point of any discussion about allusion.[16] Steven Hinds (1998) offers rich examples of how allusion works in Roman literature, and how the later alluding texts might be interpreted, but says little about discerning allusions and determining their direction. This is likely because the latter issue hardly comes into play with Latin texts, which allude to the Greek classics or Latin works that can be dated with certainty as earlier.[17] The criteria outlined in Tigay's "On Evaluating

---

A 2013 study of Q by Tripp (2013) notes that the order of the material presumed to be part of Q is different enough in the Synoptics that the hypothesis of Q is not supported by order alone. I do not believe that his approach has relevance to the cases I will examine, though his observation that order alone may not be used to prove or disprove literary dependence is important to keep in mind, and in line with Leonard.

Closer to home in terms of field, see Bakker and van Peursen (2011), which shows how, contrary to common opinion, proper statistical analysis does not support the notion that the prose of Judges 4 knows and reworks the poetry of chapter 5—though that case might be argued on different grounds. They emphasize differences as well as similarities, concluding:

> The considerable differences between these two sets of proper nouns occurring in these chapters, as well as the lack of any increased concentration of shared verbs or common nouns other than those which occur throughout the same types of stories in the book of Judges, prevent us from assuming any literary dependency between these chapters.... It is safer, therefore, to assume that the two chapters eventually go back to the same stories, but that a "textual" or "literary" dependence is unlikely. (Bakker and Peursen 2011)

According to the mathematician I consulted, this article is problematic, though looking at the issue of allusion using statistical models deserves to be explored further.

16 Two volumes have recently appeared by Dell and Kynes (2013 and 2014), which understand intertextuality very broadly, and are interested in both the phenomenon from both the modern reader and the ancient author's perspective, but neither advances the issue of discerning allusions and the directions of borrowing in a significant fashion. The seminal study of Leonard, for example, is hardly mentioned in either volume. The introductory essay by Barton (2013: 1–16) offers useful theoretical insights; he uses the term "hard intertextuality" to describe what others call "authorial intertextuality," and what I refer to as "allusion."

17 I do not refer to the many studies that are older, and thus already used by Sommer and Leonard; see especially Malul (1990). Nor have I attempted here

Claims of Literary Borrowing" in the Hallo *Festschrift* (1993), and by Wright in *Inventing God's Law* (2009: 25) are in line with Leonard's observations, especially that similarities are more important than differences. The same is true of Miller's survey "Intertextuality in Old Testament Research" (2011); he cites Leonard extensively, but does not extend his observations significantly or note anyone who does. Miller draws out and discusses the useful distinction between author vs. reader approaches to intertextuality.[18] My approach, which focuses on allusion, is from the author's perspective, and I urge all who discuss intertextuality to make clear what approach they are taking, or like Sommer, whom I follow, to avoid that term in favor of less ambiguous terms such as "allusion." I do not agree with the "radical intertextualist" scholars whom Miller quotes who see what I am trying to do as "banal source-hunting," because texts are so interwoven that "tracing lines among them becomes as meaningless as distinguishing among water drops in the ocean" (Miller 2011: 286). My interest in allusion as author-oriented intertextuality is thus the same as a recent article about intertextuality in the *Enūma Eliš* by Andrea Seri (2014), though she too does not break new ground methodologically.

Returning to the Psalms: How can we know, or at least posit, that a particular psalm knows earlier sources? More specifically, how can we prove that a particular historical psalm knew the Torah? What would such a psalm look like—or not look like?

It would seem reasonable, at least initially, that it should look like rabbinic traditions that combine the P and non-P creation story, such as texts that claim that Adam and Eve were in Eden (an element of non-P) until the first Shabbat (an element of P) (see Ginzberg 2003: 77, and 81 n. 97). Even that, however, is not a compelling criterion, since someone could combine these two stories because they deal with the same topic, much like what happens in the *Diatessaron*, which combines thematically similar material from different documents (see Peterson 2004). A better criterion for determining whether a psalm knew the redacted Torah would be the combination of materials from different sources that reflect different episodes that

---

to offer a comprehensive bibliography on allusion and intertextuality, though the issues reflected in the dialogue between Berman and Levinson and Stackert in the fourth volume of the *Journal of Ancient Judaism* (2013) deserve close examination. As the continuation of my remarks will make clear, I am more sympathetic to the perspective of Levinson and Stackert.

18 See also the useful observations in Edenburg (2010). On the other hand, I do not find satisfying the recent article by Kilchör (2013); Kilchör lacks nuance in part because he did not take into account Leonard's criteria.

are not related in terms of plot. One such example would be the mixing of the rebellion of Korah, from P, with the non-P rebellion of Datan and Abiram. This likely could only happen after the Torah was redacted into the form that it now exists, since it is unlikely that two separate people would have associated these quite different stories. (See further discussion of this particular episode below.)

To complicate matters, deviations from the biblical story do not indicate that the text under consideration does not know the Torah. This becomes especially clear from Loewenstamm, who in *The Evolution of the Exodus Tradition* brings many examples of how various Hellenistic Jews depicted the plagues in a manner that differs from Exodus (Loewenstamm 1992: 102–11). For example, Artapanus does not mention cattle pestilence, darkness, or the slaying of the first born, and in his account, the Nile inundates Egypt rather than turning to blood (Loewenstamm 1992: 103). Loewenstamm notes that many of these differences are best explained as "tendentious deviations" (1992: 104). Philo reorders the plagues beginning with those brought on by Aaron (blood, frogs, lice), followed by those brought on by Moses (hail, locusts, and darkness) (Loewenstamm 1992: 109). This is likely his innovation, despite his reliance on the LXX, which has the plagues in the same order as the MT. Josephus lacks cattle pestilence (Loewenstamm 1992: 109), and although Pseudo-Philo claims that there were 10 plagues, this may be a later copyist's correction, since he lists only 9 plagues, omitting boils, and orders them differently than MT (Loewenstamm 1992: 111). Loewenstamm brings many more such cases, both for the plague narratives and for other traditions that are part of the exodus complex, but these examples concerning the plagues are sufficient to illustrate that a later text that knows the Torah need not follow its storyline or vocabulary.

While Loewenstamm's extensive evidence suggests that deviations from the Torah do not indicate dependence on a different text, correspondences may. Various scholars have pointed out that similarities are more important than differences for determining the presence of allusions.[19]

---

19 See for example the second principle developed in Leonard 2008: 49–251, "shared language is more important than non-shared language." Of course some similarities may be explained by claiming the psalm and the Torah source both depended on a common earlier source, but I see no reason to invoke this possibility.

ALLUSIONS TO INDEPENDENT PENTATEUCHAL SOURCES

Some previous studies have explored the use of Torah sources in various psalms. For example, Leonard has shown that Psalm 78 knew particular pentateuchal sources (Leonard 2008).[20] I have examined the plague narratives in Psalm 105 (Brettler 2007), and believe that a more complete examination of the entire psalm substantiates my general claim that the Psalmist knew non-P and P as separate sources, and relied predominantly on non-P.[21] The author uses the non-P order of the plagues, and his style is characterized by non-P terminology—though some P terminology is present. Had the author of Psalm 105 known the redacted Torah, this psalm would have looked different.

In Brettler 2007, I examined the psalm, asking the following question: Is it likely that a psalmist, who knew the Torah as we have it, would have written this psalm in this form? My answer was no, since in the redacted Torah as we have it, P's voice is about as strong as non-P, while in the psalm, non-P greatly overshadows P. P and non-P traditions are rarely intertwined in the psalm as they are in the plague narrative in Exodus. I can see how that could have happened if the psalm's author had non-P in front of him, and was familiar with some of the traditions now found in P. The deviations from non-P may be explained quite easily; for example, *dever* was left out for "tendentious reasons," to use Loewenstamm's term. I doubt, however, that someone with the redacted Torah in front of him would have created Psalm 105—with darkness as its first plague along with many other deviations, some even more radical than the types described by Loewenstamm from the Jewish Hellenistic sources that knew the Torah (mostly via the LXX).

More recently I discussed "Psalm 136 as an Interpretive Text" (Brettler 2013). In this psalm, the author uses material now found in the Torah in a manner similar to the psalmists who composed Psalm 78 and 105: this author also used one Torah source as a base text, which the author interpreted in detail, while showing some awareness of other sources found in different parts of the Torah. Specifically, this psalmist used Deut 10:12–11:19 as his main text. He cites from that text in order, engaging in what Leonard in this volume calls "narrative tracking"—and citing or quoting

---

20 For a different view, see Emanuel (2007: 315).

21 I use non-P as the most general term; it is not relevant if this material is J, as many assume, or E, as suggested by Propp (1998: 314–15), JE, or some other source or set of sources. See also Leonard in this volume.

some unusual words. While Deut 10:12–11:19 was the main base text that our psalmist used, he employed other sections in Deuteronomy as well. In the same way the authors of Psalms 78 and 105 were broadly non-P cen-tered, and had non-P as the main written text in front of them, the author of Psalm 136 was Deuteronomy-centered.

Yet, just as the authors of Psalms 78 and 105 used material beyond non-P, the author of Psalm 136 used, to a small extent, non-D traditions, most prominently the death of the firstborn, which is never found in D. Thus, here as well it is likely that the psalmist had a main written source, which he may have even consulted as he wrote, while not forgetting other material that he may have known. Against the prevailing opinion, I do not believe that the author of Psalm 136 knew the entire Torah; it is signifi-cant that he nowhere uses *bara'*, the key word of the P creation story, and, furthermore, the similarities between the psalm and P are minor (Brettler 2013: 381–384). Had the author of Psalm 136 known the redacted Torah, it would be difficult to understand why the psalm is so D-centric, and why P hardly has a voice at all, especially concerning the creation narrative, where P's voice is strong and initial.

ALLUSIONS TO EXTRA-PENTATEUCHAL MATERIAL AND TO THE PENTATEUCHAL SOURCES

It is clear that some of the historical psalms knew sources outside of the Torah.[22] For example, many of these psalms allude to some reworked form of the Canaanite Baal Epic; this is true, for example, in Psalm 148:7, which mentions *taninim* and is preceded by a verse that notes וַיַּעֲמִידֵם לָעַד לְעוֹלָם חָק־נָתַן וְלֹא יַעֲבוֹר: ("He made them endure forever, establishing an order (or: boundary) that shall never change").[23] But such material could certainly be used in addition to the complete Torah text, which raises the question of whether or not we can be reasonably certain that any psalms contain allusions to the complete, redacted Torah. As the following three examples show, this is a difficult question to answer.

---

22 I consider the following among the Historical Psalms, having at least some his-torical material: Psalms 44, 66, 68, 74, 77, 78, 80, 81, 83, 89, 95, 99, 103, 105, 106, 107, 111, 114, 132, 135, 136, 137, and 144.

23 For a general treatment of this issue, see Smith (2002: 80–101); see more recently the bibliography in Flynn (2013: 66–67).

Ps. 95.8-11 reads

אַל־תַּקְשׁוּ לְבַבְכֶם כִּמְרִיבָה כְּיוֹם מַסָּה בַּמִּדְבָּר׃
אֲשֶׁר נִסּוּנִי אֲבוֹתֵיכֶם בְּחָנוּנִי גַּם־רָאוּ פָעֳלִי׃
אַרְבָּעִים שָׁנָה אָקוּט בְּדוֹר וָאֹמַר עַם תֹּעֵי לֵבָב הֵם וְהֵם לֹא־יָדְעוּ דְרָכָי׃
אֲשֶׁר־נִשְׁבַּעְתִּי בְאַפִּי אִם־יְבֹאוּן אֶל־מְנוּחָתִי׃

(95:8) Do not be stubborn as at Meribah, as on the day of Massah, in the wilderness,
(9) when your fathers put Me to the test, tried Me, though they had seen My deeds.
(10) Forty years I was provoked by that generation; I thought, "They are a senseless people; they would not know My ways."
(11) Concerning them I swore in anger, "They shall never come to My resting-place!"[24]

It is difficult to figure out to which Torah texts, if any, these verses are alluding. Massah and Meribah are mentioned together—but in reverse order of the psalm—only in Exod 17:7, which is non-P, and in the song preserved in Deut 33:8. Is it fair to assume that our psalm is alluding to one of these, or not? Does the difference in order imply lack of allusion—no narrative tracking—or is this a case of Seidel's law, which suggests that a later author may invert elements of an earlier source that he is quoting to mark it as a quotation (see Brettler 1995: 212 n. 63)—and how can we know? Is the use of *nissah* enough to show dependence on Exodus, which uses that verb in verse 7,

וַיִּקְרָא שֵׁם הַמָּקוֹם מַסָּה וּמְרִיבָה עַל־רִיב בְּנֵי יִשְׂרָאֵל וְעַל נַסֹּתָם אֶת־יְהוָה לֵאמֹר הֲיֵשׁ יְהוָה
בְּקִרְבֵּנוּ אִם־אָיִן׃

"The place was named Massah and Meribah, because the Israelites quarreled and because they tried the LORD, saying, 'Is the LORD present among us or not?'"? Alternatively, did it come from Deut 6:16 לֹא תְנַסּוּ אֶת־יְהוָה אֱלֹהֵיכֶם כַּאֲשֶׁר נִסִּיתֶם בַּמַּסָּה׃ ("Do not try the LORD your God, as you did at Massah")?

These two possibilities may be begging the question. What should be asked first is whether or not the root *nun-samekh-yod* is of any value for determining allusions, since it occurs thirty-four times, and thus is not unusual (see note 14 above). To complicate matters, the tradition of God punishing a generation for forty years is found in the Torah, but in relation

24 Translations generally follow the NJPS *Tanakh*, sometimes with slight modifications.

to the scout tradition, not the Massah and Meribah tradition. Indeed, Num 32:13, which is in the P spy narrative, is closest in terms of clustering of words:

וַיִּחַר־אַף יְהוָה בְּיִשְׂרָאֵל וַיְנִעֵם בַּמִּדְבָּר אַרְבָּעִים שָׁנָה עַד־תֹּם כָּל־הַדּוֹר הָעֹשֶׂה הָרַע בְּעֵינֵי יְהוָה:

> "The LORD was incensed at Israel, and for forty years He made them wander in the wilderness, until the whole generation that had provoked the LORD's displeasure was gone."

Only our psalm, Num 32, and the end of Job use these three words שׁנה, ארבעים, and דור together. This represents unusual shared language (Leonard criterion 3 in note 14 above) that blends into Leonard's fourth criterion of "shared phrases suggest a stronger connection than do individual shared items." Does that mean that this psalm's verse knows Num 32:13, and has intentionally and creatively combined the Massah and Meribah tradition with that of the spies to suggest that the forty years of wandering was a result of that event, and not the scouts' report of the land—even though the Torah explicitly states otherwise several times?[25] How can I decide between these three options: (1) The Psalmist knew the Torah as we have it, and combined Massah and Meribah with the scout tradition; (2) The Psalmist knew (some of) the sources or traditions that were eventually redacted into the Torah, and combined these into his account; or, (3) The Psalmist did not make up this tradition at all, but based himself on an earlier tradition or source no longer extant, which had already combined Massah and Meribah with the forty-years tradition. It is very striking that commentaries do not deal with this issue in detail.

Ps 114:8 also contains a tradition that might be related to Massah and Meribah: הַהֹפְכִי הַצּוּר אֲגַם־מָיִם חַלָּמִישׁ לְמַעְיְנוֹ־מָיִם ("who turned the rock into a pool of water, the flinty rock into a fountain"). Nowhere else in the Bible, however, is a rock turned into water—rather, water comes out of the rock! (In Exod 17:3-7 and Num 20:8-11, Moses strikes a rock and water comes out of it.) Is our psalmist playing with the Torah tradition, and renovating it? Is he merely being poetic?

The situation with Psalm 114 is unusually complex, since it is not only this verse that differs significantly from Torah traditions (Brettler, forthcoming). The psalm claims the Jordan moved backwards during the exodus (vv. 3b, 5b), mountains danced (vv. 4a, 6a), and (v. 1) Israel became

---

25 In Num 14:33-34; 32:13, the sin of the spies is responsible for the forty years of wandering.

God's people at the time of the exodus, not with Abraham or Sinai. In other words, Ps 114 contains significant non- or even anti-Torah traditions. It is difficult to determine if they are non-Torah or anti-Torah. If the psalm is allusive, they are anti-Torah; if not, they are merely non-Torah traditions. But the criteria Leonard and others have suggested are not very helpful for determining allusions in such cases, where the later text may be disputing the earlier one, and thus uses very different language than its putative source.[26]

ALLUSIONS TO THE REDACTED PENTATEUCH

To the best of my knowledge, Ps 106 provides evidence for the only likely case of a psalmist who knows the entire redacted Torah.[27] It shares significant material from the different Torah sources and DtrH; the following observations are suggestive, rather than complete. Verse 19 refers to Horeb, known in E and D.[28] Verse 9 uses the language of J, and the Song of the Sea, embedded within J.[29] In several places it knows P—for example, verses 30-31 concerning Phinehas, a tradition only found in P, or in the preceding verse 28, which closely matches Num 25:3, which is again P.[30] As Römer (2011: 485) notes, verses 34-35 resembles Dtr. In particular, verses 16-18 provide the strongest evidence that this psalm likely knew the redacted Torah as we have it:

וַיְקַנְאוּ לְמֹשֶׁה בַּמַּחֲנֶה לְאַהֲרֹן קְדוֹשׁ יְהוָה:
תִּפְתַּח־אֶרֶץ וַתִּבְלַע דָּתָן וַתְּכַס עַל־עֲדַת אֲבִירָם:
וַתִּבְעַר־אֵשׁ בַּעֲדָתָם לֶהָבָה תְּלַהֵט רְשָׁעִים:

(16) There was envy of Moses in the camp, and of Aaron, the holy one of the LORD.

26 To complicate matters further, if it is anti-Torah, is it clear that it knew the Torah as we more or less have it—or might it have known P and D as separate documents, and not known JE? Of course, if we knew for sure whether P was a source or a redactional layer, we might be able to resolve this issue. On P as a source and/or redactional layer, see Kislev (2011).

27 See the discussions in Emanuel 2007: 223-25 and in Anderson (1972: 736) who already saw Psalm 106 as a post-exilic psalm that likely knew the redacted Torah.

28 E—Exod 3:1; 17:6; 33:6; D—Deut 1:2, 6, 19; 4:10, 15; 5:2; 9:8; 18:16; 28:69.

29 The account of the Sea of Reeds in Ps 106:7-12 draws from the language of E in the narrative found in Exod 14:11-12, 21, and also draws from the Song of the Sea in Exod 15:5, 6, 8.

30 The Phinehas episode alluded to in verses 30-31 is found in Num 25:6-9 (P).

(17) The earth opened up and swallowed Dathan, closed over the party of Abiram.

(18) A fire blazed among their party, a flame that consumed the wicked.

These verses mix language found in both the Priestly Korah, and the non-Priestly Datan and Abiram story. For example, verse 17 mentions Datan and Abiram, and the verse very closely parallels the non-P Num 16:32a: וַתִּפְתַּח הָאָרֶץ אֶת־פִּיהָ וַתִּבְלַע אֹתָם וְאֶת־בָּתֵּיהֶם ("and the earth opened its mouth and swallowed them up with their households"). Yet, that rebellion in non-P was only against Moses, while Korah's rebellion in P was against both Moses and Aaron, as in verse 16; cf. Numbers 16:3: וַיִּקָּהֲלוּ עַל־מֹשֶׁה וְעַל־אַהֲרֹן וַיֹּאמְרוּ אֲלֵהֶם רַב־לָכֶם כִּי כָל־הָעֵדָה כֻּלָּם קְדֹשִׁים וּבְתוֹכָם יְהוָה וּמַדּוּעַ תִּתְנַשְּׂאוּ עַל־קְהַל יְהוָה: ("They combined against Moses and Aaron and said to them, 'You have gone too far! For all the community are holy, all of them, and the LORD is in their midst. Why then do you raise yourselves above the LORD's congregation?'"). Furthermore, the word עדה that appears in verses 17 and 18 is a well-known indicator of P (see Milgrom 1978), and is used in P's Korah story (see especially Num 16:5, 22). Finally, according to Num 16:31-32a, Datan and Abiram died in a swallow hole,

וַיְהִי כְּכַלֹּתוֹ לְדַבֵּר אֵת כָּל־הַדְּבָרִים הָאֵלֶּה וַתִּבָּקַע הָאֲדָמָה אֲשֶׁר תַּחְתֵּיהֶם:
וַתִּפְתַּח הָאָרֶץ אֶת־פִּיהָ וַתִּבְלַע אֹתָם וְאֶת־בָּתֵּיהֶם

"Scarcely had he finished speaking all these words when the ground under them burst asunder, and the earth opened its mouth and swallowed them up with their households."

This is part of the JE account (most of Num 16:29-34 is JE with the exception of verse 32b), while Korah and his assembly were consumed by fire in Num 16:35, וְאֵשׁ יָצְאָה מֵאֵת יְהוָה וַתֹּאכַל אֵת הַחֲמִשִּׁים וּמָאתַיִם אִישׁ מַקְרִיבֵי הַקְּטֹרֶת: ("And a fire went forth from the LORD and consumed the two hundred and fifty men offering the incense"), is from the P account.

Our psalm knows the two stories in their combined form, as indicated by אֵשׁ in verse 18 and תִּפְתַּח הָאָרֶץ in verse 17. As I mentioned above, it is unlikely that a person independent of the redactor of the Torah would have combined these two stories since they do not deal with the same individuals; thus, the presence of significant vocabulary items in the same order reflecting both the P Korah story and the non-P Datan and Abiram story suggests that our psalm not only knew traditions now found in the Torah, but knew the Torah as we more or less have it. Korah's name is absent in Psalm 106, but this is best explained by Gunkel's suggestion that this psalmist did not want to besmirch his Korahite relatives or friends

(Gunkel 1986: 466).[31] As noted earlier in my discussion of Loewenstamm, later texts often leave out details from their sources.

CONCLUSIONS

These cases suggest that authors of the historical psalms may have used sources that now are part of the Torah, and perhaps even the redacted Torah itself, two possibilities that must be distinguished. Psalm 106 likely betrays the influence of the redacted Torah, but this should not be generalized to all of the historical psalms in books four and five. Careful consideration of the tradition-history work of Loewenstamm highlights how difficult it is to prove—or disprove—allusions. Yet the criteria of Leonard and Carr are very helpful in indicating the likelihood and direction of allusions, and specifically in this case, the likelihood that several historical psalms knew, at the minimum, sources that eventually were woven into the Torah—or documents or traditions that are extremely close to these sources. Scholars who work on these psalms need to consider these observations in greater detail, since one aspect of interpretation is seeing how a psalm interacts with, and reworks, its source(s).

REFERENCES

Allen, Leslie. 2002. *Psalms 101-150 Revised*. Word Biblical Commentary, 21, Nashville: Thomas Nelson.

Anderson, Albert. 1972. *The Book of Psalms*. London: Oliphants.

Bakker, Dirk and W. Th. van Peursen. 2011. "Digital Text Comparison of Ancient Hebrew Texts: A Case Study of the Two Accounts of the Battle against the Canaanite Army Captain Sisera." International Conference on Informatics and Semiotics in Organizations, https://www.academia.edu/7307410/_With_W.Th._van_Peursen_Digital_Text_Comparison_of_Ancient_Hebrew_Texts._A_Case_Study_of_the_Two_Accounts_of_the_Battle_against_the_Canaanite_Army_Captain_Sisera_Judges_4-5_2011_.

Barton, John. 2013. "Déja Lu: Intertextuality, Method or Theory?" In *Reading Job Intertextually*, edited by Katherine Dell and Will Kynes, 1–16. Library of the Hebrew Bible/Old Testament Studies, 574. New York: Bloomsbury.

Berman, Joshua. 2013. "Historicism and Its Limits: A Response to Bernard M. Levinson and Jeffrey Stackert." *Journal of Ancient Judaism* 4: 297–309.

Brettler, Marc. 1995. *The Creation of History in Ancient Israel*. London/New York: Routledge.

---

31 See similarly Kraus (1993: 319), and Hossfeld and Zenger (2005: 89).

Brettler, Marc. 2007. "The Poet as Historian: The Plague Tradition in Ps 105." In *Bringing the Hidden to Light: Studies in Honor of Stephen A. Geller*, edited by K. F. Kravitz and D. M. Sharon, 19–28. Winona Lake: Eisenbrauns.

Brettler, Marc. 2009. "The Riddle of Psalm Ps 111." In *Scriptural Exegesis: The Shapes of Culture and the Religious Imagination: Essays in Honour of Michael Fishbane*, edited by Deborah A. Green and Laura S. Lieber, 62–73. Oxford: Oxford University Press.

Brettler, Marc. 2013. "Psalm 136 as an Interpretive Text." *Hebrew Bible and Ancient Israel* 2: 373–95.

Brettler, Marc. Forthcoming. "A Jewish Historical-Critical Commentary on Psalms." *Hebrew Bible and Ancient Israel*.

Brooke, George. 2000. "Rewritten Bible." In *Encyclopedia of the Dead Sea Scrolls*, edited by Lawrence Schiffman and James VanderKam, 777–81. Oxford: Oxford University Press.

Brown-deVost, Bronson. 2015. "Commentary and Authority in Mesopotamia and Qumran." PhD diss., Brandeis University.

Carr, David. 2001. "Method in Determination of Direction of Dependence: An Empirical Test of Criteria Applied to Exodus 34, 11–26 and its Parallels." In *Gottes Volk am Sinai : Untersuchungen zu Ex 32-34 und Dtn 9-10*, edited by Matthias Köckert and Erhard Blum, 107–40. Gütersloh: Kaiser, Gütersloher Verlagshous.

Carr, David. 2011. *The Formation of the Hebrew Bible: A New Reconstruction*. Oxford: Oxford University Press.

Carr, David. 2012. "The Many Uses of Intertextuality in Biblical Studies: Actual and Potential." In *Congress Volume Helsinki 2010*, edited by Marti Nissinen, 505–35. Supplements to Vetus Testamentum, 148. Leiden: Brill.

Clifford, Richard. 1992. "Creation in the Psalms." In *Creation in the Biblical Traditions*, edited by Richard Clifford and John Collins, 57–69. CBQ Monograph Series, 24. Washington DC: Catholic Biblical Association of America.

Crawford, Sidnie. 2008. *Rewriting Scripture in Second Temple Times*. Grand Rapids: Eerdmans.

Dell, Katherine and Will Kynes. 2013. *Reading Job Intertextually*. Library of Hebrew Bible/ Old Testament Studies, 574. New York: Bloomsbury.

Dell, Katherine and Will Kynes. 2014. *Reading Ecclesiastes Intertextually*. Library of Hebrew Bible/Old Testament Studies, 587. New York: Bloomsbury.

Edenburg, Cynthia. 2010. "Intertextuality, Literary Competence and the Question of Readership: Some Preliminary Observations." *Journal for the Study of the Old Testament* 35.2: 131–48.

Emanuel, David. 2007. "The Psalmists' Use of the Exodus Motif: A Close Reading and Intertextual Analysis of Selected Exodus Psalms." Ph.D. diss., Hebrew University.

Feldman, Ariel and Liora Goldman. 2014. *Scripture and Interpretation: Qumran Texts that Rework the Bible*. Berlin: De Gruyter.

Fishman, Talya. 2011. *Becoming the People of the Talmud: Oral Torah as Written Tradition in Medieval Jewish Cultures*. Philadelphia: University of Pennsylvania Press.

Flynn, Shawn. 2013. *YHWH is King: The Development of Divine Kingship in Ancient Israel*. Leiden: Brill.

Ginzberg, Louis. 2003. *Legends of the Jews*. JPS Classic Reissues. Philadelphia: Jewish Publication Society.

Gunkel, Hermann. 1986. *Die Psalmen*. Göttingen: Vandenhoeck & Ruprecht.

Hanson, Paul. 1986. *The People Called: The Growth of the Community in the Bible*. San Francisco: Harper & Row.

Hinds, Stephen. 1998. *Allusion and Intertext: Dynamics of Appropriation in Roman Poetry*. New York: Cambridge University Press.

Hornkohl, Aaron D. 2014. *Ancient Hebrew Periodization and the Language of the Book of Jeremiah: A Case for a Sixth-Century Date of Composition*. Studies in Semitic Languages and Linguistics, 74. Leiden: Brill.

Hossfeld, Frank-Lothar and Erich Zenger. 2005. *Psalms 3: A Commentary on Psalms 101-150*. Hermeneia. Minneapolis: Fortress Press.

Hurvitz, Avi. 1972. *Ben Lashon Le-lashon: Le-toldot Leshon Ha-Miḳra Bi-yeme Bayit Sheni*. Yerushalayim: Mosad Byaliḳ.

Hurvitz, Avi. 2014. *A Concise Lexicon of Late Biblical Hebrew: Linguistic Innovations in the Writings of the Second Temple Period*. Leiden: Brill.

Japhet, Sara. 1993. *I & II Chronicles*. Louisville: Westminster John Knox.

Kilchör, Benjamin. 2013. "The Direction of Dependence between the Laws of the Pentateuch: The Priority of a Literary Approach." *Ephemerides Theologicae Lovanienses* 89.1: 1–14.

Kislev, Itamar. 2011. "P, Source or Redaction: The Evidence of Numbers 25." In *The Pentateuch*, edited by Thomas Dozeman et. al., 387–400. Tübingen, Mohr Siebeck.

Kraus, Hans-Joachim. 1993. *Psalms 60-150: A Commentary*. Minneapolis: Fortress Press.

Leonard, Jeffery. 2008. "Identifying Inner-Biblical Allusions: Psalm 78 as a Test Case." *Journal of Biblical Literature* 127.2: 241–65.

Levinson, Bernard. 2013. *A More Perfect Torah: At the Intersection of Philology and Hermeneutics in Deuteronomy and the Temple Scroll*. Critical Studies in the Hebrew Bible, 1. Winona Lake: Eisenbrauns.

Levinson, Bernard and Jeffrey Stackert. 2013. "The Limitations of 'Resonance': A Response to Joshua Berman on Historical and Comparative Method." *Journal of Ancient Judaism* 4: 310–33.

Loewenstamm, Samuel. 1992. *The Evolution of the Exodus Tradition*. Jerusalem: Magnes Press.

Malul, Meir. 1990. *The Comparative Method in Ancient Near Eastern and Biblical Legal Studies*. Alter Orient Und Altes Testament, Bd. 227. Kevelaer: Butzon and Bercker.

Milgrom, Jacob. 1978. "Priestly Terminology and the Political and Social Structure of Pre-Monarchic Israel." *Jewish Quarterly Review* 69: 65–81.

Miller, Geoffrey. 2011. "Intertextuality in Old Testament Research." *Currents in Biblical Research* 9: 283–309.

Noll, K.L. 2011. "Did 'Scripturalization' Take Place in Second Temple Judaism?" *Scandinavian Journal of the Old Testament* 25: 201–16.

Petersen, William. 2004. "The Diatessaron and the Fourfold Gospel." In *The Earliest Gospels*, edited by Charles Horton, 50–68. London/New York: T & T Clark.

Propp, William. 1998. *Exodus 1-18*. Anchor Bible, 2. New York: Doubleday.

Qimron, Elisha. 1978. "Post-exilic Language in the Book of Psalms." *Beth Mikra* 73:139-50 (Hebrew).

Rezetko, Robert and Young, Ian. 2014. *Historical Linguistics & Biblical Hebrew: Steps toward an Integrated Approach*. Winona Lake: Eisenbrauns.

Römer, Thomas. 2011. "Extra-Pentateuchal Evidence for the Existence of a Pentateuch? The Case of the 'Historical Summaries.'" In *The Pentateuch*, edited by Thomas Dozeman et. al., 471–88. Tübingen: Mohr Siebeck.

Sanders, Seth. Forthcoming. "What if There Aren't Any Empirical Models for Pentateuchal Criticism?" In *Orality and Literacy in Ancient Israel*, edited by Brian Schmidt. Atlanta: Society of Biblical Literature.

Satlow, Michael. 2014. *How the Bible Became Holy*. New Haven: Yale University Press.

Schaper, Joachim. 2011. "Torah and Identity in the Persian Period." In *Judah and the Judaeans in the Achaemenid Period*, edited by Oded Lipschits et. al., 27–38. Winona Lake: Eisenbrauns.

Schmitz, Thomas. 2007. *Modern Literary Theory and Ancient Texts: An Introduction*. Oxford: Blackwell.

Schwartz, Seth. 2011. *Imperialism and Jewish Society, 200 B.C.E. to 640 C.E.* Princeton: Princeton University Press.

Seri, Andrea. 2014. "Borrowings to Create Anew: Intertextuality in the Babylonian Poem of 'Creation' (*Enūma Eliš*)." *Journal of the American Oriental Society* 134.1: 89–106.

Shaver, Judson. 1989. *Torah and the Chronicler's History Work: An Inquiry into the Chronicler's References to Laws, Festivals, and Cultic Institutions in Relationship to Pentateuchal Legislation*. Brown Judaic Series, 196. Atlanta: Scholars Press.

Smith, Mark. 2002. *The Early History of God*. Grand Rapids: Eerdmans.

Sommer, Benjamin. 1998. *A Prophet Reads Scripture: Allusion in Isaiah 40-66*. Stanford: Stanford University Press.

Tigay, Jeffrey. 1985. *Empirical Models for Biblical Criticism*. Philadelphia: University of Pennsylvania Press.

Tigay, Jeffrey. 1993. "On Evaluating Claims of Literary Borrowing." In *The Tablet and the Scroll: Near Eastern Studies in Honor of William Hallo*, edited by Mark E. Cohen, et. al., 250–55. Bethesda: CDL Press.

Tov, Emanuel. 2012. *Textual Criticism of the Hebrew Bible*, 3rd edition. Minneapolis: Fortress Press.

Tripp, Jeffrey M. 2013. "Measuring Arguments from Order for Q: Regression Analysis and a New Metric for Assessing Dependence." *Neotesamentica* 47.1: 123–48.

VanderKam, James. 2000. "Jubilees." In *Encyclopedia of the Dead Sea Scrolls*, edited by Lawrence Schiffman and James VanderKam, 434–38. Oxford: Oxford University Press.

Wright, David. 2009. *Inventing God's Law*. Oxford: Oxford University Press.

Young, Ian and Robert Rezetko. 2008. *Linguistic Dating of Biblical Texts: An Introduction to Approaches and Problems*, 2 volumes. Sheffield: Equinox.

Zahn, Molly. 2010. "Rewritten Scripture." In *The Oxford Handbook of the Dead Sea Scrolls*, edited by Timothy Lim and John Collins, 323–36. Oxford: Oxford University Press.

Chapter 6

Identifying Subtle Allusions:
The Promise of Narrative Tracking[1]

JEFFERY M. LEONARD[*]

The author of Hebrews, convinced that Jesus was not only messiah but also a priest, faced a seemingly intractable problem: How could Jesus, a descendant of Judah, be counted among the priests, who were descendants of Levi? The author finds his solution to this problem in a bit of creative biblical interpretation. Noting that Ps 110:4 declares the king to be a priest "according to the order of Melchizedek,"[2] the author concludes it must be to this priestly order that Jesus belongs (cf. Heb 5:5-10; 7:13-14).[3] But the author of Hebrews is not content merely to assert Jesus' priestly credentials. He goes on to contend that the Melchizedekian priesthood to which Jesus belongs is, in fact, a *superior* priesthood to that of Levi. This is the case, he argues, because those who serve in the priesthood of Melchizedek do so *eternally*; unlike the Levitical priests, their priestly office does not end at their deaths (cf. Heb 7:3, 15-17, 23-24). Upon what might the author of Hebrews base such an extraordinary claim? Once more, it is to Psalm 110 that the author turns, for there the careful reader will note that the psalmist declares not only, "You are a priest according to the order of Melchizedek," but, "You are a priest *forever* according to the order of

* Jeffery M. Leonard is Assistant Professor, Department of Religion, Samford University, Birmingham, Alabama.

1 I would like to thank Marc Brettler and Ziony Zevit for the many helpful comments, questions, and suggestions they offered for this article.

2 Unless otherwise noted, all biblical translations are taken from the New Revised Standard Version.

Melchizedek." "A priest forever," for the author of Hebrews, is proof that the Melchizedekian priesthood is an eternal priesthood.

For those who might harbor doubts concerning the aforementioned claim, Hebrews obliges the reader with confirmation in the Bible's only other reference to Melchizedek, Genesis 14. Noting that the Melchizedek figure appears seemingly out of nowhere in this chapter, the author of Hebrews concludes:

> Without father, without mother, without genealogy, having neither beginning of days nor end of life, but resembling the Son of God, he remains a priest forever. (Heb 7:3)

Though we might wonder how far the author of Hebrews would be willing to push this logic if pressed, for now it is enough to observe that he finds in Melchizedek's lack of pedigree a connection with, and affirmation of, the eternal priesthood he believes Jesus possesses.[4]

Continuing his discussion of Jesus and Melchizedek, the author of Hebrews goes on to adduce yet another argument from Genesis 14 in support of Melchizedek's superiority to Levi. Noting that Abraham gave Melchizedek a tenth of the booty when he defeated the alliance of Mesopotamian kings (Gen 14:20), he opines: "See how great he is! Even Abraham the patriarch gave him a tenth of the spoils" (Heb 7:4).[5] And he

---

3 Joseph Fitzmyer (2000) provides a helpful survey of the appearances of Melchizedek in the Hebrew Bible and the New Testament. More detailed studies have been produced by Fred Horton (1976) and, more recently, Gard Granerød (2010).

4 Horton (1976: 156–63) argues that the focus of the author of Hebrews is not on Melchizedek's being without ancestors (i.e., his immortality) but on his lack of a *priestly* genealogy. The connection between Melchizedek and Jesus, he maintains, is in their lack of a Levitical pedigree. Variations of the contrary view, namely that Hebrews regards Melchizedek as a heavenly or angelic figure, are argued forcefully by Marinus de Jonge and A. S. van der Woude (1966), Harold Attridge (1989), and Paul Kobelski (1981). Eric Mason (2005) provides a valuable canvass of the issues involved as he lays out his own case for Hebrews' following the angelic Melchizedek tradition evident at Qumran.

5 While the wording of Gen 14:20 leaves some uncertainty as to who gave tithes to whom, the context weighs heavily in favor of Abraham's having given the tithe to Melchizedek. Apart from the fact that priests are generally the *recipients* not the *contributors* of tithes, the narrative as a whole works by contrasting Melchizedek with the king of Sodom and Abraham's responses to both. Melchizedek blesses Abraham and is in turn blessed by Abraham via the tithe (Gen 14:18-20); the king of Sodom speaks disrespectfully to Abraham and is

continues, "One might even say that Levi himself, who receives tithes, paid tithes through Abraham, *for he was still in the loins of his ancestor when Melchizedek met him*" (Heb 7:9-10). For the author of Hebrews, the Levitical priesthood recognized the superiority of the Melchizedekian priesthood when Levi paid tithes to Melchizedek in the person of his ancestor, Abraham.

A modern reader could hardly be blamed for questioning whether the author of Hebrews has shed new light on the enigmatic figure of Melchizedek. Of course, in this regard, the author stands in good company; a long line of interpreters has failed to shed much light on this strange character. What the author does offer, however, is a fascinating glimpse into the ways in which traditions from the Tanakh were, at least at one time and place, being interpreted by communities that inherited those traditions. Whatever these traditions may originally have meant, in the hands of skillful interpreters, they were given new life as they served to reinforce old dogmas, to lend support to new beliefs, and to establish links between these later interpretive communities and their earlier precedents.[6]

As the decades since Michael Fishbane's *Biblical Interpretation in Ancient Israel* have shown (and decades before that if we reach back to early lights in the field such as Nahum Sarna), this process of interpreting and reinterpreting earlier traditions did not appear in Melchizedekian fashion—riding in suddenly out of the mists—only once the biblical period had closed.[7] On the contrary, even within the pages of the Tanakh, we find

---

rebuked (vv. 21-24). Regardless of the original intent of Genesis 14, it is clear that the author of Hebrews understood Melchizedek to be the recipient.

6 As George Brooke's recent study, "Genre Theory, Rewritten Bible and Pesher" (2010), illustrates, the continued study of Second Temple texts from Qumran and elsewhere has tended to blur the lines between Bible, inner-biblical allusion, paraphrase, and commentary. The challenges of distinguishing these genres is reflective of the fact that there was no abrupt shift from a biblical to a post-biblical world; the latter began well before the former had ended. See further, Sidnie Crawford (2008), Ariel Feldman and Liora Goldman (2014), and Marc Brettler (1999, 2003).

7 Fishbane's *Biblical Interpretation in Ancient Israel* (1985) is rightly regarded as the seminal study of inner-biblical allusion, outlining in systematic and comprehensive fashion the approach evident in nascent form in studies such as Sarna's treatment of Psalm 89 (1963). The literature on inner-biblical allusion has grown dramatically in the decades since Fishbane's work appeared and can hardly be catalogued here. Those interested in pursuing the subject further are directed to Geoffrey Miller's invaluable survey (2011) of the literature from the last twenty years of research, both in the area of the traditional search for

one author alluding to another, responding to, reinterpreting, or simply echoing the words of those who had written before. This phenomenon of inner-biblical allusion and interpretation continues to hold unique promise for expanding our understanding of both biblical and extrabiblical texts. Its study provides an invaluable window onto the ways in which ancient readers understood their own religious heritage and helps to establish a line of continuity between the biblical period and the early inheritors of the biblical tradition. Through research into inner-biblical allusion, added insight is gained into the development of beliefs and practices over the course of the biblical period, and, importantly in a time when the former documentary consensus is now seemingly in disarray, new avenues are opened for studying the development of the textual traditions (JEDP, the Deuteronomist, the prophetic corpora, etc.) that came to form the Hebrew Bible.[8]

For the promises of inner-biblical allusion to be realized fully, though, two key items must be established: First, we must have confidence that an allusion has actually occurred. Second, we must be able to determine the direction in which the allusion runs. In the case of a quotation or explicit citation, these elements are often easily determined. To hearken back to our illustration from Hebrews, there is little doubt that the author relied on Psalm 110 and Genesis 14 or that he did so largely, if not exclusively, from the Septuagintal version of these texts. This use is evident because the author actually quotes from these texts and uses the language of citation when he does so: "the one of whom these things are said" (ἐφ' ὃν γὰρ λέγεται ταῦτα; Heb 7:13); "Moses said" (Μωϋσῆς ἐλάλησεν; Heb 7:14); and "it is declared" (μαρτυρεῖται; Heb 7:17).[9] Other allusions are less obvious, however, and require more rigorous attention to matters of methodology.

---

specific textual allusions and in the synchronic method generally described as "intertextuality."

8 This latter issue was the subject of my doctoral dissertation, in which I made the case that the psalmist who composed Psalm 78 had access to J and E, but not to D and P (2006). Marc Brettler (2007, 2013) has produced several studies considering the state of the underlying Pentateuchal traditions as evidenced by the historical psalms which appear to have relied upon them. Though reaching very different conclusions, Thomas Römer (2011) has also considered the relation of the "historical summaries" to the Pentateuch.

9 While the theological and intellectual framework of the author of Hebrews was doubtless shaped by developments within extrabiblical texts from the Second Temple period (see Mason 2005: 49–62), the author's allusions to Psalm 110 and Genesis 14 are not in dispute.

IDENTIFYING INNER-BIBLICAL ALLUSIONS VIA NARRATIVE TRACKING

I have argued that the surest guide to establishing allusions in less certain cases is the presence of shared, distinctive terminology (Leonard 2008). To the degree that shared terminology is rare and abundant—that is, that uncommon terms appear with some frequency in two texts—the existence of an allusion is more secure. And to the degree that such terminology is common and scarce—that is, that only common terms appear in texts and these only occasionally—an allusion is less certain. It is this fact that shines such a bright spotlight on the allusive nature of a historical psalm like Psalm 78. When the psalmist recounts the events leading up to the exodus from Egypt, he mentions not just miracles generally (vv. 11-12) but the seven non-priestly plagues from Exodus specifically (vv. 42-51), using the same vocabulary as the non-priestly account in each case: דם (blood), צפרדע (frogs), עָרֹב (swarms) not the priestly כִּנִּם (gnats), דֶּבֶר (pestilence) not the priestly שחין (boils), ברד (hail), ארבה (locusts), בכור (firstborn).[10] The significance of the use of this sort of terminology is underscored by the fact that terms such as ערב and צפרדע appear solely in Exodus 7-8 and Psalms 78 and 105, and nowhere else in the Hebrew Bible.[11]

Similarly, when the psalm refers to the crossing of the sea, it does so in the language of Exodus 15's *Song of the Sea*. Where *Shirat HaYam* says in verse 8, "At the blast of your nostrils, the waters piled up; the floods stood up like a heap" (וברוח אפיך נערמו מים / נצבו כמו־נד נזלים), Psalm 78:13 echoes, "the waters stood up like a heap" (ויצב־מים כמו־נד). Only in Psalm 78 and Exodus 15 is נצב used to portray the waters as standing. When the Israelites cross the Jordan in Joshua 3, עמד is used instead (cf. vv. 13, 16). And while נד may be a familiar term because of the importance attributed to Exodus 15 in biblical scholarship, the term is quite rare in the Bible, occurring in only

10 William Propp's recent commentary in the Anchor Bible series offers an excellent analysis of the sources in the plague narrative (Propp 1998: 310–21). Lemmelijn (2002) provides extensive documentation of the secondary literature surrounding the plague narratives in his study of the Priestly contribution (source or redaction) to the pericope. A notable dissenter from the traditional source-critical view (two or three sources finally joined by a redactor) is Loewenstamm (1992).

11 צפרדע is found only in Exod 7:27-8:9; Ps 78:45; 105:30. ערב occurs only in Exod 8:17-27; Ps 78:45; 105:31. I have given extensive attention to Ps 78's exclusive reliance on the non-priestly version of the plagues elsewhere (2006: 65–128). Concerning the plagues in Psalm 105, see Brettler (2007).

three texts in the Tanakh outside of Exodus 15 and Psalm 78 (Josh 3:13, 16; Ps 33:7; Isa 17:11). As I point out below, this same pattern adheres when the psalmist describes the complaint narratives in the wilderness. When Psalm 78 speaks of the Kibroth Hattaavah incident, for example, it does so specifically in the language of Numbers 11.

Although the presence of shared, distinctive terminology may provide the most certain basis for identifying textual allusions, it must surely be the case that some ancient authors drew upon other texts without obliging their future readers with strikingly rare lexical signals of their dependence. In her important discussion of literary allusion, Ziva Ben Porat (1976: 108–10) argues that an allusion requires first and foremost a "marker," an identifiable element that the alluding text uses to evoke the text from which the marker derives.[12] But as Benjamin Sommer (1998: 11) observes, this marker or sign may take a wide variety of forms: a poetic line, sentence, phrase, motif, rhythmic pattern, idea, title, or even the form of a work.[13] When the overlap of distinctive terminology is absent, when the "marker" is not a line, sentence, or phrase, other features will have to be explored to identify textual allusions. In the remainder of this study I focus on just one of these features, an allusive technique that I call *narrative tracking*.

12 Ben-Porat (1976: 109–11) argues that the marker by itself does not truly constitute a literary allusion. Instead, an allusion must involve "the activation of indirectly evoked elements from an independent text for the formation of intertextual patterns." It is only once the understanding of the *marker* (the shared element as it appears in the alluding text) and the *marked* (the shared element as it appears in the evoked text) has been modified and a "fuller interpretation" of both achieved that Ben-Porat will concede that an allusion has occurred. See also Carmela Perri 1978: 295–96. Sommer (1998: 16–17) notes, however, that in some examples of borrowing, "the meaning of the marked sign in the source has little effect on a reading of the sign with the marker in the alluding text." He labels this sort of borrowing "echo," to distinguish it from Ben-Porat's category of "allusion." This is similar to the distinction Earl Miner (1993: 39) makes between allusion and "source borrowing." Sommer also distinguishes allusion from "influence" and "exegesis." By influence, he refers to the broader effects of antecedent authors, texts, or traditions, upon a present text. Exegesis, he defines as "an attempt to analyze, explain, or give meaning to (or uncover meaning in) a text" (1998: 14–18).

13 Although Perri's categories of "proper naming" and "definite descriptions" are not helpful, the potential sorts of allusions she lists within them are (1978: 304–5). She notes direct quotation, inclusion of a proper name, echoes of content or form, repetition of a phrase, paraphrase, topical and historical echoes of persons and events, and even echoes of literary styles and conventions.

By narrative tracking, I refer to the process by which one text alludes to another by mimicking its narrative structure.[14] As I illustrate below, in cases of narrative tracking, shared terminology may sometimes signal an allusion; more important, though, are narrative parallels that highlight one text's reliance on the other.

NARRATIVE TRACKING IN MATTHEW'S NATIVITY STORY

Narrative tracking is the sort of allusive technique that is present in settings such as the account of the birth of Jesus in Matthew 1-2. Determined to cast Jesus as the new lawgiver, Matthew (and, importantly, only Matthew) draws parallels between the life of Jesus and the life of Moses.[15] Just as Moses' birth took place under the shadow of Pharaoh's edict to kill the Hebrew boys (Exod 1:15-22), so Matthew suggests, Jesus' birth elicited Herod's edict to kill the boys of Bethlehem (Matt 2:16). As Moses' life was miraculously spared in Egypt (Exod 2:1-10), so Jesus survives by fleeing to Egypt with his parents (Matt 2:13-15, 19–23). When Moses departed from Egypt, he passed through the waters of the Reed Sea (Exod 14-15). The very first story following Jesus' flight to Egypt in Matthew is the account of his passing through the waters of the Jordan at his baptism (Matt 3:1-17). Moses sojourned in the wilderness for forty years. After his baptism, Matthew's Jesus sojourns in the wilderness for forty days (Matt 4:1-11). It is on a mountain in the wilderness that Moses received the Torah

14 This process is similar to what Robert Alter (1989: 119–23) has described as "situational" allusion, the sort of allusion that occurs in passages such as the Israelites' crossing of the Jordan River in Joshua 3. While this text relies heavily on the earlier account of the sea crossing in Exodus 14-15, it does so with only a minimum of terminological overlap. The only genuinely distinctive word shared by the two texts is גֵּד, "heap" (Josh 3:13, 16). Alter identifies another example of situational allusion in William Faulkner's *Absalom, Absalom*. Although Faulkner draws heavily upon the biblical story of David in his characterization of Sutpen, the verbal connections between the two are limited almost exclusively to the novel's title. The main difference between situational allusion and narrative tracking is simply that narrative tracking relies more heavily on parallels in the overall structure and plot of allusively connected texts.

15 Concerning Matthew's portrayal of Jesus as one devoted to Torah observance, see Thomas Blanton 2013. The connections between the birth stories of Moses and Jesus are explored by Raymond Brown (1993: 112–16, 544, 557–62), R. D. Aus (2004), Allan Kensky (1993), John Dominic Crossan (1986), and especially Dale Allison (1993: 140–65).

(Exod 19-24). And in the story that follows Jesus' wilderness experience in Matthew, Jesus delivers the Sermon on the Mount, a sermon devoted largely to the continued authority of the Torah (Matt 5-7).

While the tracking of Matthew's nativity story with the life of Moses is fairly straightforward, features of this allusive connection help to provide methodological guidelines for identifying other, similar allusions. First, it is important to note that the connection between the lives of Matthew's Jesus and the Torah's Moses is not based on shared, distinctive terminology. There are isolated overlaps to be sure. In the Septuagint's rendering of Exod 4:19, for example, Moses is told to return to Egypt because "all those seeking your life are dead" (τεθνήκασιν γὰρ πάντες οἱ ζητοῦντές σου τὴν ψυχήν). Similarly, in Matt 2:20, Joseph is told to return to Israel because "those seeking the life of the child are dead" (τεθνήκασιν γὰρ οἱ ζητοῦντες τὴν ψυχὴν τοῦ παιδίου). For the most part, though, the connection between Matthew and Exodus relies on the extended narrative overlap between the two texts. It is the presence of *parallel events* placed in *parallel order* that alerts us to the fact that the later author has relied on the earlier narrative.

Second, an important signal for identifying this sort of allusion is the presence of parallels that are unusual or distinctive.[16] Much of what links the lives of Jesus and Moses in Matthew is material that is absent from the Lukan account of Jesus' birth in Luke 1-2. Luke's story does not mention Herod's decree against the boys of Bethlehem, nor does it have room for the flight to Egypt.[17] These are distinctively Matthean elements. It is the fact that Matthew stands out from Luke just at the point that he aligns with Exodus that signals his dependence on the Moses stories.

Third, once a link between two texts has been established on the basis of narrative tracking, the likelihood that less obvious parallels between the texts are allusive is naturally increased.[18] When the translators of the

---

16 I have argued elsewhere for the importance of unusual or distinctive parallels when adducing allusions on the basis of terminological overlap (Leonard 2008: 251–52).

17 In Luke's account, Joseph, Mary, and Jesus return to their home in Nazareth immediately after the purification rites for Mary had been completed, that is, only forty days after Jesus' birth (Lk 2:23-23, 39). In Matthew's account, the family is portrayed as being from Bethlehem originally and only moving to Nazareth when circumstances would not permit a return to Judea after the sojourn in Egypt (Matt 2:19-23).

18 In this regard, allusions based on narrative tracking parallel those based on lexical overlap. The accumulation of strong terminological connections between

New Revised Standard Version, for example, describe the men of Gibeah in Judg 19:22 as "a perverse *lot*," we can be sure they are calling our attention to the plight of Abraham's nephew Lot, because Judges 19 and Genesis 19 so obviously parallel one another. In the Matthean example cited above, the baptism of Jesus, when viewed in isolation, has little to commend itself as an allusive passage. Set in the context of leaving Egypt and entering the wilderness, though, the likelihood of a connection with Moses' passing through the waters as he left Egypt and entered the wilderness is greatly increased. Similarly, one cannot help but wonder if the "mount" on which Matthew places Jesus' "Sermon on the Mount" is not an allusion to Mount Sinai, particularly given the fact that Luke describes the same sermon as being delivered on a "flat place" (τόπου πεδινοῦ; Lk 6:17).[19]

NARRATIVE TRACKING IN PSALM 104

Examples of the sort of narrative tracking found in Matthew are as evident in the Tanakh as they are in later interpretive traditions. I would argue it is this allusive style that is found in the creation hymn that is Psalm 104. A connection between Psalm 104 and Genesis 1 could be argued on the basis of their substantial lexical overlap. Both texts are marked by the use of ברא (Gen 1:1, 21, 27 [3x]; Ps 104:30), תהום (Gen 1:2; Ps 104:6), חשׁך (Gen 1:2, 4, 5, 18; Ps 104:20), רוח (Gen 1:2; Ps 104:4), מקום (Gen 1:9; Ps 104:8), עשׂב (Gen 1:11, 12, 29, 30; Ps 104:14), מועדים (Gen 1:14; Ps 104:19), רמשׂ (Gen 1:24, 25, 26; cf. vv. 21, 26, 28, 30; Ps 104:25; cf. v. 20), and עוף השׁמים (Gen 1:26, 28, 30; Ps 104:12). The problem with this approach, though, is that none of the terms shared by the two texts is particularly rare, and none occurs in an extended quotation or even a shared phrase.[20] The language is nothing more than an ordinary collection of terms one would expect in a text describing the natural world.

Given the lack of definitive lexical overlap between the psalm and the priestly narrative, some have denied altogether a direct connection

---

texts weighs in favor of positing connections between other, less certain allusions (Leonard 2008: 253–55).

19 In another context, Luke's reference to a "flat place" could easily allude to the plain where Moses delivered the Law to the Israelites encamped at the foot of the mountain. Without Matthew's emphasis on the Law and his tracking of Jesus' life with the life of Moses, however, an allusion here seems unlikely.

20 While ברא is not rare, it does figure as a distinctive term in P's creation account.

between the two. Hermann Gunkel (1998: 63) conceded a connection between the psalm and Genesis 1 but maintained the psalmist's treatment of the creation theme was so free as to suggest he might have known it in an older form and not as part of the Pentateuch's priestly work. Hans-Joachim Kraus (1989: 298–99) takes this argument a step further, suggesting that the psalmist freely reproduces any number of "primeval themes of tradition" and insisting, for Genesis 1 specifically, "There can hardly be any thought of a literary consultation or even a dependence." These arguments are bolstered by the fact that there are also significant differences between the two texts, most notably the fact that both animals and humans appear much earlier in the psalm (v. 11; in what I argue is a reflex of the third day) than they do in Genesis 1 (vv. 24-31, the sixth day).

Given the lack of definitive terminological overlap, the free treatment of the creation theme by the psalmist, and the significant differences between the psalm and the priestly account, how can the dependence of the former passage on the latter be established? Here, I suggest the answer lies again in the psalmist's narrative tracking of the Genesis account. At point after point, the psalmist can be seen to mirror the structure of the creation account in Genesis 1, recasting it in an expansive poetic style but doing so in such a way that a direct connection between the texts is readily apparent.[21]

In verses 1b-2a, the psalmist echoes the creation of light on the first day of creation:

> You are clothed with honor and majesty,
>   wrapped in light as with a garment.

In verses 2b-4, Day Two's watery dome (רָקִיעַ) and the sky beneath it are recalled:

---

21 Though beyond the scope of this study, there is considerable evidence to suggest Psalm 104 has also been influenced by the Egyptian *Hymn to Aten* (a transcription of the original is available in Sandman 1938); translations are available from Miriam Lichtheim (*COS* 1.26.44-46) and John Wilson (*ANET*, 369–71). Frank Crüsemann (1969) outlines the case for a connection with the Aten hymn, particularly in vv. 20-30. Paul Dion (1991) affirms this connection but maintains the storm imagery in the earlier portions of the psalm derives from Canaanite precedents. Leslie Allen (1983: 29–31) provides a helpful summary of the issues involved.

You stretch out the heavens like a tent,
> you set the beams of your chambers on the waters,[22]

you make the clouds your chariot,
> you ride on the wings of the wind,

you make the winds your messengers,
> fire and flame your ministers.

The psalmist then turns to the creation of land described on the third day. In verses 5–9, he declares:

You set the earth on its foundations,
> so that it shall never be shaken.

You cover it with the deep as with a garment;
> the waters stood above the mountains.

At your rebuke they flee;
> at the sound of your thunder they take to flight.

They rose up to the mountains, ran down to the valleys
> to the place that you appointed for them.

You set a boundary that they may not pass,
> so that they might not again cover the earth.

In this description, the land is envisioned as first being covered with water ("You cover it with the deep as with a garment; the waters stood above the mountains") and emerging only once the waters are gathered "to the place you appointed for them." This forms an exact parallel with the divine command in Gen 1:9: "Let the waters under the sky be gathered together into one place, and let the dry land appear."[23]

---

22 I am indebted to Ziony Zevit who suggested to me in a personal communication that a further connection with Genesis 1's רָקִיעַ may well be found in the subtle aural resonance of the psalmist's כַּיְרִיעָה הַמְקָרֶה in verses 2b–3a.

23 Richard Clifford (1981) argues convincingly that the language of rising up mountains and running down valleys in verse 8 is to be understood as the personification of the waters as warriors fleeing from the divine rebuke in verse 7 to the pit prepared for them (cf. Pss 114:3-6; 77:17). This corresponds perfectly with the depiction in Gen 1:9 of the waters being gathered into one place in response to the divine command. Note that there are also echoes in the psalmist's description of the priestly version of the deluge. The divine blast (גְּעָרָה) and thunder (רַעַם) that drive away the waters in the psalm suggest the wind from God that dries the waters in the priestly Gen 8:1. The psalmist's assurance that the waters will never again cover the earth (בַּל־יְשׁוּבוּן לְכַסּוֹת הָאָרֶץ) connects with the promises, again found only in P, that "never again will there be a flood to destroy the earth" (Gen 9:11) and "the waters shall never again

The parallel with Genesis continues as the psalmist couples the appearance of land with the provision of plants to sustain creation (vv. 14-16):

> You cause the grass to grow for the cattle,
>> and plants for people to use,
> to bring forth food from the earth,
>> and wine to gladden the human heart,
> oil to make the face shine,
>> and bread to strengthen the human heart.
> The trees of the LORD are watered abundantly,
>> the cedars of Lebanon that he planted.

In verse 19, the psalmist moves on to the creation of the heavenly lights, found on the fourth day in Genesis:

> You have made the moon to mark the seasons;
>> the sun knows its time for setting.

Next come the sea and its creatures in verses 25–26, matching the fifth day:

> Yonder is the sea, great and wide,
>> creeping things innumerable are there,
>> living things both small and great.
> There go the ships,
>> and Leviathan that you formed to sport in it.

The creation of animals and humans on the sixth day is less explicit in the psalm, because the psalmist has proleptically included these and the blessings they receive from creation all along the way. Even here, though, the psalmist echoes Genesis 1. In this sixth section of the psalm, verses 27–30, the poet muses:

> These all look to you
>> to give them their food in due season;
> when you give to them, they gather it up;
>> when you open your hand, they are filled with good things.
> When you hide your face, they are dismayed;
>> when you take away their breath, they die and return to their dust.

---

become a flood to destroy all flesh" (Gen 9:15). The fact that this complex of echoes derives solely from priestly materials may suggest the psalmist was working from a priestly text that was not yet joined to the Torah's non-priestly traditions.

> When you send forth your spirit, they are created;
>> and you renew the face of the ground.

Nearly every line of this section parallels language from the sixth day. Describing the plants God has made, Gen 1:29 declares, "*You shall have them for food*," and v. 30 repeats, to these "*I give all the green plants for food*." Psalm 104:27-28 echoes, "These all look to you *to give them their food*." In Gen 1:24, God commands, "Let the *earth* bring forth living creatures of every kind," and verse 30 describes God's creatures as those "in which there is *the breath of life*." Psalm 104 echoes, "When you take away *their breath*, they die and return to *their dust*."

Given the sustained parallels between Psalm 104 and Genesis 1 on the first six days of creation, one cannot help but wonder whether verses 33-35 of the psalm were also part of this allusive pattern:

> I will sing to the LORD as long as I live;
>> I will sing praise to my God while I have being.
> May my meditation be pleasing to him,
>> for I rejoice in the LORD.
> Let sinners be consumed from the earth,
>> and let the wicked be no more.
> Bless the LORD, O my soul. Praise the LORD.

Might these references to singing, meditation and rejoicing be yet another allusion, this time to the otherwise unmentioned seventh day of creation? Might these echo the observance of Shabbat?[24]

The fact that Psalm 104 so precisely mirrors the structure of Genesis 1 argues strongly in favor of a direct connection between the two texts. There are other features, though, which, like the previous example of Matthew's birth narratives, serve to confirm the allusive connection. One of the great distinctives of Genesis 1's creation account is its separation of the creation of light, on day one (v. 3), from the creation of the celestial objects—sun, moon, and stars—on day four (vv. 14-16). The reasons for this separation in Genesis 1 are both structural (the days of Genesis 1's creation are arranged in two parallel panels) and polemical (the God of Israel creates light without the help of the celestial deities of sun, moon, and star).[25]

---

24 Fishbane (1971: 154) makes a similar point concerning a potential allusion to the Sabbath in Job 3's parallel of the priestly creation account (cf. Job 3:13; Gen 2:1-3).

25 See Nahum Sarna (1989: 4-10) who notes both these features.

These features are entirely absent from Psalm 104, yet Genesis 1's unusual order is still preserved.[26]

Psalm 104's mention of Leviathan provides a similar piece of evidence. The defeat of the sea or sea monster is treated as the *precursor* to creation both among Israel's neighbors (e.g., Enuma Elish) and in the biblical literature itself (cf. Pss 74:12-17; 89:7-13). Quite strikingly, Genesis 1 mentions the great sea monsters (הַתַּנִּינִם הַגְּדֹלִים) but waits until Day Five (v. 21) to do so. This unusual placement of these creatures is duplicated in Psalm 104, as the psalmist recalls the creation of Leviathan but not until the fifth section of the psalm (v. 26), paralleling the order in Genesis.[27]

There can be little question that Psalm 104 is written in a more expansive style than Genesis 1, that it differs from Genesis 1 in several respects (such as its allowing animals and humans to enjoy creation almost from the very beginning of creation), or that parts of the psalm appear to have been influenced by the Egyptian Hymn to Aten. As I have argued elsewhere, however, these differences do not—indeed, *cannot*—undermine the potential presence of allusions in areas where psalm does *not* differ from Genesis (Leonard 2008: 249-51).

A psalmist intent on alluding to Genesis 1 would be under no obligation whatsoever to mimic the style of the priestly text, to limit his or her hymnic composition to just those features mentioned there, or to refrain from drawing upon source materials outside of Genesis 1. Further, in a hymn so intently focused on the blessings creation showers upon its creatures, it is no real scandal that the psalmist might choose to narrate the enjoyment

26 As Gerhard von Rad's study of onomastic texts in the biblical orbit (Psalm 148, Ben Sira 11, the Song of the Three Children) and in Egypt (the *Onomasticon* of Amenope) demonstrates, sun, moon, and stars are almost always grouped with heaven and placed at the very beginning of the catalogues of creation's features (von Rad 1966: 282-83). Job 38 departs from this order, but it alludes to the sun only as "morning" (v. 12), "dawn" (v. 12), and "light" (vv. 15, 19), ignores the moon altogether, and includes the constellations, improbably, among meteorological phenomena such as clouds and rain (vv. 25-38). Proverbs 8:22-30 lists features of creation (mountains, hills, depths, etc.) but with little discernable order.

27 Fishbane (1971: 153-54) draws attention to the matter of textual order in his argument that Job 3 relies upon and seeks to undo the account of creation in Genesis 1: "These verses do not constitute a disjunctive lament; their sequence and rhythm are exactly paralleled by the archetypal cosmic pattern of Genesis." By his reckoning, the mention of Leviathan in Job 3:8 is intended to parallel the mention of הַתַּנִּינִם on Day Five of creation.

of those blessings on each day of creation rather than just the sixth. To deny outright the presence of allusions in Psalm 104, it would be necessary to demonstrate that the psalmist either could not or did not draw upon Genesis 1. In the absence of any definitive information concerning the date of the psalm's composition, it cannot be argued that the psalmist *could not have* drawn upon the priestly account. There remains then only the question of whether there is enough evidence *in the areas where these texts do overlap* to affirm or deny a connection between them. It is my contention that the demonstrable narrative tracking of the psalm with the Genesis account, even in areas such as the priestly text's improbable placement of the celestial objects and sea monsters, can only be explained by positing a direct link between the two.

NARRATIVE TRACKING IN PSALM 78

The long rehearsal of Israel's historical traditions found in Psalm 78 provides several instances of narrative tracking. As the following selection of parallels indicates, the terminological overlap between Ps 78:23-31 and Numbers 11 is strong enough to establish the psalmist's direct dependence on the Kibroth Hattaavah narrative:

Psalm 78	Numbers 11
לִשְׁאָל־אֹכֶל לְנַפְשָׁם (v. 18)	מִי יַאֲכִלֵנוּ בָּשָׂר (v. 18) נַפְשֵׁנוּ יְבֵשָׁה (v. 6)
יַסַּע קָדִים בַּשָּׁמָיִם (v. 26)	וְרוּחַ נָסַע מֵאֵת ה׳ (v. 31)
וַיַּפֵּל בְּקֶרֶב מַחֲנֵהוּ סָבִיב לְמִשְׁכְּנֹתָיו (v. 28)	סְבִיבוֹת הַמַּחֲנֶה (v. 31)
וְתַאֲוָתָם יָבֹא לָהֶם לֹא־זָרוּ מִתַּאֲוָתָם (v. 29-30)	Various uses of תאוה (vv. 4, 31, 34)
עוֹד אָכְלָם בְּפִיהֶם (v. 30)	הַבָּשָׂר עוֹדֶנּוּ בֵּין שִׁנֵּיהֶם (v. 33)
וְאַף אֱלֹהִים עָלָה בָהֶם (v. 31)	וְאַף ה׳ חָרָה בָעָם (v. 33)

Importantly though, the order of events in the psalm suggests the psalmist has, like Numbers 11, prefaced the Kibroth Hattaavah story with a reference to the incident at Taberah.

Immediately prior to the psalm's description of the blessing (and curse) that was the provision of meat, we find in verse 21 the psalmist's declaration:

לָכֵן שָׁמַע ה׳ וַיִּתְעַבָּר / וְאֵשׁ נִשְּׂקָה בְיַעֲקֹב / וְגַם־אַף עָלָה בְיִשְׂרָאֵל

Therefore, when the LORD heard, he was full of rage;
  a fire was kindled against Jacob,
  His anger mounted against Israel.

Viewed in isolation, this verse might be regarded as nothing more than one of the Psalter's many poetic descriptions of divine wrath. Tracking with the narrative in Numbers 11, however, the echoes of the Taberah incident are unmistakable:

וַיִּשְׁמַע ה׳ וַיִּחַר אַפּוֹ וַתִּבְעַר־בָּם אֵשׁ ה׳ וַתֹּאכַל בִּקְצֵה הַמַּחֲנֶה

And YHWH heard and was incensed, and a fire from YHWH burned against them and consumed the outskirts of the camp. (Num 11:1; my translation)

It is because the psalmist and the tradent in Numbers 11 place the same events in the same order that a connection between the two can be established. Further, the narrative tracking of the psalm with Numbers 11 points to an allusion even in the texts' shared common terms שָׁמַע, אַף, and אֵשׁ, and gives us near certainty that the psalm's וַיִּתְעַבָּר (עבר*) is a wordplay on Numbers' וַתִּבְעַר and תַּבְעֵרָה (בער*).

In this particular instance, the psalmist who composed Psalm 78 appears to have joined the Taberah and Kibroth Hattaavah incidents together as a means of resolving a dilemma inherent in the Numbers text. While many translations of Numbers 11 offer some variation of "the people complained *about their misfortunes*," the JPS translation is nearer the mark when it says merely, "The people took to complaining *bitterly*." The substance of the people's complaint is never mentioned. What Numbers omits, however, Ps 78:18-20 is only too happy to provide. The psalmist fleshes out the people's bitter complaints to say:

> They tested God in their heart
>   by demanding the food they craved.
> They spoke against God, saying,
>   "Can God spread a table in the wilderness?
> Even though he struck the rock
>   so that water gushed out and torrents overflowed,
> can he also give bread,
>   or provide meat for his people?"

It is this question that the psalmist suggests provoked the fires of Taberah (vv. 21-22):

Therefore, when the LORD heard, he was full of rage;
>> a fire was kindled against Jacob,
>> his anger mounted against Israel,
> because they had no faith in God,
>> and did not trust his saving power.

Though we have the advantage in this passage of distinctive terminological overlap, at least in the Kibroth Hattaavah description, the unusual features in the psalm again underscore the allusive connection. Only here in all of Psalm 78 does the psalmist supply direct speech from the people whose rebellious history he narrates. That this sort of speech would be supplied at the very moment when the corresponding text so obviously needs clarification supports the claim for a textual allusion in this passage.[28]

Narrative tracking also alerts us to Psalm 78's allusion to the so-called Ark Narrative in 1 Samuel 4-6 and 2 Samuel 6. While terminological overlap with the Ark Narrative is almost entirely missing in the relevant portion of the psalm (vv. 59-72), the narrative parallels between the two passages point strongly toward an allusive connection. Verses 59–62 of the psalm track with the Israelites' defeat and loss of the Ark of the Covenant at Ebenezer in 1 Sam 4:1-11a:

> When God heard, he was full of wrath,
>> and he utterly rejected Israel.
> He abandoned his dwelling at Shiloh,
>> the tent where he dwelt among mortals,
> and delivered his power to captivity,
>> his glory to the hand of the foe.
> He gave his people to the sword,
>> and vented his wrath on his heritage.

Verses 63–64 echo the deaths of Hophni and Pinchas and the mourning of Pinchas' wife that was cut short by her death in premature childbirth (1 Sam 4:11b-22):

> Fire devoured their young men,
>> and their girls had no marriage song.
> Their priests fell by the sword,
>> and their widows made no lamentation.

28 This attempt by the psalmist to fill a gap in the underlying source text fits well with the criteria David Carr (2001) proposes for determining the direction of an allusion. Carr draws special attention to expansions in the form of direct speech.

Verses 65–66 match the humiliation of the Philistines in 1 Sam 5:1-12:

> The Lord awoke as from sleep,
>> like a warrior shaking off wine.
> He struck his foes behind,
>> dealing them lasting disgrace. (JPS)

The tracking of the psalmist's account with the narrative in 1 Samuel high-lights his clever allusion, וַיַּךְ־צָרָיו אָחוֹר, to the hemorrhoids visited upon the Philistines (1 Sam 5:9, 12).

Verses 67–68 reflect the detail that though the ark was returned by the Philistines to Israel in 1 Samuel 6, it did not return to Shiloh. Instead its bovine porters carried it to Beth Shemesh, where it awaited David's trans-fer to Jerusalem (2 Sam 6).

> He rejected the tent of Joseph,
>> he did not choose the tribe of Ephraim;
> but he chose the tribe of Judah,
>> Mount Zion, which he loves.
> He built his sanctuary like the high heavens,
>> like the earth, which he has founded forever.
> He chose his servant David,
>> and took him from the sheepfolds.

Importantly, the fact that Psalm 78 includes this transfer to Judah lends support to Leonhard Rost's suggestion (1982: 6–34) that the Ark Narrative originally extended to include 2 Samuel 6 as well.[29]

CONCLUSION

There can be little doubt that allusions based on shared distinctive ter-minology will continue to stand out as those most confidently identified in terms of their presence and most confidently traced in terms of their direction of dependence. A focus on features such as narrative tracking

---

29 See also Martin Noth (1991: 76–85), P. Kyle McCarter (1980: 14–17), and Frank Moore Cross (1973: 274–89). John Van Seters (1983: 346–53) and K. A. D. Smelik (1989) are among those who challenge the notion of a separate Ark Narrative. Patrick Miller and J. J. M. Roberts (1977) acknowledge the independence of the Ark Narrative but deny that 2 Samuel 6 was joined to 1 Samuel 4-6 as part of this early work. Erik Eynikel (2000: 88–106) surveys the arguments for and against the Ark Narrative's dependence on 1 Samuel 1-3.

can nevertheless draw attention to other, less obvious textual allusions, and can lend support to allusive connections based only on common terms or wordplays.

While the historical psalms remain a fruitful area of research for these sorts of connections, narrative tracking holds promise for tracing or suggesting connections in other areas of biblical and extrabiblical literature as well. The clear parallel to the exodus in Gen 12:10-20, for example, could easily be categorized as an example of narrative tracking.[30] A less certain but more tantalizing suggestion would be the possibility that the Yahwist's primeval history tracks with the Epic of Gilgamesh. The similarities between the stories are well-known: the loss of immortality, the complicity of a serpent in that process, the story of the flood, the release of raven and dove to test the receding waters, the presence of heroes and heroic deeds—all of these suggest some sort of connection between the two corpora. The parallel manner in which the two works conclude also points toward an allusive relationship. The Yahwist's Primeval History culminates with the building of Babel, not the Tower—though this feature generally garners the most attention—but the city. In Gen 11:4 the people call out, "Come let us build *a city* and a tower" (v. 4). The narrator then describes the divine response as, "And YHWH went down to see *the city* and the tower" (v. 5). And when the people are scattered, the author notes, "And they ceased building *the city*" (v. 8). The city is mentioned without the tower; the tower is never mentioned without the city. This is because it is the city—not the tower—that the people build to make a name for themselves. The Yahwist's primeval narrative culminates in humanity's misplaced hopes in a city.

Importantly, it is in a city that the Gilgamesh Epic ends as well. Having lost his bid for immortality to the serpent, Gilgamesh wanders back home disconsolate. The epic narrates:[31]

> Then Gilgamesh sat down and wept,
> down his cheeks the tears were coursing.

---

30 Abraham Malamat (1970: 1-16) makes a similar case for understanding the account of the Danites' migration to northern Canaan as "a sort of diminutive model of a campaign of inheritance, which pattern appears on the national scale in the Exodus and pan-Israelite Conquest cycles" (1970: 1). The extensive parallels Malamat draws between the Danite migration and the Israelites' departure from Egypt could readily be considered under the heading of narrative tracking.

31 Translation adapted from Andrew George (2003: 99).

> He spoke to Ur-shanabi the boatman:
> "For whom, Ur-shanabi, toiled my arms so hard,
> for whom ran dry the blood of my heart?
> Not for myself did I find a bounty,
> for the 'Lion of the Earth' I have done a favour!"

The hero's mood changes just a few lines later, however, when at last Gilgamesh spies the city of Uruk which he built:

> When they arrived in Uruk-the-Sheepfold,
> said Gilgamesh to him, to Ur-shanabi the boatman:
> "O Ur-shanabi, climb Uruk's wall and walk back and forth!
> Survey its foundations, examine the brickwork!
> Were its bricks not fired in an oven?
> Did the Seven Sages not lay its foundations?
> A square mile is city, a square mile date-grove, a square mile is
> clay-pit, half a square mile the temple of Ishtar"

In this scene, Gilgamesh finally finds his immortality; he finds it in the city of Uruk that he built. But this is an immortality the Yahwist rejects. The Yahwist's narrative tracks with the Gilgamesh Epic, but it offers a contrary message in its vision of how humans were meant to live.

The connections between the Gilgamesh Epic and Genesis 1-11 constitute ground that has been regularly plowed while yielding only very tentative results. The culmination of these two works in a story of hopes placed in a city may well turn out to be just another disappointing coincidental overlap. Whether this proves to be the case or not, however, there can be little question that the lens of narrative tracking opens up new and potentially important avenues for researching the issue.

BIBLIOGRAPHY

Allen, Leslie C. 1983. *Psalms 101-150*. Word Biblical Commentary, 21. Waco: Word Books.

Allison, Dale C. 1993. *The New Moses: A Matthean Typology*. Minneapolis, MN.: Fortress Press.

Alter, Robert. 1989. *The Pleasures of Reading: In an Ideological Age*. New York: Simon and Schuster.

Attridge, H. W. 1989. *The Epistle to the Hebrews: A Commentary on the Epistle to the Hebrews*. Hermeneia. Philadelphia: Fortress.

Aus, R. D. 2004. *Matthew 1-2 and the Virginal Conception: In Light of Palestinian and Hellenistic Judaic Traditions on the Birth of Israel's First Redeemer, Moses*. Studies in Judaism. Lanham, MD: University Press of America.

Ben-Porat, Ziva. 1976. "The Poetics of Literary Allusion." *PTL: A Journal for Descriptive Poetics and Theory* 1: 105–28.

Blanton, Thomas R. 2013. "Saved by Obedience: Matthew 1:21 in Light of Jesus' Teaching on the Torah." *Journal of Biblical Literature* 132: 393–413.

Brettler, Marc Z. 1999. "Judaism in the Hebrew Bible? The Transition from Ancient Israelite Religion to Judaism." *Catholic Biblical Quarterly* 61: 429–47.

Brettler, Marc Z. 2003. Review of James W. Watts, ed., *Persia and Torah: The Theory of Imperial Authorization of the Pentateuch* and Gabriel Boccaccini, *Roots of Rabbinic Judaism: An Intellectual History, from Ezekiel to Daniel. Journal of Religion* 83: 317–19.

Brettler, Marc Z. 2007. "The Poet as Historian: The Plague Tradition in Psalm 105." In *Bringing the Hidden to Light: The Process of Interpretation: Studies in Honor of Stephen A. Geller*, edited by Kathryn F. Kravitz and Diane M. Sharon, 19–28. Winona Lake, IN: Eisenbrauns.

Brettler, Marc Z. 2013. "Psalm 136 as an Interpretive Text." *Hebrew Bible and Ancient Israel* 2: 373–95.

Brooke, George J. 2010. "Genre Theory, Rewritten Bible and Pesher." *Dead Sea Discoveries* 17: 332–57.

Brown, Raymond Edward. 1993. *The Birth of the Messiah: A Commentary on the Infancy Narratives in the Gospels of Matthew and Luke.* Anchor Bible Reference Library. New York: Doubleday.

Carr, David M. 2001. "Method in Determination of Direction of Dependence: An Empirical Test of Criteria Applied to Exodus 34, 11–26 and its Parallels." In *Gottes Volk am Sinai: Untersuchungen zu Ex 32-34 und Dtn 9-10*, edited by Matthias Köckert and Erhard Blum, 107–140. Gütersloh: Chr. Kaiser.

Clifford, Richard J. 1981. "A Note on Ps 104:5-9." *Journal of Biblical Literature* 100: 87–89.

Crawford, Sidnie White. 2008. *Rewriting Scripture in Second Temple Times.* Studies in the Dead Sea Scrolls and Related Literature. Grand Rapids: Eerdmans.

Cross, Frank Moore. 1973. *Canaanite Myth and Hebrew Epic: Essays in the History of the Religion of Israel.* Cambridge, MA: Harvard University Press.

Crossan, J. D. 1986. "From Moses to Jesus: Parallel Themes." *Bible Review* 2: 18–27.

Crüsemann, Frank. 1969. *Studien zur Formgeschichte von Hymnus und Danklied in Israel.* Edited by Günther Bornkamm and Gerhard von Rad. Wissenschaftliche Monographien zum Alten und Neuen Testament, 32. Neukirchen-Vluyn: Neukirchener Verlag.

Dion, Paul E. 1991. "YHWH as Storm-god and Sun-god: The Double Legacy of Egypt and Canaan as Reflected in Psalm 104." *Zeitschrift für die alttestamentliche Wissenschaft* 103: 43–71.

Eynikel, Erik. 2000. "The Relation between the Eli Narratives (1 Sam. 1-4) and the Ark Narrative (1 Sam. 1-6; 2 Sam. 6:1-19)." In *Past, Present, Future: The Deuteronomistic History and the Prophets*, edited by Johannes C. De Moor and Harry F. van Rooy, 88–106. Leiden: Brill.

Feldman, Ariel, and Liora Goldman. 2014. *Scripture and Interpretation: Qumran Texts that Rework the Bible.* Edited by John Barton, Reinhard G. Kratz and Markus Witte. Beihefte zur Zeitschrift für die alttestamentliche Wissenschaft, 449. Berlin: Walter de Gruyter.

Fishbane, Michael A. 1971. "Jeremiah 4:23-26 and Job 3:3-13: A Recovered Use of the Creation Pattern." *Vetus Testamentum* 21: 151–67.

Fishbane, Michael A. 1985. *Biblical Interpretation in Ancient Israel*. Oxford: Clarendon.

Fitzmyer, Joseph A. 2000. "Melchizedek in the MT, LXX, and the NT." *Biblica* 81: 63–69.

George, Andrew R. 2003. *The Epic of Gilgamesh: The Babylonian Epic Poem and Other Texts in Akkadian and Sumerian, translated and with an introduction by Andrew George*. Penguin Classics. London/New York: Penguin Books.

Granerød, Gard. 2010. *Abraham and Melchizedek: Scribal Activity of Second Temple Times in Genesis 14 and Psalm 110*. Beihefte zur Zeitschrift für die alttestamentliche Wissenschaft, 406. Berlin: Walter de Gruyter.

Gunkel, Hermann, and Joachim Begrich. 1998. *Introduction to the Psalms: The Genres of Religious Lyric of Israel*. Translated by James D. Nogalski. Mercer Library of Biblical Studies. Macon, GA: Mercer University Press. [Original edition: *Einleitung in die Psalmen: die Gattungen der religiösen Lyrik Israels*. In Göttingen Handkommentar zum Alten Testament. Göttingen: Vandenhoeck and Ruprecht, 1985, 1933.]

Horton, Fred L. 1976. *The Melchizedek tradition: A Critical Examination of the Sources to the Fifth Century A.D. and in the Epistle to the Hebrews*. Society for New Testament Studies Monograph Series, 30. Cambridge: Cambridge University Press.

de Jonge, Marinus, and Adam S. van der Woude. 1966. "11Q Melchizedek and the New Testament." *New Testament Studies* 12: 301–26.

Kensky, Allan. 1993. "Moses and Jesus: The Birth of the Savior." *Judaism: A Quarterly Journal of Jewish Life and Thought* 42: 43–49.

Kobelski, Paul J. 1981. *Melchizedek and Melchireša'*. Catholic Biblical Quarterly Monograph Series, 10. Washington, D.C.: Catholic Biblical Association of America.

Kraus, Hans-Joachim. 1989. *Psalms 60-150: A Continental Commentary*. Translated by Hilton C. Oswald. Minneapolis: Fortress. [Original edition: *Psalmen*, Teilband 2, Psalmen 60-150, in the Biblischer Kommentar series. Neukirchen-Vluyn: Neukirchener Verlag, 1961/1978.]

Lemmelijn, Bénédicte. 2002. "The So-Called 'Priestly' Layer in Exod 7,14-11,10: 'Source' and/or/nor 'Redaction'?" *Revue Biblique* 109: 481–511.

Leonard, Jeffery M. 2006. "Historical Traditions in Psalm 78." Ph.D. diss., The Near Eastern and Judaic Studies Department, Brandeis University, Waltham, MA.

Leonard, Jeffery M. 2008. "Identifying Inner-Biblical Allusions: Psalm 78 as a Test Case." *Journal of Biblical Literature* 127: 241–65.

Loewenstamm, Samuel E. 1992. *The Evolution of the Exodus Tradition*. Translated by Baruch J. Schwartz. Jerusalem: Magnes.

Malamat, Abraham. 1970. "The Danite Migration and the Pan-Israelite Exodus-Conquest: A Biblical Narrative Pattern." *Biblica* 51: 1–16.

Mason, Eric F. 2005. "Hebrews 7:3 and the Relationship between Melchizedek and Jesus." *Biblical Research* 50: 41–62.

McCarter, P. Kyle. 1980. *I Samuel*. Anchor Bible, 8. Garden City, NJ: Doubleday.

Miller, Geoffrey D. 2011. "Intertextuality in Old Testament Research." *Currents in Biblical Research* 9: 283–309.

Miller, Patrick D., Jr., and J. J. M. Roberts. 1977. *The Hand of the Lord: A Reassessment of the "Ark Narrative" of 1 Samuel*. Johns Hopkins Near Eastern Studies. Baltimore: Johns Hopkins University Press.

Miner, Earl. 1993. "Allusion." In *The New Princeton Encyclopedia of Poetry and Poetics*, edited by Alex Preminger and T. V. F. Brogan, 38–40. Princeton, NJ: Princeton University Press.

Noth, Martin. 1991. *The Deuteronomistic History*, 2nd edition. Journal for the Study of the Old Testament: Supplement Series, 15. Sheffield: Sheffield Academic Press. [Original edition, *Überlieferungsgeschichtliche Studien*, pp. 1–110 in the 2nd edition. Tübingen: Max Niemeyer Verlag, 1957.]

Perri, Carmela. 1978. "On Alluding." *Poetics* 7: 289–307.

Propp, William H. C. 1998. *Exodus 1-18*. Anchor Bible, 2. New York: Doubleday.

Römer, Thomas C. 2011. "Extra-Pentateuchal Biblical Evidence for the Existence of a Pentateuch? The Case of the 'Historical Summaries,' especially in the Psalms." In *The Pentateuch*, edited by Thomas B. Dozeman, Konrad Schmid and Baruch J. Schwartz, 471–88. Tübingen: Mohr Siebeck.

Rost, Leonhard. 1982. *The Succession to the Throne of David*. Translated by Michael D. Rutter and David M. Gunn. Edited by J. W. Rogerson. Historic Texts and Interpreters in Biblical Scholarship. Sheffield: The Almond Press.

Sandman, Maj. 1938. *Texts from the Time of Akhenaten, Bibliotheca ægyptiaca*. Bruxelles: Édition de la Fondation égyptologique Reine Élisabeth.

Sarna, Nahum M. 1963. "Psalm 89: A Study in Inner Biblical Exegesis." In *Biblical and Other Studies*, edited by Alexander Altmann, 29–46. Cambridge, MA: Harvard University Press.

Sarna, Nahum M. 1989. *Genesis / Be-reshit: The Traditional Hebrew Text with New JPS Translation*. JPS Torah Commentary. Philadelphia: Jewish Publication Society.

Smelik, K. A. D. 1989. "The Ark Narrative Reconsidered." In *New Avenues in the Study of the Old Testament*, edited by A. S. van der Woude, 128–44. Leiden: Brill.

Sommer, Benjamin D. 1998. *A Prophet Reads Scripture: Allusion in Isaiah 40-66*. Stanford: Stanford University Press.

Van Seters, John. 1983. *In Search of History: Historiography in the Ancient World and the Origins of Biblical History*. New Haven, London: Yale University Press.

von Rad, Gerhard. 1966. "Job xxxviii and Ancient Egyptian Wisdom." In *The Problem of the Hexateuch and Other Essays*, 281–91. Edinburgh: Oliver and Boyd. [Original edition: *Gesammelte Studien zum Alten Testament*. Munich: Kaiser Verlag, 1958.]

Chapter 7

Literary Allusions and Assumptions about Textual Familiarity

JOEL S. BADEN[*]

INTRODUCTION

Those of us engaged in the literary-historical investigation of the Hebrew Bible are the world champions of discovering and defending, often quite vigorously, various claims of textual dependence: the argument that a given text could not have existed without, was written in relation to, and, often, cannot be understood without reference to, an earlier text. The first of these claims, that one text could not have existed without another preceding it, is often the most straightforward to make, if not necessarily the easiest to defend. I am perfectly willing to posit that the priestly account of creation in Genesis 1 could not have existed without Enuma Elish, in either its written or oral form. Yet when it comes to the second claim of dependence, I have to abandon ship: I do not think, as many scholars do, that Genesis 1 was written in conscious relation to Enuma Elish, as political or theological polemic.[1] On the other hand, I am certainly willing to embrace that possibility when it comes to the relationship between the Covenant Code and the Laws of Hammurabi. Although I may not be entirely convinced, I think it quite plausible that not only could the Covenant Code not

* Joel S. Baden is Professor of Hebrew Bible at Yale University Divinity School, New Haven, Connecticut.

1 See, for example, the fairly standard view as classically articulated by Kapelrud 1974. The basic statement is this: "In P's creation story the whole frame is of Babylonian origin, but the main ideas are markedly of another kind, consciously set up against the polytheistic account in Enuma elish" (1974: 186).

have existed without Hammurabi having existed first, but the Covenant Code may well have been composed with Hammurabi, the literary document, explicitly in mind (Wright 2009).

The first claim, that an earlier text necessarily preceded the one in question, is argued and defended largely on broad grounds: the story is so similar that there must be some sort of relationship, or there are aspects of the text that are uniquely suited to one cultural background such that when the text appears elsewhere we can assume some sort of borrowing, that sort of thing. No one in Canaan was terrified of destruction by means of excess water; hence the Flood story must have been borrowed from some culture that was. The second claim, that one text was written in relation to another, is argued and defended on closer literary grounds: there is such structural parallelism that, as has been argued for the Covenant Code and Hammurabi, it is hard to imagine the two arising independently; or the narrative is so close, or the wording so nearly verbatim, et cetera.

Though we may argue about what constitutes dependence, we are generally arguing over specific and identifiable features of our respective texts, be they broad features or closely delimited ones. But when it comes to that third claim—that one text cannot be understood without reference to the text upon which it is dependent—there is, I think, far less "objective" evidence on which to rely. Because what is at stake here is the question not of what the text says, but of how the text works.

I am not interested here in the question of whether we, as scholars, can understand the composition and history and cultural background and whatever else about a text we may be interested in. No scholar would try to understand the history of the Covenant Code, for instance, without at least engaging the parallels in form and structure and content with Hammurabi, and indeed with all sorts of other ancient legal materials too. The question I am interested in is not about scholarly inquiry, but about the audience imagined by the original author or authors. We, with our historical interests, were never the intended target of these texts.

And yet it is increasingly observed that we try far too often to make the intended audience of a given text into the ancient equivalent of a modern-day biblical scholar. This is the well-known problem of the ideal reader: we imagine that the ancient audience (or, for that matter, even the modern non-scholarly audience) comes to the text armed with BDB, and ABD, and Even-Shoshan.[2] But we know that this ideal reader never existed. Indeed, we are pushing the edges of probability when we imagine

---

2 On the problem of the ideal reader, see the classic work of Iser 1978.

even the ideal author: the author who produces a text that can be indexed against all of the knowledge of the ancient world that we moderns have accumulated.

But let us, for this purpose at least, assume a near-ideal author. What kind of text would an ancient author produce? What kinds of references would that author make, and to what ends? And, of those references, what would that author expect the audience of the work to appreciate? To put it in a sentence: what should we expect an ancient author to have expected his or her audience to have known, and how do those expectations change our scholarly evaluations of the literary relationships between the text in question and its literary referents?

TEXTUAL DEPENDENCE AND ALLUSION IN D

Although such questions could be asked about Genesis 1 and Enuma Elish, or about the Covenant Code and Hammurabi, I want to concentrate on a different and broader corpus: the pentateuchal document D and its relationship to non-priestly texts in Genesis–Numbers.[3] The fact of D's dependence on its non-priestly textual antecedents, both in terms of those non-priestly texts being necessary prerequisites and in terms of D's composition in intentional relationship with the non-priestly texts, has been demonstrated, amply and convincingly to my mind, both for the legal and the narrative portions of D.[4] This allows us to turn directly to the third issue of textual dependence mentioned above: what sort of knowledge of the non-priestly pentateuchal texts did the author of D imagine, or require, his readership to have in order to understand his new literary product?

---

3 Of all the many points of disagreement among pentateuchal scholars, the existence and broad identification of the D document, which comprises the vast majority of the biblical book of Deuteronomy, is thankfully not one of them. Nor is the existence of identifiably priestly material in Genesis-Numbers— which is also to say the existence of identifiably non-priestly material in Genesis-Numbers. Beyond such platitudes, unfortunately, the happy consensus evaporates rather quickly. Whether D is unified or layered, and how many layers there may be, and when it/they is/are to be dated, and whether the non-priestly texts are unified or layered, and how many layers or sources there may be, and when they are to be dated, both with respect to each other and with respect to the priestly and deuteronomic writings—these (barely) deeper issues remain unresolved within the field.

4 For legal texts, see Levinson 1988; for narrative, see the following discussion.

There are, generally speaking, three levels of literary reference in D to the preexisting non-priestly texts. There is broad retelling of the non-priestly story—for example, the D re-narration of the theophany and law-giving at Horeb (Deut 4:10-13; 5:1-28; 9:8-21, 25-10:5). There is ostensibly direct reference to that which has already and only taken place in that nonpriestly account; for example, when Moses says to the Israelites, "May Yahweh bless you as he said to you" (כאשר דבר לכם) (Deut 1:11). And there is allusion to events that have taken place only in the nonpriestly account; for example, the simple mention of the events that took place at Taberah, Massah, and Kivrot-hatta'avah (Deut 9:22). Each of these types of reference entails a different potential set of assumptions and expectations.

THE HOREB NARRATIVE

The deuteronomic presentation of the Horeb episode is unambiguously dependent on the nonpriestly story of the theophany in the wilderness, or, more accurately, on the one of the nonpriestly stories of the theophany in the wilderness that I and a handful of others call E, but which is identifiably distinct from the priestly and nonpriestly Sinai strands in any case.[5] D in this narrative is not only dependent on but also written in direct relationship to the nonpriestly Horeb story, as the structural identity and manifold near-verbatim clauses make clear.[6] Perhaps even more compelling in this regard is not the similarity between the two, but the major difference: whereas in the story in Exodus the culmination of the encounter is the transmission and reception of the law of the Covenant Code (Exod 20:19-23:32; 24:3-8), in Deuteronomy this major moment is effectively elided. God does give Moses a set of laws—"I will give you all the *mitzvot* and the *huqqim* and the *mishpatim* that you will teach them" (Deut 5:28)—but they are not transmitted to the people at Horeb, and there is no covenant ceremony to seal the deal. All of Exodus 21-24, essentially, is condensed into that single verse in Deut 5:28.

5 For the argument for the existence of E, see Baden 2012: 103–28. For those working from the perspective that there is no such source as E, but who still recognize the distinctiveness of the Horeb narrative in Exodus 19-24, 32-34 over against the priestly and nonpriestly Sinai traditions, see, e.g., Blum 2011.

6 There are those scholars who view the dependence as working the other way, with the nonpriestly passage in Exodus–Numbers being dependent on the passages in D; see, e.g., Rose 1981; Johnstone 1998; Perlitt 1990. For a response to such arguments, see Baden 2011.

As most everyone from the halls of Montezuma to the shores of Tripoli has recognized, the effect of this condensation is to replace the laws of the Covenant Code with those of D: the story is now changed so that the laws that God gave to Moses at Horeb were held by Moses until this moment, in the plains of Moab, on the last day of Moses's life, before Israel enters the promised land.[7] This rather clear rejection of the central claim of the Exodus account speaks strongly in favor of D being a consciously dependent composition. We with our diachronic scholarly understandings of these sorts of things look at this and say, "Aha! The author of D is rejecting the claims of the nonpriestly author in Exodus; this is polemical, and that polemic is, in fact, the agenda here: the denial of the Covenant Code is the object of this retelling of the narrative."[8]

But I would suggest that we are too quick to identify polemic with literary intent. Or, at the very least, we are too quick to read arguments as negative rather than as positive. Imagine being a reader of D with no knowledge of the existence of the Covenant Code whatsoever. Would D's argument be incomprehensible? Hardly. Any reader of D will come to the correct conclusion that what this author wants us to think is that the laws provided here, in Deuteronomy 12–26, are the laws that were given by God to Moses at Horeb: these and no others. After all, God says to Moses at Horeb, "I will give you the mitzvot and the huqqim and the mishpatim that you will teach them for them to observe in the land that I am giving them to possess" (Deut 5:28); and then when Moses begins his legal discourse in the plains of Moab in Deuteronomy 12, he begins with: "These are the huqqim and mishpatim that you must be careful to observe in the land that Yahweh, the God of your fathers, is giving you to possess" (Deut 12:1). Who could conclude anything other than that these laws in Deuteronomy are the laws given at Horeb?

---

7 See, for example, Weinfeld 1991: 19: "[The author of Deuteronomy] makes quite clear that at Sinai the Decalogue was proclaimed, whereas the law proper was given to Israel by Moses on the plains of Moab. In other words, Deuteronomy would be seen as replacing the old book of the covenant and not as complementing it."

8 See, for example, Eissfeldt 1965: 220–23. See his statement: "These historical examples [i.e., the repetitions of the narratives from Exodus–Numbers, including the description of the events of Horeb] are certainly intended to strengthen the exhortations too, but the compiler is in them following yet another purpose, namely to make the older Pentateuch narrative in which B [i.e., the Covenant Code] is embedded superfluous, or at any rate to correct it and to lead to its being understood in a particular sense" (1965: 221).

The positive argument of D is present and immediately perceptible even without its negative counterpart: the claim that the laws of the Covenant Code were not given at Horeb. For any reader who is familiar with the Covenant Code and its narrative framework, of course, the polemic will be striking and unavoidable. But we must remember that the polemic, here and, I suggest, almost everywhere, exists not for its own sake, but in service of a positive program.

And note too that as clear as the anti-Covenant Code polemic might seem to us, it is entirely implicit in D. Nowhere does D acknowledge that there is an alternative view; D simply states that its claims are the right ones (to the implicit exclusion of any others that might be out there). Similarly, at no point in this paper have I made reference to those scholars who might think that in fact D is comprehensible only when read alongside the Covenant Code, the very story and legal block that it is trying to replace. I think that my arguments are strong enough that I need not attempt to tear down any alternative claims. But if you happen to have read some other scholarship, you might recognize that I am implicitly arguing against a position even while I am couching the entire discourse as an argument in favor of a position.[9]

THE כאשר CLAUSE

The type of full-scale narrative retelling that we find in the Horeb episode in D is perhaps the easiest sort of literary reference to deal with; after all, the story is told again essentially in full, so that there is no need for a reader to know any previous versions of the story to understand what is happening. The author, in other words, need have no expectations regarding the reader's knowledge. But what about a case like Deut 1:11: "May Yahweh, the God of your fathers, increase your numbers a thousandfold, and bless you as he promised you" (כאשר דבר לכם)?

This verse ostensibly assumes that the reader is familiar both with the fact that Yahweh had once promised that Israel would be a numerous people and with the circumstances of that promise. The seeming casualness of the reference here might lead us to suspect that the author of D

---

9 I am now at liberty to provide references to such scholarship, which argues that we understand D correctly only if we read it alongside and as a sort of commentary on the Covenant Code. See, most prominently, the work of Eckart Otto, conveniently summarized in a recent article (Otto 2013).

not only knows the patriarchal narratives himself, but expects his readers also to know them. After all, the כאשר clause does appear to demand a known referent, as it does, for instance, in the very next use, Deut 1:19: "we set out from Horeb ... as Yahweh our God had commanded us" (כאשר צוה יהוה אלהינו אתנו), an undeniable reference back to God's command in Deut 1:6-7, "Yahweh our God spoke to us at Horeb, saying, 'You have stayed long enough at this mountain; set out and go to the hill country of the Amorites."

It would seem a stretch to argue that the reference back to the patriarchal promise in Deut 1:11 does not entail some expectation that the reader is familiar with that patriarchal promise.[10] Then again, there are other places where a כאשר clause seems to be creating narrative, rather than simply recalling it. In Deut 10:8-9, we learn that "at that time"—that is, either at Jotbath, the last stop from Deut 10:7, or at Horeb, where the main part of the story in this chapter takes place—it was decided that the Levites would carry the ark and serve Yahweh and bless in Yahweh's name, and that they would receive no inheritance because Yahweh is their portion: "as Yahweh your God said concerning them," (כאשר דבר יהוה אלהיך לו). If this כאשר clause refers to the decision to separate out the Levites, then it is difficult to pin down the prior narrative to which it might point. Parts of this statement look similar to bits of P, but other parts are emphatically not so.[11] The timing, if at Horeb, might align it with the nonpriestly

10 The only circumstance in which such familiarity is not assumed is if one holds to the theory that the entire notion of the patriarchal promise as expressed in Genesis is a post-D development, and that when D refers to the "fathers" it means the generation of the Exodus; see the standard argument for this position by Römer 1990.

11 Similar to P is the claim that it is the responsibility of the Levites to carry the ark (cf. Numbers 4), the notion that the Levites have received no hereditary lands in Israel (cf. Num 18:23-24), and some of the language: הבדיל (cf. Num 8:14); לעמוד לפני...לשרת (cf. Num 16:9); חלק and נחלה (cf. Num 18:20). Contrasts with P include the idea that the Levites as a whole will carry the ark, rather than specifically the Kohathites; the designation of the ark as "the ark of the covenant of Yahweh" rather than the "ark of the עדות"; the shift from standing לפני העדה to minister to the community in Num 16:9 to standing לפני יהוה to minister to Yahweh himself in Deut 10:8, a notion that P could hardly tolerate; the description of the Levites as blessing in Yahweh's name, a role that in P is reserved for Aaron and his sons (6:23-27); and the idea that Yahweh is the replacement for the Levites' territorial inheritance, which stands in significant opposition to the claim of P that for the Levites it is the tithe that replaces their inheritance (Num 18:24), while Yahweh is the replacement only for Aaron and his sons (Num 18:20).

narrative in Exod 32:26-29, but the content is entirely mismatched.[12] If, somewhat more restrictively, we take the כאשר clause to refer only to the immediately preceding clause, the statement that the Levites would not inherit because Yahweh is their portion, we are faced with a similar problem: nowhere in the text prior to this has such a claim been made for the Levites, by D or anyone else.[13] In other words, what D says happened here כאשר דבר יהוה is in fact not narrated anywhere else. This is a D innovation, couched in כאשר language.

This is not to suggest, of course, that in Deut 1:11 D is innovating the patriarchal promise. It is, however, to point out that there need not be any known literary antecedent for such a reference. If we did not have the patriarchal narratives, if all we had was D, would we find the statement in Deut 1:11 to be utterly confusing? Surely not: we would take it as a point of new information. At some point in the past, Yahweh must have promised the Israelites that they would increase greatly.[14] It is worth noting that the

---

12 According to Exod 32:26-29, the Levites were selected for their cultic service in the period between Moses's destruction of the first set of tablets (Exod 32:19) and his return up the mountain for the second set (34:1). Although the chronology of Deut 10:1-11 is decidedly convoluted, the coordination of the installation of the Levites in 10:8-9 with the ascent of Moses to receive the second set of tablets in 10:10 (which summarizes the events narrated in more detail in 10:1-5) is at the very least suggestive. Deuteronomy never recounts the episode of Exod 32:26-29, even while it rehashes virtually every detail of the surrounding story. If this brief narrative allusion in Deut 10:8-9 is in fact to the pseudo-ordination of the Levites as a result of their zealotry, we may wonder whether D is intentionally downplaying the violent origins of Levite service, in part perhaps because the elevation of the Levites is a central part of the deuteronomic program. See Weinfeld 1991: 420: "vv. 8-9 here seem to presuppose the events as presented in Exod 32"; cf. also Nelson 2002: 128 and Tigay 1996: 106. At the same time, however, Deut 10:8-9 does not allude in any way to the events described in Exod 32:26-29, in which the Levites rally to Moses and slaughter their fellow Israelites; nor does Exod 32:26-29 make any mention of their role carrying the ark or their hereditary disenfranchisement.

13 The closest parallel is Num 18:20, where the priests—Aaron's descendants, not the Levites, a distinction clear in the P source and famously elided in D—are told that Yahweh is their portion.

14 It is worth noting that, for those scholars who believe that the "fathers" in D to whom the promise of land was given are not the patriarchs of Genesis but rather the generation of the Exodus, this is precisely what is assumed: these references to the promise are not referring the reader back to the promise texts in Exodus–Numbers, but rather serve to tell the reader that this promise was in fact given to the previous generation. See the comment of Römer with

references to the patriarchal promise in D always serve a clear rhetorical purpose: they support, in virtually every case, the deuteronomic demand for covenantal obedience.[15] In this sense, כאשר authorizes a new narrative claim in the same way that, in Chronicles and Ezra-Nehemiah, ככתוב or כמשפט authorizes a new legal claim.[16] Functionally, כאשר phrases, like all types of analepsis, do not direct the reader back to a previous narrative, even when such a narrative exists; they serve to exempt the reader from having to make recourse to a previous narrative.[17] They may refer to something that has in fact been narrated—and indeed they most often do—but they need not do so.

When D makes reference to the patriarchal promise, we might note, it is never in the style of "Remember what Yahweh your God promised your ancestors," full stop. Whether the reference is to progeny, or possession of the land, or blessing of various sorts, the content of the promise is always restated. D tells the reader what God promised the patriarchs—indeed, D sometimes tells us that God promised the patriarchs things that, in the text of Genesis-Numbers, God never really promises the patriarchs—wealth, for example.[18] D's references need not be tied back to a particular preexisting

---

regard to Deut 1:11: "Ob man dieses כאשר דבר לכם auf einen bestimmten Text beziehen soll, ist mehr als fraglich" (1990: 109).

15 Cf. Deut 4:1, 31; 6:3, 10, 18, 23; 7:8, 12-13; 8:1, 18; 9:5; 11:9, 21; 13:18; 19:8; 26:15; 27:3; 29:12; 31:20.

16 On this phenomenon, see Fishbane 1985: 107-43, 209-16.

17 Note the definition of analepsis in the *Oxford Dictionary of Literary Terms* (Baldrick 2008): "Analepsis enables a storyteller to fill in background information about characters and events. A narrative that begins *in media res* will include an analeptic account of events preceding the point at which the tale began." This is precisely what we find in Deuteronomy, which on the level of the narrative framework begins on the last day of Moses's life, and on the level of Moses's recollection begins (in terms of the speech) with the departure from Horeb or (in terms of the history rehearsed) with the events of Horeb itself. See Stackert 2007: 219 n. 18: "In all cases of 'citation' in Deuteronomy, the author does not intend for his readers/audience to check his sources." Indeed, though we as scholars know that the author did have sources—sources that we are able to check because they have been preserved for us in the compiled Pentateuch—Deuteronomy does not directly cite sources, in the manner of Kings, for example, that would lead a reader of an independent Deuteronomy to think that such sources must have existed.

18 See Deut 8:18: "Remember Yahweh your God, for he gives you the power to get wealth, in order to fulfill the covenant that he swore with your fathers." Neither חיל nor כח ever appears in any of the patriarchal promise texts in

pentateuchal text, but belong rather to the broad tradition of the patriarchal promise, a tradition that is found, after all, in every pentateuchal
source and outside the Pentateuch as well (Baden 2013).[19] The author may
assume some knowledge on the part of the reader, but it is not necessarily
knowledge of a literary composition—even while D is, indisputably, writing with full knowledge of those literary compositions.[20]

I might point out that earlier in this paper I too made oblique reference
to some earlier writings. I wrote: "The fact of D's dependence on its non-
priestly predecessor texts, both in terms of those nonpriestly texts being
necessary prerequisites and in terms of D's composition in intentional
relationship with the nonpriestly texts, has been demonstrated, amply
and convincingly to my mind, both for the legal and the narrative portions of D." Those readers familiar with the work of Bernard Levinson will
recognize the legal reference immediately. But for those who do not know
Levinson's work, is the sentence somehow impossible to understand? I
should hope not. I am alluding to a specific literary work, but doing so
in terms that describe only a generalized scholarly argument, and doing
so not for the purposes of retelling or re-authenticating that argument
but in order to establish a groundwork for the claims that I really want to
make. To be honest, from a rhetorical standpoint, I could have completely
invented the scholarship I am "referring to" here. And at least with the
reference to that scholarship that has demonstrated "convincingly to my
mind" the dependence of D's narratives on nonpriestly texts, to a certain
extent I have invented it, in the sense that the work I referred to there is
my own (Baden 2009: 99–195).

Genesis-Numbers. Yahweh does bless the patriarchs with wealth, but does so
in their lifetimes, not as part of a future promise; cf. Gen 26:12-13. The closest
possible parallel to the concept expressed here is Gen 15:14, the prediction that
the descendants of Abraham who leave Egypt will do so גדול ברכש. This is not,
however, quite the same thing as Yahweh promising that Israel will have the כה
to acquire חיל.

19 On the notion that כאשר clauses can have oral traditions as their referents, see
    Hulst 1963–64.

20 Thus it is possible to uphold the claim of Milgrom (1978), that most of the כאשר
    clauses in Deuteronomy are consciously nodding to the nonpriestly literary
    sources on which D was dependent, and still recognize that such self-conscious
    citation on the part of the author need not translate into explicit textual refer-
    ence for the reader.

THE WILDERNESS EPISODES

Perhaps the most difficult of the three categories is that exemplified by Deut 9:22: "At Taberah and at Massah and at Kibrot-hatta'avah you provoked Yahweh." This verse refers to three locations, all of which appear only in the nonpriestly parts of the Pentateuch, each of which appear only once in the nonpriestly story (Num 11:1-3; Exod 17:1bβ-7; Num 11:4-34*), and all of which belong, in my opinion, to the same nonpriestly literary strand.[21] There is, in my mind, no doubt that the author of D knew the text from which all of these locations were taken, nor is there any question that the author of D was alluding to what took place in the stories of these locations, all of which involve Israelite complaining.[22] It is easy enough to say that for those readers familiar with the nonpriestly narratives of Exodus and Numbers the mere mention of these three locations would conjure up the full stories. But what about those readers unfamiliar with the nonpriestly narratives? Would this verse be meaningless? Is it possible that the author of D could have written this verse thinking that anyone in his intended audience would not have read those parts of what is now Exodus and Numbers?

Again: it's not impossible. The verse tells us that at three different places the Israelites provoked Yahweh. Even for those who know the nonpriestly stories, they are boiled down to their barest essence here: you people provoke Yahweh repeatedly. The details of the stories are eviscerated, quite intentionally, for the purpose of making this larger point. And the verse makes that larger point even without the reader knowing the details of the stories to which it refers.[23] It is the enumeration of provocations that is the rhetorical function of the verse, not the description of those provocations, nor even necessarily any "reality" to which they might refer. Those who know the stories will get a fuller experience from reading the verse, but those who do not will still appreciate the force of the statement, even if their literary experience is somewhat diminished.

This verse may fall into the category of the erudite authorial allusion: that is, a reference that is pitched at a level really appropriate only for some insider group. Such references still serve a purpose for those who

---

21 For the literary division of Numbers 11, and on the relationship of all three stories as part of a continuous J narrative, see Baden 2012: 82–102.

22 See Baden 2012: 173–79.

23 Contra Nelson 2002: 126: "The text counts on the reader's familiarity with tradition"; and Tigay 1996: 102: "Moses relies on his audience's familiarity with the events."

are not insiders: not only is the basic thrust of the statement clear, but the very fact of a reference that they do not understand can add authority to the author. Hosea refers to Israel's fortresses being "destroyed as Shalman destroyed Beth-arbel" (Hos 10:14). It's a reference that has no referent of which we are aware.[24] Surely Hosea knew what he was referring to. Perhaps some elite members of his audience did as well. Perhaps almost all of his audience did.[25] But we, who have no idea what is being referred to here, have no problem understanding Hosea's sentence, and Hosea surely would have known that his sentence would be fully comprehensible even to the ignorant. Whoever Shalman was, and wherever Beth-arbel was, we know that the former destroyed the latter, and it was awful, and that's all the information we need in order to understand the threat that the simile poses.[26] Indeed, Hosea could well have invented both Shalman and Beth-arbel out of whole cloth, and it would change nothing.

Earlier in this paper, in describing the breadth of scholarship that recognized D's polemic against the Covenant Code, I used the phrase "from the halls of Montezuma to the shores of Tripoli." Now it is almost certain that almost no one reading this paper knows exactly what "the halls of Montezuma" are, or what historical event that phrase refers to.[27] The same hold true, I would think, for "the shores of Tripoli," though more people might be able to name the country in which Tripoli could be found.[28] More

---

24 See Andersen and Freedman 1980: 570: "Neither the person [Shalman], nor the place Beth-Arbel, nor the incident, has been identified with any confidence."

25 See Mays 1969: 149: "To intensify their awareness of the scope and terror of the coming devastation, Hosea compares it to an event which must have been well known to his audience." Cf. Wolff 1974: 187–88.

26 See Andersen and Freedman 1980: 562: "Since the line cites a byword for destruction on an enormous scale, and is used only as a simile, our ignorance is more irksome than restricting." This is made evident by the significant amount of space that commentators still devote to expounding on the prophetic message of the verse, even as they admit that its referents remain mysterious. Note the line from Mays quoted in the previous note, in which Mays clearly understands exactly what Hosea is attempting to communicate even as he simultaneously seems to make that understanding dependent on familiarity with the unfamiliar events at Beth-Arbel.

27 Evidently it is a reference to the Battle of Chapultepec, an American victory in the Mexican-American war in 1847. It is safe to say that most Americans would be unable even to confirm that there had ever been such a thing as the Mexican-American war.

28 Libya. The reference is to the Battle of Derne, a Marine victory in the First Barbary War of 1805.

people, I would wager, will know that the phrase comes from the Marines' Hymn, and might even hear the continuation of the phrase: "we will fight our country's battles on the land and on the sea." But I would also bet that few people could finish the song—I know I can't. This is akin, roughly, to a reader of D recognizing that the allusions to Taberah, Massah, and Kibrot-hatta'avah are from the stories of the Israelites in the wilderness, but perhaps without actually remembering what exactly happened there, and without being able to tell the rest of the story surrounding those episodes. My use of the Marines' Hymn was evocative and rhetorical, not a literal reference to whatever took place at the halls of Montezuma or the shores of Tripoli. So too, I would suggest, for the references in D.

Moreover, there are surely those readers, especially non-Americans, for whom the reference to the United States' Marines' Hymn conjured absolutely nothing at all. I knew that before I wrote it, and I wrote it anyway, because I knew, as every author does, that not everyone will catch every reference. I knew also that if I structured my sentence correctly it wouldn't matter, because the purpose of the phrase—the use of a merism to describe the scope of scholarly agreement—would be evident even without having to fill in the content of the references. And for those who did not catch the citation, for whom the words meant nothing, I may, perhaps, have made it seem as if I had access to some relatively restricted knowledge, some cultural reference available only to the few. That is why people drop names: it conveys a certain level of knowingness. As D is widely recognized as one of the great rhetoricians of the Bible, we should be wary of assuming that there are rhetorical strategies that were beyond his literary capacities (see, e.g., Tigay 1996: xviii–xix).

CONCLUSION

It is, I hope I have made clear, my belief that the kinds of intertextual allusions, references, and citations that we find in D provide no evidence whatsoever that the author of D expected or required his readership to be familiar with the literary texts upon which he indisputably relied and to which he was certainly responding. A few final thoughts, then, on some related issues.

It is often suggested that the act of citation, allusion, or reference is, even in polemical discourse, an act of authorization. Even when arguing against something, we credit it with being worthy of argument.[29] I think not. In this case, I think that D wants those of us who are familiar with its literary predecessors to stop reading them. And those of us who are not, D wants to keep it that way.[30] The author of D may value the earlier non-priestly writings—but he does not want us to value them.[31] Allusion is not authorization, at least not universally, because allusion does not demand

29 See, for example, Pakkala 2013: 84: "Regardless of the intentional challenge, the author of the *Urdeuteronomium* implies that the Covenant Code possessed some authority in the community he was writing in. This is seen in the way he formulated parts of his own document with the older document in view. The Covenant Code may have possessed some authority in the context in which the author of the *Urdeuteronomium* wrote so that it had to be taken into consideration."

30 See Stackert 2007: 219: "Regarding his intent toward the Covenant Collection, the most plausible conclusion is that the Deuteronomic author takes a pragmatic approach: if some who encounter it are persuaded on the basis of this new legal collection's similarity with its prestigious source, Deuteronomy is a success. If others are won over on the merits of Deuteronomy alone, its authors likewise achieve their goal. In either case, Deuteronomy's intent is to make its own distinctive vision the authoritative view and to marginalize the Covenant Collection and other sources to whatever extent possible." Even given the strongly negative presentation of D's view of the Covenant Code here, there are, I think, two points on which it is possible to be stronger. First: the idea that the Covenant Code is a "prestigious source" is, it seems, still dependent on the idea that D's use of the Covenant Code can be explained only on the grounds that the earlier work was authoritative somehow. As far as I can see, there is no reason to assume so; the Covenant Code need not have been authoritative, either for the broader community or even for the author of D, in order for D or any other author to have used it and refuted it. Every scholar has taken the time to rebut an argument that is made only in one little-noted article in an obscure collection somewhere. Though we bring it to attention by mentioning it, we do not thereby recognize its inherent prior authority; nor do we particularly want anyone to go find it and read it for themselves. Second: the phrase "to whatever extent possible" makes it sound as if this marginalization is in fact the goal of the D author, with that process in mind at every turn. But I think this overstates the concern that D had for the Covenant Code. It is marginalized, no doubt; but the author of D could certainly have done more had that been his primary concern.

31 See Sommer 1998: 27: "Even if the old text is preserved, the new text attempts to relegate the old one to a noneffective status. It is worth noting, however, that replacement is not identical to rejection. The core ideas of the older text are preserved in the new one along with various improvements. Precisely because that core remains, however, the older text no longer serves any practical role (at least in the view of the author of the new text)."

recognition. There are biblical allusions that we will never understand—not because we don't know the referent, as in the example from Hosea, but because we don't know that they are allusions in the first place.

Recognition that references can convey rhetorical meaning even when devoid of recognizable content, and that references can in fact be completely invented, problematizes the notion that we as scholars can use references to speak about the authority or canonicity of an earlier text to which reference is being made.[32] The fact that D refers to the nonpriestly pentateuchal sources means only that those sources existed, not that they were authoritative, for D or for anyone else. Though, for that matter: if we did not have those sources preserved for us in the canonical Pentateuch, would we presume that they existed just because D makes references that we then would not understand? Would we assume that there must be a document, a written source, somewhere out there that told the stories of Taberah, Massah, and Kibroth-hatta'avah? Do we assume that for Hosea?

The desire among pentateuchal scholars to identify those places where D and the nonpriestly pentateuchal laws and narratives are related is common and unproblematic on its own. From such studies we can learn what the author of D may have been familiar with, which aspects of which earlier texts he found valuable, and which of his claims may be innovations. But what we may learn from these readings of D should not be confused with what the author of D wanted his audience to learn. References, citations, and allusions are used by the scholar to grasp the history of the literature. But we scholars are not the audience for the biblical authors. No biblical author wrote in order that his readers should be able to trace the Bible's literary history, nor is knowledge of that literary history a necessary precondition for understanding any biblical writings.

REFERENCES

Andersen Francis I. and David Noel Freedman. 1980. *Hosea*. Anchor Bible, 24. New York: Doubleday.

Baden, Joel S. 2013. *The Promise to the Patriarchs*. New York: Oxford University Press.

Baden, Joel S. 2012. *The Composition of the Pentateuch*. New Haven: Yale University Press.

Baden, Joel S. 2011. "The Deuteronomic Evidence for the Documentary Theory." In *The Pentateuch: International Perspectives on Current Research*, edited by Thomas B. Dozeman, Konrad Schmid, and Baruch J. Schwartz, 327–44. Forschungen zum Alten Testament, 78. Tübingen: Mohr Siebeck.

32   On this scholarly phenomenon, see Moss 2013 (esp. 121).

Baden, Joel S. 2009. *J, E, and the Redaction of the Pentateuch.* Forschungen zum Alten Testament, 68. Tübingen: Mohr Siebeck.

Baldrick, Chris. 2008. *Oxford Dictionary of Literary Terms,* 3rd edition. Oxford: Oxford University Press.

Blum, Erhard. 2011. "The Decalogue and the Composition History of the Pentateuch." In *The Pentateuch: International Perspectives on Current Research,* edited by Thomas B. Dozeman, Konrad Schmid, and Baruch J. Schwartz, 289–301. Forschungen zum Alten Testament, 78. Tübingen: Mohr Siebeck.

Eissfeldt, Otto. 1965. *The Old Testament: An Introduction.* New York: Harper & Row

Fishbane, Michael. 1985. *Biblical Interpretation in Ancient Israel.* Oxford: Clarendon.

Hulst, A. R. 1963–64. "Opmerkingen over de Ka'ašer-Zinner in Deuteronomium." *Nederlands theologisch tijdschrift* 18: 337–61.

Iser, Wolfgang. 1978. *The Act of Reading: A Theory of Aesthetic Response.* Baltimore: Johns Hopkins University Press

Johnstone, William. 1998. *Chronicles and Exodus: An Analogy and Its Application.* Journal for the Study of the Old Testament Supplement Series, 275. Sheffield: Sheffield Academic.

Kapelrud, Arvid S. 1974. "Mythological Features in Genesis Chapter 1 and the Author's Intentions." *Vetus Testamentum* 24: 178–86.

Levinson, Bernard M. 1998. *Deuteronomy and the Hermeneutics of Legal Innovation.* New York: Oxford University Press.

Mays, James Luther. 1969. *Hosea.* Old Testament Library. Philadelphia: Westminster.

Milgrom, Jacob. 1978. "A Formulaic Key to the Sources of D." *Eretz-Israel: Archaeological, Historical and Geographical Studies* 14: 42–47 [Hebrew].

Moss, Candida R. 2013. "Nailing Down and Tying Up: Lessons in Intertextual Impossibility from the Martyrdom of Polycarp." *Vigiliae Christianae* 67: 117–36.

Nelson, Richard D. 2002. *Deuteronomy.* Old Testament Library. Louisville: Westminster John Knox.

Otto, Eckart. 2013. "The History of the Legal-Religious Hermeneutics of the Book of Deuteronomy from the Assyrian to the Hellenistic Period." in *Law and Religion in the Eastern Mediterranean: From Antiquity to Early Islam,* edited by Anselm C. Hagedorn and Reinhard G. Kratz, 211–50. Oxford: Oxford University Press.

Pakkala, Juha. 2013. *God's Word Omitted: Omission in the Transmission of the Hebrew Bible.* Forschungen zur Religion und Literatur des Alten und Neuen Testaments, 251. Göttingen: Vandenhoeck & Ruprecht.

Perlitt, Lothar. 1990. *Deuteronomium.* Biblischer Kommentar: Altes Testament, 5. Neukirchen-Vluyn: Neukirchener Verlag.

Römer, Thomas. 1990. *Israels Väter: Untersuchungen zur Väterthematik im Deuteronomium und in der deuteronomistischen Tradition.* Orbis biblicus et orientalis, 99. Freiburg: Univeresitätsverlag.

Rose, Martin. 1981. *Deuteronomist und Jahwist: Untersuchungen zu den Berührungspunkten beider Literaturwerke.* Abhandlungen zur Theologie des Alten und Neuen Testaments, 67. Zurich: Theologischer Verlag.

Sommer, Benjamin D. 1998. *A Prophet Reads Scripture: Allusion in Isaiah 40-66.* Stanford: Stanford University Press.

Stackert, Jeffrey. 2007. *Rewriting the Torah: Literary Revision in Deuteronomy and the Holiness Legislation*. Forschungen zum Alten Testament, 52. Tübingen: Mohr Siebeck.

Tigay, Jeffrey H. 1996. *The JPS Torah Commentary: Deuteronomy*. Philadelphia: Jewish Publication Society.

Weinfeld, Moshe. 1991. *Deuteronomy 1-11*. Anchor Bible, 5. New York: Doubleday.

Wolff, Hans Walter. 1974. *Hosea*. Hermeneia. Philadelphia: Fortress.

Wright, David P. 2009. *Inventing God's Law: How the Covenant Code Used and Revised the Laws of Hammurabi*. Oxford: Oxford University Press.

Chapter 8

Isaiah 60-62 in Intertextual Perspective[1]

MARVIN A. SWEENEY[*]

I

Isaiah 60-62 is a well-known *crux interpretum* in discussion of the compositional history of the book of Isaiah. Although this text is included in the chapters assigned to Trito-Isaiah, its affinities with Deutero-Isaiah, including the so-called Servant Songs, have prompted scholars to present a number of hypotheses concerning its compositional setting and function. Many note the affinities of these chapters with Deutero-Isaiah while arguing that they constitute the core of Trito-Isaiah (Westermann 1969: 296–308; Childs 2001: 493–96; Smith 1995: 22–49; Stromberg 2011: 11–13, 27–30); others argue that there is no Trito-Isaiah and that Isa 56-66 as a whole must be considered as an extension of Isa 40-55 (Paul 2012; Sommer 1998); and still others argue that Isa 60-62 constitute part of a redactional stratum that edited Proto- and Deutero-Isaiah into a sixth century edition of the book (Steck 1991: 1–166; cf. Sekine 1989).

This paper contends that intertextual considerations aid in addressing the debate. It considers the current state of intertextual studies, including both its synchronic and diachronic dimensions, such as the degree to which intertextual relationships may be the result of intentional authorial citation or allusion or the result of reader-oriented association. A formal overview of Isa 60-62 then establishes the literary coherence of

* Marvin A. Sweeney is Professor of Hebrew Bible at Claremont School of Theology, Claremont, California.
1 I am indebted to my Research Assistant, Dr. Pamela J. W. Nourse, for her meticulous reading of my manuscript. All remaining errors are my own.

this text and provides the basis for considering its intertextual relationships with its various contexts, including Trito-Isaiah, Deutero-Isaiah, Proto-Isaiah, as well as works beyond Isaiah, such as Haggai, Zechariah, and Ezra-Nehemiah. As a result of these considerations, the paper argues that Isa 60-62 deliberately cites and reconceptualizes earlier Proto- and Deutero-Isaian texts. Isaiah 60-62 presents a servant figure who is not a king, prophet, nor Israel, but who is instead is a priest from the Jerusalem Temple. Isaiah 60-62 thereby gives expression to the concerns of the late-sixth century edition of the book of Isaiah as well as its final late-fifth century form.

II

Intertextuality is the study of texts in relation to their literary contexts, including the citation of or allusion to other literary works, the placement of a text in relation to its immediate literary context(s), and the interpretation of a text in relation to other literary compositions.

Current methodological overviews of intertextual interpretation indicate that its roots lie in earlier diachronic or author-centered conceptions of redaction-criticism and inner-biblical exegesis employed throughout much of the twentieth century (Sommer 1998: 6–31; Tull 1999: 156–80; Green 2000; Newsom 2003: 3–31; Mandolfo 2007: 1–28). Such work was considered to be the product of later tradents or redactors of an earlier text who deliberately added their own comments in an effort to reinterpret earlier narratives or prophetic oracles to serve their own later interests. Examples of such work from the latter twentieth century appear in efforts to define an Assyrian or Josianic edition of the book of Isaiah by scholars such as Clements (1980), Barth (1977), Vermeylen (1977–78), and Sweeney (1996), based on the observation of texts in Isa 1-39 designed to condemn the Assyrian empire and posit a Judean restoration following the projected Assyrian downfall. Such work remains valid, but it places the onus on the interpreter to reconstruct the authors of the texts and their particular viewpoints based on a combination of formal, lexical, and hermeneutical criteria (cf. Stackert 2007: 18–29). In the case of Isaiah, such criteria would include: 1) the presence of a literary context in which a later text would have access to an earlier text, e.g., later Isaian texts such as Trito-Isaiah appear as part of the larger book of Isaiah which includes earlier materials in Proto- and Deutero-Isaiah; 2) a lexical correspondence between the later text and the earlier text, e.g., later Isaian texts such as Trito-Isaiah cite words and phrases that appear in Proto- or Deutero-Isaiah; and 3) a hermeneutical perspective in the later text that demonstrates an attempt to interpret the earlier citations in relation to the concerns expressed in the later text, e.g., later Isian texts such as Trito-Isaiah demonstrate an interest in interpreting or reinterpreting the earlier citation from Proto- or Deutero-Isaiah.

But current intertextual work is also rooted in contemporary literary criticism, particularly the recognition of the role played by readers in the construction and interpretation of a text. With the rise of reader-response criticism and the subsequent development of synchronic literary perspectives in biblical exegesis, interpreters have come to recognize the role of the reader in the construction of biblical texts. Such work posits that texts are entities in and of themselves that stand independently of the author or authors who produced them (cf. Barton 1996: 140–236; Morgan with Barton 1988: 203–268). With only the text as evidence, it is impossible to know the mind of the author, either on the part of the interpreter of the text or even of the author who wrote it. Interpreters construct an image of the author based upon their own subjective readings of texts and then use that construct as a basis for giving expressions to their own concerns. Duhm's identification of the so-called Servant Songs of Deutero-Isaiah is a case in point (Duhm 1968: 19). Duhm's identification and isolation of the songs presupposes his view that ancient authors were only able to express themselves in short, self-contained units. Furthermore, Duhm argued that a suffering messiah figure must be the subject of the songs. Later interpreters have observed, however, that the songs are closely interrelated to their larger literary context in Isa 40-55 which identifies Jacob/Israel as YHWH's servant (Mettinger 1983; cf. Orlinsky 1967). Contemporary theorists, based especially in the work of Mikhail Bakhtin, posit that authors and interpreters draw upon the larger world of language and text that they inhabit, often subconsciously, so that it is impossible for the scholar to know if an intertextual association is the deliberate work of an original author or the observation of a reader who reads her or his own ideas into the text (e.g., Green 2000). In such a view, texts do not convey the meanings intended by their authors as it is impossible to know what an author intended, either by the interpreters or even by the author him- or herself. Meaning is thereby ascribed to texts by their readers, and the validity of the interpretation is decided by the numbers of other readers willing to accept it. And so we must ask if it is possible to account for such subjectivity in assessing potential intertextual relationships between and among texts.

Although the field is often polarized by author- and reader-centered theorists who deny the validity of the others' work, contemporary interpreters must recognize that textual interpretation calls for a synthesis of these views. Texts are indeed the products of authors who wrote them with a specific set of intentions that readers may or may not recognize and correctly reconstruct. At the same time, texts are read by readers who bring their own worldviews to bear in their interpretation—and therefore construction—of the texts at hand. But the extent to which later readers correctly discern the presumed intentions of a text's author must be judged in relation to the criteria presented above.

III

With these considerations in mind, analysis may now turn to Isa 60-62, beginning with its formal structure and generic characteristics. Isaiah 60-62 has long been recognized by interpreters of the Book of Isaiah as a coherent text that appears in the form of a prophetic announcement of the restoration of Jerusalem (Stromberg 2011: 11–13; for a detailed analysis of Isaiah 60-62, see Sweeney 2016; for discussion of form critical methodology, see Sweeney 1999: 58–89). The passage is clearly demarcated by the initial announcement in Isa 60:1 ("Arise, shine, for your light has come"), with the focus throughout on Zion's restoration, and the concluding announcements in Isa 62:10-12 concerning the arrival of the deliverer and the restoration of Zion. Isaiah 63:1 begins a new unit that focuses on YHWH's return from victory over Edom. The basic structure of the passage is easily established by the prophet's presentations of the words of two different speakers: YHWH's words to Zion in Isa 60:1-22 and the Speech of the Anointed Priest in Isa 61:1-62:12. The two sub-units are interrelated by the role played by the priest in the Temple as spokesperson to the people on behalf of YHWH; i.e., YHWH makes the initial announcement of Zion's restoration and the priest reiterates and elaborates upon YHWH's words.

The prophet's presentation of YHWH's words to Zion in Isa 60:1-22 concerning the return of Zion's exiles and the restoration of Zion comprises two elements. The first is the prophet's address to Zion in Isa 60:1-3 to rise and see the shining presence of YHWH. The second is the prophet's presentation of YHWH's address to Zion in Isa 60:4-22 that announces Zion's restoration. This unit in turn comprises three elements, namely, the command to Zion to see both the approach of her children and the wealth from the nations in Isa 60:4-7, the announcement proper of the restoration of

Zion in Isa 60:8-18, and the prophet's presentation of YHWH's promise for eternal possession of the land in Isa 60:19-22. The prophet's presentation in Isa 61:1-62:12 of the Speech of the Anointed Priest comprises five basic elements, including: the Anointed One's statement of his commission to release the captives so that they might serve in Jerusalem as priests to the nations in Isa 61:1-9; the Anointed One's psalm of rejoicing over the restoration of YHWH's righteousness before the nations in Isa 61:10-11; the Anointed Priest's pledge to Jerusalem to enable her righteousness and deliverance to be realized in Isa 62:1-7; the announcement of YHWH's oath of protection for Jerusalem in Isa 62:8-9; and the announcement and signal that the deliverer has arrived in Isa 62:10-12.

The structure of the passage may be diagrammed as follows:

Prophetic Announcement of the Restoration of Jerusalem
Isaiah 60:1-62:12

I. The Prophet's Presentation of YHWH's Words to Zion: Return of Zion's Exiles and Restoration of Zion	60:1-22
A. Prophet's address to Zion: Rise and see shining presence of YHWH	60:1-3
B. Presentation of YHWH's address to Zion: Announcement of Zion's restoration	60:4-22
1. Command to Zion to see the approach of children and wealth from the nations	60:4-7
2. Announcement of the restoration of Zion	60:8-18
3. Prophet's presentation of YHWH's promise for eternal possession of land	60:19-22
II. The Prophet's Presentation of the Speech of the Anointed Priest	61:1-62:12
A. The Anointed One's statement of his commission to release the captives so that they might serve in Jerusalem as priests to the nations	61:1-9
B. The Anointed One's psalm of rejoicing over the restoration of YHWH's righteousness before the nations	61:10-11
C. The Anointed Priest's pledge to Jerusalem to enable her righteousness and deliverance to be realized	62:1-7
D. Announcement of YHWH's oath of protection for Jerusalem	62:8-9
E. Announcement and signal that the deliverer has arrived	62:10-12

IV

Consideration of the intertextual dimensions of Isaiah 60-62 may begin with its immediate literary context in Isaiah 56-66, the so-called Trito-Isaiah, as well as the Book of Isaiah as a whole. (For earlier intertextual work on Isaiah 60-62, see Fishbane 1985: 495-99; Sommer 1998: 80-88; Lau 1994: 1-117.) Scholars have long recognized Isaiah 56-66 as a major component of the book of Isaiah, most commonly as a diachronically defined component of prophecies from the early Persian period ranging from the late-sixth through the fourth centuries BCE. Considered synchronically, my previous work has shown that these chapters portray the restoration of Jerusalem and the obligations of the people to YHWH's covenant (Sweeney 1988: 87–92).

The intertextual relationship between Isaiah 60-62 and its context in Isaiah 56-66 appears to be constituted not in this instance by the citation of earlier texts, but by its place with the structure and sequence of texts within Isaiah 56-66, which are concerned with Jerusalem's restoration. Although Jerusalem's restoration is a major concern of Isaiah 56-66 as a whole, Isaiah 60-62 appears to be differentiated from its immediate literary context in Isaiah 56-66. In portraying the restoration of Jerusalem, Isaiah 60-62 makes no differentiation among the restored people, i.e., all are restored in the understanding of this text. But when one considers Isaiah 60-62 in relation to its context within Isaiah 56-59 and 63-66, a major difference appears insofar as Isaiah 56-59 and 63-66 are interested in differentiating the righteous and the wicked within the people. Isaiah 56-59 begins in Isa 56:1-8 by announcing that foreigners and eunuchs are included in the restored people, but it continues by stipulating the covenant obligations of the people, especially observance of the Shabbat. Other texts in Isaiah 56-59 take up the issue of covenant observance and repentance for those who had failed to observe YHWH's will: Isa 56:9-57:21 focuses on YHWH's willingness to forgive those who repent; Isa 58:1-14 presents an admonition to repent; and Isa 59:1-23 presents a lament concerning YHWH's willingness and ability to forgive those who repent. Isaiah 63-66 focuses on judgment against those who are considered wicked and restoration for those who are righteous: Isa 63:1-6 focuses on YHWH's punishment of Edom as a symbol of wickedness among the nations; Isa 63:7-64:11 presents the prophet's lament and appeal for mercy on behalf of the people; and Isa 65:1-66:24 presents a scenario of restoration for the righteous and death for the wicked. Isaiah 60-62 does not share in the differentiation between the righteous and the wicked, although it does portray the scenario of restoration. Such considerations indicate that Isaiah 60-62 and Isaiah 56-59, 63-66 were not written by the same authors.

Turning to the intertextual relationship between Isaiah 60-62 and Isaiah 40-55 or Deutero-Isaiah, we need to reassess their synchronic and diachronic relationship. It is important to recognize that, although Isaiah 55 constitutes the culmination of Deutero-Isaiah in the view of most dia-chronically-oriented scholars, Isaiah 55, with its concern for redefining Israel as the recipient of YHWH's eternal Davidic covenant, introduces Isaiah 56-66 (Sweeney 2014: 94-113; 2016). Isaiah 56-66 thereby defines the expectations of those who would take part in YHWH's covenant. We have already observed that Isaiah 60-62 does not share in the differentiation of the righteous and the wicked characteristic of Isaiah 56-59 and 63-66, which raises the question of the relationship between these textual blocks and Isaiah 60-62. Given its shared concerns with Isaiah 40-55 with the res-toration of the exiles to Jerusalem, we may ask to what extent is Isaiah 60-62 related intertextually to Isaiah 40-55? Is Isaiah 60-62 a part of Isaiah 40-55? Or is it somehow closely related?

The intertextual interrelationship between Isaiah 60-62 and Isaiah 40-55 or Deutero-Isaiah appears to be close, although there is indeed differenti-ation between the two bodies of text. The portrayal in Isaiah 60-62 of the restoration of Jerusalem shares a basic concern with that of Deutero-Isaiah, i.e., the city will be restored and the exiles restored to the city without con-sideration of their righteous or wicked character. Likewise, Isaiah 60-62 portrays a servant figure who speaks in Isa 61:1-7 much as Deutero-Isaiah presents a servant figure throughout Isaiah 40-55. But whereas Deutero-Isaiah portrays a suffering servant who is to be identified with Jacob/Israel, the servant figure in Isaiah 60-62 displays a different character.

The servant figure in Isa 61:1-7 is not Jacob/Israel. This servant's tasks, to proclaim the release of the captives, to comfort the mourners of Zion, and to call upon them to oversee the restoration of Jerusalem, indicate that this servant is to address and exhort the exiles, but that this servant is not to be equated with them even metaphorically. Many scholars there-fore argue that the servant figure in Isa 61:1-7 must be a prophet or a royal figure.

The bases for identifying this figure as a prophet are (1) his role in addressing Israel like a prophet, (2) the statement in verse 1 that "the spirit of my L-rd YHWH is upon me," and (3) the use of two key verbs from Isa 6 and Isa 40:1-11, two key texts that have been recognized as the prophetic commissioning narratives for Proto-Isaiah and Deutero-Isaiah respec-tively (e.g., Seitz 1990). The statement concerning "the spirit of YHWH" is a corollary of the figure's anointed status and may be discounted as we will see below (see, e.g., 1 Sam 16:13).

But we now encounter the deliberate intertextual citation of terms that appear in Isa 6:1-13 and Isa 40:1-11, which portray the prophetic commissioning of Isaiah ben Amoz in Isa 6:1-13 and Deutero-Isaiah in Isa 40:1-11.

The first verb is *šělāḥanî* ("he has sent me") in Isa 61:1, which relates intertextually to Isaiah's response, *šělāḥēnî*, "send me!" to YHWH's request for a prophet to speak to the people on YHWH's behalf in Isa 6:8. The second verb is *lěbaśśēr* ("to proclaim good tidings") also in Isa 61:1 which appears as a key term in Deutero-Isaiah's prophetic commission in Isa 40:9 to serve as the *měbaśśeret ṣîyôn* ("herald of Zion") or the *měbaśśeret yěrûšālāim* ("herald of Jerusalem"). Such intertextual references indicate a sense of continuity with the prophet, Isaiah ben Amoz, as portrayed in Isa 6, and the anonymous prophet, Deutero-Isaiah, as portrayed in Isa 40:1-11. Insofar as Isa 6:1-13 and Isa 40:1-11, from which the intertextual lexical citations are drawn, are both generally considered to be prophetic commissioning or call narratives, many interpreters simply presume that the servant figure in Isa 61:1-7 must be a prophet.

But there is a problem with the presumption that Isa 61:1-7 must be a prophet. The servant figure in Isa 61:1-7 is described as anointed by YHWH. Prophets are typically called or summoned to service by YHWH, but we must recognize that prophets are not typically anointed in ancient Israel or Judah. Our servant figure in Isa 61:1-7, therefore, cannot be a prophet. Consequently, other scholars identify him as a royal or messianic figure in keeping with the royalist perspective of the book of Isaiah. Kings in ancient Israel and Judah are anointed, and so the argument carries some merit. Surely, such identification is attractive when one considers the intertextual relationships with Proto-Isaiah's oracles concerning the ideal Davidic monarch in Isa 9:1-6, 11:1-16, and 32:1-8. Indeed, the emphasis on the great light that will shine from Zion at the outset of the passage in Isa 60:1-3 to herald the restoration of Zion clearly has intertextual links with Isa 9:1 that speaks of the people who have walked in darkness but now see a great light as the ideal Davidic king emerges. Proto-Isaiah is heavily invested in Davidic ideology when viewed in diachronic perspective (Sweeney 1996). Isaiah 9:1-6 portrays the ideal righteous Davidic monarch identified as "the prince of peace" who will bring peace to his people. Isaiah 11:1-16 identifies the wise and righteous monarch who will restore the unity of Israel and Judah and subdue their enemies. Isaiah 32:1-8 is the ideal king who will reign in righteousness and appoint ministers who will govern with justice. But when viewed in synchronic perspective, identification with an ideal Davidic monarch is hardly satisfactory insofar as Deutero-Isaiah identifies Cyrus as YHWH's messiah and Temple builder in Isa 44:28 and 45:1, and reassigns the Davidic covenant from the house of David to the people of Israel as a whole in Isaiah 55. When viewed in synchronic intertextual perspective, Davidic ideology changes markedly in the book of Isaiah. There is no longer a Davidic monarch in Isaiah 40-66, much less in Isaiah 56-66.

Monarchs are not the only figures who are anointed in ancient Israel and Judah; priests are anointed as well, and in the absence of the Davidic—or any other Judean or Israelite—monarchy at the close of the Babylonian exile and outset of the Persian period, we must look to literature beyond the book of Isaiah to consider another possibility. Priests are anointed in ancient Israel and Judah, but priests are in short supply in the book of Isaiah until Isa 66:18-22 which announces that YHWH will select priests and Levites from the exiles returning to Jerusalem from the nations.

When we consider intertextual evidence of the larger literary world of the Bible outside of the book of Isaiah, it seems likely that our servant figure is indeed a priest (cf. Grelot 1990), perhaps to be identified with Joshua ben Jehozadak, who returned to Jerusalem in 522 BCE with Zerubbabel ben Shealtiel and who was ordained as high priest for the newly reconstructed Temple completed in ca. 515 BCE. Joshua ben Jehozadak's role is described briefly in Ezra 3 and especially in the visions of Zechariah ben Berechiah ben Iddo in Zech 1-6. I have already discussed the intertextual relationship between the book of Zechariah and the book of Isaiah in detail, noting particularly that Zechariah is composed as a response and counterpoint to Isaiah (Sweeney 2005: 222-35; cf. Sweeney 2000: 559–709). Whereas Isaiah maintains that Jerusalem and Judah must submit to Cyrus and the Persian empire in keeping with YHWH's will, Zechariah—and indeed the book of the Twelve as a whole—calls for the rise of a new Davidic king who will play a role in YHWH's defeat of the nations and the nations' recognition of YHWH at Zion. Joshua ben Jehozadak plays a key role in Zechariah, i.e., he is ordained in Zechariah 3; portrayed as an anointed figure alongside the royal Zerubbabel in Zechariah 4; and he sits crowned on the Jerusalem throne with a priest by his side in place of the absent Zerubbabel in Zechariah 6. Joshua is the de facto Judean ruler (under Persian sovereignty) of Judah until the rise of the new Davidic monarch in Zechariah 9-14.

Closer attention to the portrayal of the servant figure in Isa 61:1-7 points to his role as a priest. He is anointed, and he is tasked to proclaim release (Hebrew, *děrôr*) to the captives, liberation to the prisoners, a year of YHWH's favor, and a day of vindication for our G-d in Isa 61:1-2. The proclamation of release, *dĕrôr*, is indeed a priestly function that is identified with the proclamation of the Jubilee year in Lev 25:10, and the sabbatical year in Jer 34:8, 15, 17 and Ezek 46:17. The year of release occurs every seven years when fields are allowed to lie fallow so that the poor might glean (Exod 23:10-11), so that slaves might be released (Exod 21:2-11; Jer 34:8-16), and so that debts might be forgiven (Deut 15:1-18). With the passage of seven sabbatical years, a year of Jubilee is proclaimed in which land is returned to its tribal owners in addition to the other provisions (Leviticus 25). The rebuilding of the Jerusalem Temple in 520–515 BCE would at the very least mark the reinstitution of the sabbatical system in Jerusalem, and Joshua ben Jehozadak as High Priest would be the figure who would oversee its implementation. Furthermore, as high priest, Joshua would oversee the ordination of other priests to serve under him in the newly restored Temple, which would explain the comments in Isa 61:1-7 that our servant figure would clothe the mourners of Zion with turbans, the oil of rejoicing, and a garment of praise before naming them as priests of YHWH who would oversee the influx of wealth brought to the Temple by the nations at large (cf. the description of the priestly garments in Exodus 28-29).

Such a description and such a role suggest that our servant figure in Isa 61:1-7 is a priest, perhaps Joshua ben Jehozadak, High Priest of the rebuilt Jerusalem Temple in 520–515 BCE, and the restoration of Jerusalem as portrayed in Isa 60-62 is in fact based upon the restoration of the Jerusalem Temple as the holy center of the city and of creation at large in ancient Judean thought (Levenson 1984; 1985).

V

The preceding discussion points to the crucial role of intertextuality in the interpretation of Isaiah 60-62. Here, intertextuality must be understood in three dimensions: the deliberate citation of or allusion to other biblical texts; the interpretation of texts in relation to their immediate literary contexts; and the interpretation of texts in relation to the broader literary world. Isaiah 60-62 constitutes an element of Isaiah 56-66, which defines the obligations to YHWH's covenant by those who would be considered righteous in the restored Jerusalem in the final form of the book. But our discussion also points to a diachronic dimension of Isaiah 60-62 as a potential culmination for an earlier edition of the book that included Deutero-Isaiah together with Proto-Isaiah. There are indeed differences between

Isaiah 60-62 and Isaiah 40-55, which suggests that Isaiah 60-62 was composed as part of a sixth-century redaction of the book of Isaiah—written at the time of the reconstruction of the Jerusalem Temple—that could easily have played a role in the dedication of the new Temple. Such a redaction would have played a role in facilitating the transition of Judean authority from the royal house of David to a combination of the Persian monarchy and the Jerusalem priesthood, all under the umbrella of YHWH's role as sovereign monarch of creation. Isaiah 60-62 thereby had a hand in providing the religio-political foundations for Jewish life throughout much of the Second Temple period.

REFERENCES

Barth, Hermann. 1977. *Die Jesaja-Wörte in der Josiazeit*. Wissenschaftliche Monographien zum Alten und Neuen Testament, 48. Neukirchen-Vluyn: Neukirchener Verlag.

Barton, John. 1996. *Reading the Old Testament: Method in Biblical Study*, 2nd edition. Louisville: Westminster John Knox.

Blenkinsopp, Joseph. 2003. *Isaiah 56-66*. Anchor Bible, 19B. New York: Doubleday.

Childs, Brevard S. 2000. *Isaiah: A Commentary*. Old Testament Library. Louisville: Westminster John Knox.

Clements, Ronald E. 1980. *Isaiah 1-39*. New Century Bible. Grand Rapids: Eerdmans.

Duhm, Bernard. 1968. *Das Buch Jesaia*, 5th edition. Göttingen: Vandenhoeck & Ruprecht.

Fishbane, Michael. 1985. *Biblical Interpretation in Ancient Israel*. Oxford: Clarendon.

Green, Barbara. 2000. *Mikhail Bakhtin and Biblical Scholarship: An Introduction*, SBL Semeia Studies, 38. Atlanta: Society of Biblical Literature.

Grelot, P. 1990. "Sur Isaïe LXI: La Première consecration d'un grand prêtre." *Revue Biblique* 97: 414-31.

Lau, Wolfgang. 1994. *Schriftgelehrte Prophetie in Jes 56-66*, Beihefte zur ZAW, 225. Berlin: Walter de Gruyter.

Levenson, Jon D. 1984. "The Temple and the World." *Journal of Religion* 64: 275-98.

Levenson, Jon D. 1985. *Sinai and Zion: An Entry into the Jewish Bible*. Minneapolis: Winston.

Mandolfo, Carleen R. 2007. *Daughter Zion Talks Back to the Prophets: A Dialogic Theology of Lamentations*. SBLSemeia Studies, 58; Atlanta: Society of Biblical Literature.

Mettinger, T. N. D. 1983. *A Farewell to the Servant Songs: A Critical Examination of an Exegetical Axiom*. Lund: Gleerup.

Morgan, Robert, with John Barton. 1988. *Biblical Interpretation*. The Oxford Bible Series. Oxford: Oxford University Press.

Newsom, Carol. 2003. *The Book of Job: A Contest of Moral Imaginations*. Oxford: Oxford University Press.

Orlinsky, Harry M. 1967. *Studies in the Second Part of the Book of Isaiah: The So-Called "Servant of the L-rd" and "Suffering Servant" in Second Isaiah*. Vetus Testamentum Supplement, 14. Leiden: Brill.

Paul, Shalom M. 2012. *Isaiah 40-66*. Grand Rapids: Eerdmans.

Seitz, Christopher R. 1990. "The Divine Council: Temporal Transition and New Prophecy in the Book of Isaiah." *Journal of Biblical Literature* 109: 228–47.

Sekine, Seizo. 1989. *Die tritojesajanische Sammlung (Jes 56-66) redaktionsgeschichtliche Untersucht.* Beihefte zur ZAW, 175. Berlin: Walter de Gruyter.

Smith, P. A. 1995. *Rhetoric and Redaction in Trito-Isaiah: The Structure, Growth and Authorship of Isaiah 56-66.* Vetus Testamentum Supplement, 62. Leiden: Brill.

Sommer, Benjamin D. 1998. *A Prophet Reads Scripture: Allusion in Isaiah 40-66.* Stanford: Stanford University Press.

Stackert, Jeffrey. 2007. *Rewriting the Torah: Literary Revision in Deuteronomy and the Holiness Legislation.* Forschungen zum Alten Testament, 52. Tübingen: Mohr Siebeck.

Steck, Odil Hannes. 1991. *Studien zu Tritojesaja.* Beihefte zur ZAW, 203. Berlin: Walter de Gruyter.

Stromberg, Jacob. 2011. *Isaiah after Exile: The Author of Third Isaiah as Reader and Redactor of the Book.* Oxford Theological Monographs. Oxford: Oxford University Press.

Sweeney, Marvin A. 1988. *Isaiah 1-4 and the Post-Exilic Understanding of the Isaianic Tradition.* Beihefte zur ZAW, 171. Berlin: Walter de Gruyter.

Sweeney, Marvin A. 1996. *Isaiah 1-39, with an Introduction to Prophetic Literature.* Forms of Old Testament Literature, 16. Grand Rapids: Eerdmans.

Sweeney, Marvin A. 1999. "Form Criticism." In *To Each Its Own Meaning: Biblical Criticisms and their Application,* edited by S. L. McKenzie and S. R. Haynes, 158–90. Louisville: Westminster John Knox.

Sweeney, Marvin A. 2000. *The Twelve Prophets.* Berit Olam. Collegeville: Liturgical.

Sweeney, Marvin A. 2005. "Zechariah's Debate with Isaiah." In *Form and Intertextuality in Prophetic and Apocalyptic Literature,* 222–35. Forschungen zum Alten Testament, 45. Tübingen: Mohr Siebeck.

Sweeney, Marvin A. 2014. "The Reconceptualization of the Davidic Covenant in Isaiah." In *Reading Prophetic Books: Form, Intertextuality, and Reception in Prophetic and Post-Biblical Literature,* 94–113. Forschungen zum Alten Testament, 89. Tübingen: Mohr Siebeck.

Sweeney, Marvin A. 2016. *Isaiah 40-66.* Forms of Old Testament Literature, 17. Grand Rapids: Eerdmans.

Tull, Patricia K. 1999. "Rhetorical Criticism and Intertextuality." In *To Each Its Own Meaning: Biblical Criticisms and their Application,* edited by S. L. McKenzie and S. R. Haynes, 156–80. Louisville: Westminster John Knox.

Vermeylen, Jacques. 1977–87. *Du prophète d'Isaïe à l'apocalyptique,* 2 volumes. Echter Bibel. Paris: Gabalda.

Westermann, Claus. 1969. *Isaiah 40-66: A Commentary.* Old Testament Library. Philadelphia: Westminster.

Chapter 9

The Book of Job and Mesopotamian Literature: How Many Degrees of Separation?[1]

EDWARD L. GREENSTEIN[*]

INTRODUCTION

The Book of Job, as is well known, belongs to an ancient Near Eastern literary tradition of texts about pious sufferers (see, e.g., Weinfeld 1988; Mattingly 1990; Gorea 2007: ch. 2; Klein 2011: 559–63). Perhaps the texts closest in content to Job are the two Akkadian poems, "Let Me Praise the Lord of Wisdom" (Annus and Lenzi 2010; Oshima 2014: 3–114, 169–342, 376–438) and the so-called Babylonian Theodicy (Oshima 2013; 2014: 115–67, 343–75, 439–64). The former was already known in an abbreviated form among the Syro-Canaanite scribes of the second millennium BCE (Arnaud 2007: 110–14; Cohen 2013: 165–75).[2] However, in spite of many similarities between these Akkadian texts and Job (see below), one would be hard-pressed to establish a direct dependency (cf. Dhorme 1967: cx–cxi; Andersen 1975: 26–29; Longman 2012: 51). That is because without very

* Edward L. Greenstein is Professor of Biblical Studies at Bar-Ilan University, Ramat-Gan, Israel.
1 The present article is an elaboration on a presentation made at a session of the National Association of Professors of Hebrew held at the annual meeting of the Society of Biblical Literature, 19 November 2012. I thank Ziony Zevit for inviting me to make the presentation and for including this article in the present volume.
2 Since the full *Ludlul* poem would seem to have been composed no earlier than the Ras Shamra version, the latter would seem to be related to a precursor of *Ludlul* (Cohen 2013: 172; Oshima 2014: 25).

specific motifs and language in common, a unique connection between two texts cannot be demonstrated. Nevertheless, the poetry of Job can be shown to display a direct acquaintance with *some* Babylonian literature and language. Without being able to claim that the poet of Job had a direct acquaintance with the Mesopotamian texts concerning the pious sufferer, we can, I shall argue, demonstrate the Joban poet's familiarity with other genres of Babylonian literature, and with the Akkadian language (see Greenstein 2008 with the references there).

By contrast, the narrative framework of Job, written, like all biblical narrative, in prose (Greenstein 2014), relates a tale of testing that has no parallel in Mesopotamian literature or, so far as I know, in ancient Near Eastern literature in general (see Greenstein 2007b).[3] Nor am I aware of any specifically Babylonian language in the prose framework, which has been dated to the exilic or post-exilic period (Hurvitz 1974; Joosten 2013). Accordingly, the present discussion focuses exclusively on the poetic core of the book of Job.

CRITERIA FOR ESTABLISHING TEXTUAL DEPENDENCE

Before turning to the substance of my claim, that the Joban poet knew some Babylonian, I would comment on the criteria by which scholars tend to support their assertions that a particular author was aware of, influenced by, or even dependent upon some other corpus or work. In the absence of a specific reference or allusion of one work to another,[4] scholars often marshal a set of criteria, or tests, in order to establish an allusion or other form of intertextual connection between two texts. For Hays (1989), whose criteria are probably those most often cited today, a textual allusion must be, for example, historically plausible—i.e., the text alluded to must have been accessible to the author who is presumably alluding to it—and the allusion needs to make literary sense in context.

I think that what often happens is that, in the absence of an explicit reference, critics first get a sense of textual dependence and then attempt, after the fact, to establish a basis for that sense on grounds that others might accept (cf. Greenstein 1989). We formulate our sense of an intertextual relationship as a theory, and then we put our theories out there for

---

3   The closest parallel in ancient Near Eastern literature is the biblical story of the Binding of Isaac (Genesis 22), a comparison that was made already in ancient times; see, e.g., Ruiten 2002.

4   On allusion in biblical literature, see especially Sommer 1998.

others to consider. It is analogous to a claim of similarity between works: "Do people group things together because they are similar, or do they conceive them to be similar because they group them together?" (Handler 2013: 271). In any event, others will be better convinced of our claims when we support them with specific data: (1) similar themes, preferably in similar contexts; (2) similar motifs; (3) a similar sequence in the parallels that are adduced; and, wherever possible, (4) similar wording.[5] By drawing on seemingly visible exhibits, we try to convince others that our sense of a connection—our associations—are well-founded. It all boils down to an argument from specificity. The more specific the connections we draw, the more convincing will our arguments be (cf. Berman 2008). We will also want to establish, *pace* Hays (cf. Greenstein 1996a: 26–31), a plausible scenario by which our author might have known the proposed intertext.

GENERIC RESEMBLANCE

As said at the outset, the book of Job belongs to an array, perhaps a tradition, of ancient Near Eastern texts that deal with the distress of a pious sufferer. The texts that have seemed closest to Job are from Mesopotamia (e.g., Gray 2010: 5–20; Seow 2013: 51–56): the Sumerian poem "Man and His God"; an Old Babylonian poem of a pious sufferer, *Ludlul bel nēmeqi* ("Let Me Praise the Lord of Wisdom"—often referred to by moderns as "the Babylonian Job"); and the Babylonian "Theodicy," which, like Job, is composed in dialogical form (for basic bibliography see Sparks 2005: 61–63). A shorter work with strong resemblances to *Ludlul* was, as said above, found at Ras Shamra (Ugarit; see above, n. 2).[6] It would seem to reflect a prototype of the *Ludlul* poem—which is as much as hymn to Marduk as the complaint of a confounded sufferer.

Since an Akkadian poem of the pious sufferer type was known in Syria in the late second millennium BCE, it may be assumed that this literary type was part of the general cultural heritage of ancient Israel (cf. Greenstein 2012b). However, this likelihood does not enable us to determine whether or not the poet of Job, writing some time during the Persian period, knew the Ras Shamra version of *Ludlul*, or the Babylonian *Ludlul*, or the Babylonian "Theodicy."

  5 Compare the criteria adopted in Greenstein (1996a) for establishing a historical textual link between passages in Ugaritic and biblical literature, drawing on the work of Malul (1990) and Talmon (1978).
  6 For a comparison with the full Babylonian *Ludlul* poem, see Cohen 2013: 172–74.

There is a family resemblance between *Ludlul* and Job (for more detailed comparisons, see Gray 2010: 8–10; Seow 2013: 52–54): both protagonists complain of physical afflictions and social stigmatization; both fail to comprehend the divine causes of their suffering; both experience visions of a divine being (assuming that the hair-raising vision in Job 4:12–21 belongs to Job; see especially Greenstein 2005 and now Brown 2015). On the level of the literary motif and—for me—the crucial one of language, however, the parallels are not very specific. The closest parallel of this sort that I can find is a vague one between the Ras Shama *Ludlul* and one couplet in Job (cf. Seow 2013: 54):

([d]Marduk adallal) [š]a imḫaṣanni u irēmanni (Cohen 2013: 168, line 34')

(I will praise the god Marduk) who has stricken me
and (then) had compassion on me.

כִּי הוּא יַכְאִיב וְיֶחְבָּשׁ / יִמְחַץ וְיָדָיו תִּרְפֶּינָה

For he (God) gives pain and then binds (the wound);
Strikes and then heals with his own hands. (Job 5:18)

Only the verb *maḫāṣu* / מחץ, a not uncommon verb in BH poetry (cf. Held 1959: 170–71), is shared between the two sources. Moreover, Job 5:18 is more clearly dependent on a verse from earlier Hebrew poetry, Deut 32:39b (Greenstein 2013c: 73):

אֲנִי אָמִית וַאֲחַיֶּה / מָחַצְתִּי וַאֲנִי אֶרְפָּא

I slay and I revive; I strike and I myself heal.

In fact, there is, to my mind, a closer parallel to the line cited from *Ludlul* in Lam 3:32:

כִּי אִם-הוֹגָה וְרִחַם / כְּרֹב חֲסָדָיו

For when he (God) afflicts, he then shows compassion—
In accordance with his great devotion.

In this verse we also find רחם, the Hebrew cognate of Akkadian *rēmu* (Sperling 1989; Tawil 2009: 361); but because the parallel is of a general thematic nature, I would not press for a specific connection between the passage in *Ludlul* and Lam 3:32.[7]

---

7   Berlin (2002: 94) does well to compare Job 5:17–18 but does not refer to *Ludlul* or any other extra-biblical sources.

From both a formal and a thematic perspective, the closest literary parallel to the poem of Job in the ancient world is the Babylonian "Theodicy," a highly structured dialogue between a sufferer and his sympathetic friend, running to 27 stanzas of eleven lines each, each line beginning with same cuneiform sign (Oshima 2013; 2014).[8] The friend admonishes the sufferer in a manner reminiscent of Eliphaz in the first cycle of speeches in Job (Gray 2010: 10–11; Seow 2013: 55–56).

In both the "Theodicy" (lines 61–62) and Job (4:10–11) the comforting friend points out to the sufferer that the savage lion, symbolizing the wicked (Greenstein 2013b: 188), thrives only temporarily. In the final analysis, the deity does not allow the wicked to prosper—the lion is trapped, according to the "Theodicy," or starved, according to the poem of Job. However, these parallels, and others that could be adduced (see Mattingly 1990: 325–36; Van der Toorn 1991: 67–68; Gray 2010: 10–14), are differently formulated and share no distinctive language in common.

LINGUISTIC LINKS

In order to find a Mesopotamian text with both thematic and linguistic linkages to the book of Job, one must leave the genre of pious sufferer complaints and turn to the creation myth, *Enūma elish*. There we find a strong parallel in the evocation in Job of the storm god's combat with the sea (see Greenstein 2008: 54–55):

בְּכֹחוֹ רָגַע הַיָּם וּבִתְבוּנָתוֹ מָחַץ רָהַב:
בְּרוּחוֹ שָׁמַיִם[שם ים]‏[9] **שִׁפְרָה** חֹלֲלָה יָדוֹ נָחָשׁ בָּרִחַ:

Using his power he stilled/aroused[10] the sea,
And using his skill he smote Rahab;
Using his wind he put Yamm in his net;
His hand pierced the elusive[11] serpent. (Job 26:12–13)

ušparrirma bēlu(m) **saparrašu** *ušalwēši*

---

8 There are, of course, some large gaps (e.g., stanzas IX–XI); but the overall structure is clear.

9 For this widely accepted reading, see Tur-Sinai 1957: 383–84; for discussion and further bibliography see Cohen (1978: 50, 97–98) and Greenstein (1982: 207–8 with notes).

10 For the artful ambiguity of the verb, see Gordis (1936: 55); Greenstein (2007: 95).

11 For ברח 'fleeting', see, for example, Koehler and Baumgartner 2001: 156b.

The Lord[12] spread his net and engulfed her (IV 95; Lambert 2013: 90; translation mine).

In both passages the god of the storm ensnares the sea in a net, and in both the word for "net" is the Akkadian word *saparru*. It is true that the slightly revocalized Hebrew word שִׂפְרֹה "his net" has a Hebrew cognate סְפֹרָה "bag" in Ps 56:9. However, the Joban spelling with *sin* rather than *samekh* makes it doubtful that Job and Psalms are drawing on the same word; and if the reconstructed word in Job has an archaic 3 masculine singular possessive suffix, as suggested, it would make the term masculine, unlike the Hebrew cognate but just like the proposed Akkadian counterpart.

Now if the Joban poet, who displays a broad knowledge of foreign (non-Hebrew) language (see Greenstein 2003b; 2008; 2012a) and wide-reaching literary reach (see Dell and Kynes 2013), knew at least part of *Enūma elish*, tablet IV in particular, we might find another parallel to Job in the reference to pulling a bar across the sky and damming up the celestial waters (Greenstein 2006: 4; 2008: 55–56):

וַיָּסֶךְ בִּדְלָתַיִם יָם בְּגִיחוֹ מֵרֶחֶם יֵצֵא׃
בְּשׂוּמִי עָנָן לְבֻשׁוֹ וַעֲרָפֶל חֲתֻלָּתוֹ׃
וָאֶשְׁבֹּר עָלָיו חֻקִּי וָאָשִׂים בְּרִיחַ וּדְלָתָיִם׃

He[13] hedged with double-doors (the god) Sea,
As he was gushing out of the womb;
When I gave him cloud as a garment,
Raincloud as his swaddling clothes;
And I imposed[14] upon him my boundary,
Setting a bolt across double-doors. (Job 38:8-10)

išdud parka[15] *maṣṣara ušaṣbit*

He pulled across a bar, he set in place a guard. (IV 139; Talon 2005: 56; my translation)

---

12 Lambert (2013: 91) renders "Bel."

13 The third person unusually replaces the first person discourse in this verse. Many scholars resort to emendation; see the discussion in Clines 2009: 16. However, note the third person references to the deity by himself in Job 38:41; 39:17; 40:9, 19; as well.

14 Reading ואשמר "I set as a guard" in keeping with the image in 7:12 (Greenstein 2008: 55 n. 23).

15 Reading *parka* with Talon instead of *maška* "leather" with Lambert (2013: 94), precisely on account of the parallel. The cuneiform sign is the same.

Here there are no words used in common, but the image of restraining the personified sea behind barred doors is remarkably similar (so already Ball 1922: 416; Gordis 1978: 443–44; Greenstein 2008: 55–56).

MORE GENERIC RESEMBLANCES

The Job passage, of course, also evokes the image of a fetus being held in the womb behind bolted doors, which is familiar from Babylonian incantation literature (see Greenstein 2008: 55–56; Langton 2012).[16] Compare, for example, this excerpt:

> Assuluhi, Enki's son, saw him. / He loosed his tight-tied bonds, /
> He set him on the way, / He opened him the path...
> She has spoken to the doorbolt, it is released.
> "The lock is [fre]ed, / The doors thrown wide...." (Foster 2005: 171–72)

Job's opening discourse, in which he curses the day of his birth and the night of his conception, makes use of a similar image:

$$\text{כִּי לֹא סָגַר דַּלְתֵי בִטְנִי וַיַּסְתֵּר עָמָל מֵעֵינָי:}$$

> For it (or he) did not shut the doors of my womb,
> And hid not suffering from my eyes. (Job 3:10)[17]

Although Job throughout this discourse makes use of incantation literature, apart from such general images as the doors closing the womb and the light at the end of the birth passage, there are no specific parallels. On the basis of first millennium CE and other evidence, there is reason to suspect that the poet of Job draws on Aramaic rather than Babylonian sources (see Greenstein 2003b: 654–55; 2007a: 86–87).

---

16 Langton (2012: 54–55) accredits the 2008 presentation at the annual meeting of the Society of Biblical Literature on which Greenstein (2008) is based. Paul (2013: 171–74) adds some comparative material but fails to acknowledge preceding studies. Job's use of motifs from incantation literature in order to lay a retroactive curse on his birth is highly ironic; in the ancient world women would frequently seek incantations in order to ease their birthing and protect their fetuses (see Greenstein 2003a: 67). This rhetorical reversal is characteristic of Job's opening speech.

17 For a literary explanation of Job's reference to the womb as his own, see Greenstein 2007: 84–85.

Another generic parallel between the poem of Job and Mesopotamian literature is found in first millennium BCE Assyrian and Babylonian descriptions of gods. The limbs and other body parts of a god are identified with trees, plants, animals, and metals that are somehow felt to resemble them (see Livingstone 1986: 92–112). Consider the following excerpts:

> His top-knot is tamarisk.... / ...[His] whiskers are a frond.
> His knees are [cedar]. His ankle bones are an apple...
> His tongue is a whet-stone...
> His larger limbs are a lion. His smaller limbs are a dog...
> [His] stature is a poplar...
> His skull is silver. His sperm is gold.... (text 1: 1–3, 7, 9–10, 12;
> Livingstone 1986: 94–95)

> [His] stature is a cypress...
> [His] thighs are juniper.
> His knees are cedar...
> [His] sides are oak.
> His sperm is gold.... (text 2: 2–4, 6, 7; ibid.: 94–97)

We find a similar array of components in the descriptions of the behemoth and leviathan in the God-speeches in Job, for example:

עֲצָמָיו אֲפִיקֵי נְחֻשָׁה / גְּרָמָיו כִּמְטִיל בַּרְזֶל

His (behemoth's) limbs are pipes of bronze,
His bones like an iron rod. (Job 40:18)

לִבּוֹ יָצוּק כְּמוֹ-אָבֶן / וְיָצוּק כְּפֶלַח תַּחְתִּית

His (leviathan's) heart is cast hard, like stone;
Cast hard like the underneath millstone. (Job 41:16)[18]

The biblical descriptions of the quasi-mythological creatures are not the same as those in the Mesopotamian texts;[19] nor are any of the Hebrew words discernibly Babylonian. Accordingly, from my perspective there is

---

18 Cf. the JPS *Tanakh* translation.
19 At least since the path-breaking work of Gunkel (2006: especially 32–43), the behemoth and leviathan in the second divine discourse in Job have generally been regarded as mythological creatures bearing a resemblance to the hippopotamus and crocodile, respectively; see, for example, Fyall (2002: especially chs. 6 and 8); Whitney (2006: especially 28 with notes).

no literary dependence between them. However, their generic similarity makes it clear that these terrifying creatures are semi-mythological and not natural, as Gordis (1978: 569–72), for example, has contended.[20]

There does seem to be a special relationship between the structure of Job's lawsuit against God and the procedures of Babylonian jurisprudence (see, e.g., Roberts 1973; Scholnick 1977; Greenstein 1996b; Hoffman 2007; and Magdalene 2007). The claim that the legal argument in Job depends on Babylonian law can be supported by appeal to the Joban use of the phrase שים דברה "to set a word / matter / case" in 5:8 (see Paul 1979: 235–36):

אוּלָם אֲנִי אֶדְרֹשׁ אֶל־אֵל / וְאֶל־אֱלֹהִים אָשִׂים דִּבְרָתִי

> Rather I would seek out El,
> Before God would I lodge my complaint.

In standard biblical Hebrew the term for a legal case in not דברה but דבר (Greenstein 1999: 161–62).The unique locution שים דברה appears to be a calque of Babylonian *āwata šakānu* (*CAD* Š/1: 136), where the term for a legal case is a feminine noun—reflected in Hebrew דברה—and the verb *šakānu* is precisely rendered by Hebrew שים.[21]

Another Joban image that may be illuminated by Babylonian legal procedures is found in Job 14:17 (Holtz 2012):

---

20 Gordis's arguments have already been answered point by point by Fyall (2002: 127–28). There would seem to be several generic parallels between the descriptions of the behemoth and leviathan in Job and some monstrous figures known from the Gilgamesh epic tradition. Compare, for example, Job 41:17 ("Even gods dread his (Leviathan's) august demeanor") with Gilgamesh II 176 ("Who, even among the gods, could attack him") (Humbaba; Foster 2001: 19; cf. II 252, p. 21). Or Job 41:11 ("From his (Leviathan's) mouth issue torch-flames") (and cf. v. 13) with Gilgamesh IV 47 ("Whose maw was fire, whose breath was death") (said of Humbaba; Foster 2001: 34). If Job 40:23—a notoriously difficult verse (see Clines 2009: 1190–21 for many alternate readings)—is rendered, "If the river stops up, he (Behemoth) will not be alarmed; he will feel secure even if the Jordan rushes into his mouth!" (cf. Kahana 1928: 220), we find a parallel in the description of the divine Bull of Heaven, who (in the Sumerian account) "drank up the water of the Agilu canal. Though the Agilu canal reaches a double league in length, its thirst was not quenched" (trans. Douglas Frayne in Foster 2001: 124); cf. the Standard Babylonian Gilgamesh Epic VI 118 (Foster 2001: 49).

21 For another expression in which there is a semantic equivalence between שים and *šakānu*, see Gabbay (2014).

חָתֻם בִּצְרוֹר פִּשְׁעִי וַתִּטְפֹּל עַל-עֲוֹנִי:

Seal[22] my transgression in a pouch,
And plaster over my crime!

Job entreats the deity to set aside the crimes for which he presumes the deity is holding him accountable by sealing them in a pouch. Sealing in a pouch was a juridical mechanism for safeguarding evidence until it was needed (see also Hos 13:12 and the discussion in Holtz 2012). Although the Joban image may be directly related to the attested Babylonian practice, because the terminology is unrelated (the Akkadian term for "sealing" is *kanāku*), there is no way of establishing a specifically Babylonian nexus.

The attentive reader will have observed that in my view, textual influence cannot be demonstrated by generic and thematic parallels alone but must be supported by a linguistic link—a Babylonian word or phrase that might best explain the peculiar Hebrew of Job. It is my impression that, while it is hard to confirm the dependence of Job on Mesopotamian literature, we would do well to assume a strong familiarity of the Joban poet with at least some Babylonian language.

KNOWLEDGE OF AKKADIAN

Examples of the poet's use of Akkadian in Job have been adduced for about a century. I have treated a number of examples, most of them identified before, in Greenstein (2008; see also Greenstein 2012a: 350–53). For example, in 6:25 Job describes the discomfort that his words cause his companions (cf. Greenstein 2008: 60–62):

מַה-נִּמְרְצוּ אִמְרֵי-יֹשֶׁר / וּמַה-יּוֹכִיחַ הוֹכֵחַ מִכֶּם

Why do my honest words provoke (you)?
Why do they prompt you to reproach?

Elsewhere in the Bible (e.g., 1 Kgs 2:8; Mic 2:10) the verb/adjective נמרץ means something like "severe". But in the two places in Job where a form of מרץ is used (see also 16:3), the meaning "severe" or "grievous" does not provide a suitable sense. In 6:25 Job refers to (his own) "honest words"

---

22 In parallel with the verb in the following clause, this verb should be read not as vocalized—as a passive participle (*ḥātūm*)—but as an imperative: *ḥătóm*.

that disturb and provoke his friends. A fitting sense is obtained by adopting the hypothesis that the poet is employing נמרץ in its Akkadian usage of disturbing speech. Consider the following example from a Babylonian inscription of the Persian monarchy:

awēlu ša (d)Aḫurmazda uta'ama ina muḫḫīka lā imarruṣ

O man, that which (the god) Ahurmazda has commanded, may it not be difficult for you! (Weissbach 1911: 91, line 35)

Here the Akkadian verb *marāṣu* denotes the distress that is caused by discourse, just as in our example from Job 6.[23] It is most reasonable to conclude that the Joban poet draws on an Akkadian usage.

A relatively new example of the Joban poet's acquaintance with Akkadian may be found in 8:14 (Greenstein 2013a: 345–46). Here Bildad contrasts the fate of the wicked with that of the righteous. Whereas the home of the wicked is liable to collapse, the home of the righteous is very well secured. Bildad describes the wicked's abode as follows:

אֲשֶׁר־יָקוֹט כִּסְלוֹ / וּבֵית עַכָּבִישׁ מִבְטַחוֹ

His stronghold is gossamer,
and his trust a spider's house.

Based on the apparent synonymity of כסלו and מבטחו Saadia Gaon (Goodman 1988: 216) already concluded that the word יקוט is not, as many (e.g., Hartley 1988: 159) think, a verb, but rather a noun roughly synonymous with בית עכביש "spider's web". Saadia ventured an etymology from Aramaic קיט "summer", the season when spiders' webs would be most visible. However, in light of the number of plausible Akkadian loans one can find in the poetry of Job, I have suggested that the word יקוט is nothing but a contracted, or distorted, form of the Akkadian expression for a spider's web—*qē ettūti* (CAD Q, p. 288b). The expression is employed, for example, in the Babylonian poem of the destructive deity Erra (Cagni 1969: 66 line 88), which Bodi (1991) suggests had an influence on Ezekiel, and in the inscriptions of Sennacherib (Grayson and Novotny 2014: 313 lines 6–7). I see no reason that it should not be found in the linguistically rich poetry of Job.

---

23 Tawil (2009: 225) does not distinguish a nuance of "provocative" language, rendering "severe" in our context as well.

CONCLUSION

The poetry of Job makes use of a variety of literary elements that are known from Mesopotamian literature from diverse periods. We find the theme of theodicy and the topos of the complaining pious sufferer. We find the motif of the womb that is figured like a barred door and of semi-mythological creatures made of metal, stone, and other components. I have also joined earlier scholars in discerning a possible dependence of Job on a passage or two from *Enūma elish* tablet IV. In this last instance I based my contention on the presence of a linguistic link between the Babylonian source and Job. When applying the standard of identifying shared words and phrases, one may suggest that the poet of Job knew some Babylonian language and may have had some acquaintance with some Babylonian literature as well. The more one can establish a dependence on the level of language, the better one can hypothesize a familiarity with Mesopotamian literature in a more general way. Even so, I have not yet found a sure basis for claiming a direct knowledge of pious sufferer texts from Mesopotamia by the poet of Job. My judgment is that ancient Hebrew authors became familiar with pious sufferer texts, as they did with many other types of wisdom literature, from local sources (cf. Greenstein 2012b).

REFERENCES

Andersen, Francis I. 1975. *Job: An Introduction and Commentary*. Tyndale Old Testament Commentaries. Downer's Grove, IL: Inter-varsity.

Annus, Amar, and Lenzi, Alan. 2010. *Ludlul bēl nēmeqi: The Standard Babylonian Poem of the Righteous Sufferer*. State Archives of Assyria Cuneiform Texts, 7. Helsinki: Neo-Assyrian Text Corpus Project.

Arnaud, Daniel. 2007. *Corpus des textes de bibliothèque de Ras Shamra-Ougarit (1936–2000)*. *Aula Orientalis* Supplement, 23. Barcelona: Editorial Ausa.

Ball, C. J. 1922. *The Book of Job: A Revised Text and Version*. Oxford: Clarendon.

Berlin Adele. 2002. *Lamentations: A Commentary*. Old Testament Library. Louisville: Westminster John Knox.

Berman, Joshua. 2008. "Establishing Narrative Analogy in Biblical Literature: Methodological Considerations." *Beit Mikra* 53: 31–46 [Hebrew].

Bodi, Daniel. 1991. *The Book of Ezekiel and the Poem of Erra*. Orbis Biblicus et Orientalis. Fribourg: Academic Press.

Brown, Ken. 2015. *The Vision in Job 4 and Its Role in the Book*. Forschungen zum Alten Testament, 75. Tübingen: Mohr Siebeck.

Cagni, Luis. 1969. *L'epopea di Erra*. Studi semitici, 34. Rome: Universita di Roma.

Clines, David J. A. 2009. *Job 38–42*. Word Biblical Commentary, 18B. Nashville: Thomas Nelson.

Cohen, Harold R. (Chaim). 1978. *Biblical Hapax Legomena in the Light of Akkadian and Ugaritic*. Society of Biblical Literature Dissertation Series, 37. Missoula, MT: Scholars Press.

Cohen, Yoram. 2013. *Wisdom from the Late Bronze Age*. Writings from the Ancient World, 34. Atlanta: Society of Biblical Literature.

Dell, Katharine, and Kynes, Will, eds. 2013. *Reading Job Intertextually*. Library of Hebrew Bible / Old Testament Studies, 574. New York/London: Bloomsbury.

Dhorme, Edouard. 1967. *A Commentary on the Book of Job*. Translated by Harold Knight. London: Thomas Nelson and Sons.

Foster, Benjamin R. 2001. *The Epic of Gilgamesh*. New York/London: Norton.

Foster, Benjamin R. 2005. *Before the Muses: An Anthology of Akkadian Literature*, 3rd edition. Bethesda, MD: CDL Press.

Fyall, Robert S. 2002. *Now My Eyes Have Seen You: Images of Creation and Evil in the Book of Job*. Downers Grove, IL: Apollos-InterVarsity Press.

Gabbay, Uri. 2013. "Hebrew *śôm śekel* (Neh. 8:8) in Light of Aramaic and Akkadian." *Journal of Semitic Studies* 59: 47–51.

Gordis, Robert. 1936. "Hebrew Roots of Contrasted Meanings." *Jewish Quarterly Review* 27: 33–58.

Gordis, Robert. 1978. *The Book of Job: Commentary, New Translation, and Special Studies*. New York: Jewish Theological Seminary.

Gorea, Maria. 2007. *Job: Ses precursors et ses epigones ou comment faire du nouveau avec de l'ancien*. Paris: De Boccard.

Gray, John. 2010. *The Book of Job*. Edited by David J. A. Clines. Sheffield: Sheffield Phoenix.

Grayson, A. Kirk, and Novotny, Jamie. 2013. *Royal Inscriptions of Sennacherib, King of Assyria (704–681 BC), Part 2*. Royal Inscriptions of the Neo-Assyrian Period, 3/2. Winona Lake, IN: Eisenbrauns.

Greenstein, Edward L. 1982. "The Snaring of Sea in the Baal Epic." *Maarav* 3: 195–216.

Greenstein, Edward L. 1989. "Theory and Argument in Biblical Criticism." In *Essays on Biblical Method and Translation*, 53–68. Brown Judaic Studies, 92. Atlanta: Scholars Press.

Greenstein, Edward L. 1996a. "The Canaanite Literary Heritage in Ancient Hebrew Writing." In *Scribes, Schools and Libraries in Antiquity*, edited by Nili Shupak, 19–38. Michmanim, 10. Haifa: University of Haifa [Hebrew].

Greenstein, Edward L. 1996b. "A Forensic Understanding of the Speech from the Whirlwind." In *Texts, Temples, and Traditions: A Tribute to Menahem Haran*, edited by Michael V. Fox et al., 241–58. Winona Lake, IN: Eisenbrauns.

Greenstein, Edward L. 1999. "Jethro's Wit: An Interpretation of Wordplay in Exodus 18." In *On the Way to Nineveh: Studies in Honor of George M. Landes*, edited by Stephen L. Cook and Sara C. Winter, 155–71. Atlanta: Scholars Press.

Greenstein, Edward L. 2003a. "Interpreting the Bible by Way of Its Ancient Cultural Milieu." In *Studies in Jewish Education IX: Understanding the Bible in Our Times, Implications for Education*, edited by Marla L. Frankel and Howard Deitcher, 61–73. Jerusalem: Magnes [Hebrew].

Greenstein, Edward L. 2003b. "The Language of Job and Its Poetic Function." *Journal of Biblical Literature* 122: 651–66.

Greenstein, Edward L. 2006. Review of *Before the Muses*, 3rd edition. *Review of Biblical Literature* (on-line), July. 4 pp.

Greenstein, Edward L. 2007a. "Features of Language in the Poetry of Job." In *Das Buch Hiob und seine Interpretationen*, edited by Thomas Krüger et al., 81–96. Abhandlungen zur Theologie des Alten und Neuen Testaments, 88. Zurich: Theologischer Verlag.

Greenstein, Edward L. 2007b. "God's Test of Job." In *Shai le-Sara Japhet: Studies in the Bible, Its Exegesis and Its Language*, edited by Moshe Bar-Asher, Dalit Rom-Shiloni, and Nili Wazana, 263–72. Jerusalem: Mossad Bialik [Hebrew].

Greenstein, Edward L. 2006. "The Poetic Use of Akkadian in the Book of Job." In *The Avi Hurvitz Festschrift*, edited by S. Fassberg and A. Maman, 51–68. Meḥqarim be-Lashon, 11–12. Jerusalem: Institute of Jewish Studies of the Hebrew University of Jerusalem [Hebrew with English abstract].

Greenstein, Edward L. 2012a. "On the Use of Akkadian in Biblical Hebrew Philology." In *Looking at the Ancient Near East and the Bible through the Same Eyes: A Tribute to Aaron Skaist*, edited by Kathleen Abraham and Joseph Fleishman, 335–53. Bethesda, MD: CDL Press.

Greenstein, Edward L. 2012b. "Wisdom in Ugaritic." In *Language and Nature: Papers Presented to John Huehnergard on the Occasion of His Sixtieth Birthday*, edited by Rebecca Hasselbach and Na'ama Pat-El, 69–89. Chicago: Oriental Institute of the University of Chicago.

Greenstein, Edward L. 2013a. "The Invention of Language in the Poetry of Job." In *Interested Readers: Essays on the Hebrew Bible in Honor of David J. A. Clines*, edited by James K. Aitken, Jeremy M. S. Clines, and Christl M. Maier, 331–46. Atlanta: Society of Biblical Literature.

Greenstein, Edward L. 2013b. "Some Metaphors in the Poetry of Job." In *Built by Wisdom, Established by Understanding: Essays on Biblical and Near Eastern Literature in Honor of Adele Berlin*, edited by Maxine L. Grossman, 179–95. Bethesda, MD: CDL Press.

Greenstein, Edward L. 2013c. "Parody as a Challenge to Tradition." In *Reading Job Intertextually*, edited by Katharine Dell and Will Kynes, 66–78. New York/London: Bloomsbury.

Greenstein, Edward L. 2014. "Direct Discourse and Parallelism." In *Discourse, Dialogue and Debate in the Bible: Essays in Honour of Frank Polak*, edited by Athalya Brenner-Idan, 79–91. Sheffield: Sheffield Phoenix.

Gunkel, Hermann. 2006 [1895]. *Creation and Chaos in the Primeval Era and the Eschaton*. Translated by William Whitney Jr. Grand Rapids, MI: Eerdmans.

Handler, Richard. 2013. "The Uses of Incommensurability in Anthropology." In *Comparison: Theories, Approaches, Uses*, edited by Rita Felski and Susan Stanford Friedman, 271–91. Baltimore: Johns Hopkins University Press.

Hartley, John E. 1988. *The Book of Job*. New International Commentary on the Old Testament. Grand Rapids, MI: Eerdmans.

Hays, Richard B. 1988. *Echoes of Scripture in the Letters of Paul*. New Haven: Yale University Press.

Held, Moshe. 1959. "*mḫṣ/*mḫš* in Ugaritic and Other Semitic Languages (A Study in Comparative Semitic Lexicography)." *Journal of the American Oriental Society* 79: 169–76.

Hoffman, Yair. 2006. "The Book of Job as a Trial: A Perspective from a Comparison to Some Relevant Ancient Near Eastern Texts." In *Das Buch Hiob und seine Interpretationen*, edited by Thomas Krüger et al., 21–31. Abhandlungen zur Theologie des Alten und Neuen Testaments, 88. Zurich: Theologischer Verlag.

Holtz. Shalom E. 2012. "Why Are the Sins of Ephraim (Hos 13,12) and Job (Job 14,17) Bundled?" *Biblica* 93: 107–15.

Hurvitz, Avi. 1974. "The Date of the Prose-Tale of Job Linguistically Reconsidered." *Harvard Theological Review* 67: 17–34.

Joosten, Jan. 2012. "Linguistic Clues as to the Date of the Book of Job: A Mediating Position." In *Interested Readers: Essays on the Hebrew Bible in Honor of David J. A. Clines*, edited by James K. Aitken, Jeremy M. S. Clines, and Christl M. Maier, 437–57. Atlanta: Society of Biblical Literature.

Kahana, Abraham. 1928. *The Book of Job*. Torah, Prophets, Writings with a Scientific Commentary. Tel Aviv: Meqorot [Hebrew].

Klein, Jacob. 2011. "Mesopotamian Literature—Genesis Traditions, Wisdom Literature, and Lamentations." In *The Literature of the Hebrew Bible: Introductions and Studies*, edited by Zipora Talshir, 523–79. Jerusalem: Yad Yitzhak Ben-Zvi [Hebrew].

Koehler, Ludwig, and Baumgartner, Walter. 2001. *The Hebrew and Aramaic Lexicon of the Old Testament*. Revised by Walter Baumgartner and Johann J. Stamm. Translated and edited by M. E. J. Richardson. Leiden: Brill.

Lambert, W. G. 2013. *Babylonian Creation Myths*. Winona Lake, IN: Eisenbrauns.

Langton, Karen. 2012. "Job's Attempt to Regain Control: Traces of a Babylonian Birth Incantation in Job 3." *Journal for the Study of the Old Testament* 36: 53–63.

Livingstone, Alasdair. 1986. *Mystical and Mythological Explanatory Works of Assyrian and Babylonian Scholars*. Oxford: Clarendon.

Longman, Tremper III. 2011. *Job*. Baker Commentary on the Old Testament. Grand Rapids, MI: Baker Academic.

Magdalene, F. Rachel. 2007. *On the Scales of Righteousness: Neo-Babylonian Trial Law and the Book of Job*. Brown Judaic Studies, 348. Providence: Brown University.

Malul, Meir. 1990. *The Comparative Method in Ancient Near Eastern and Biblical Legal Studies*. Alter Orient und Altes Testament 227. Neukirchen-Vluyn: Butzon & Bercker Kevalaer.

Mattingly, Gerald L. 1991. "The Pious Sufferer: Mesopotamia's Traditional Theodicy and Job's Counsellors." Pp. 305–48 in *The Bible in the Light of Cuneiform Literature = Scripture in Context III*. Ed. William W. Hallo, Bruce W. Jones, and Gerald L. Mattingly. Lewiston, NY: Edwin Mellen.

Oshima, Takayoshi. 2013. *The Babylonian Theodicy*. State Archives of Assyria Cuneiform Texts, 9. Helsinki: Neo-Assyrian Text Corpus Project.

Oshima, Takayoshi. 2014. *Babylonian Poems of Pious Sufferers: Ludlul Bēl Nēmeqi and the Babylonian Theodicy*. Orientalische Religionen in der Antike. Tübingen: Mohr Siebeck.

Paul, Shalom M. 1979. "Unrecognized Biblical Legal Idioms in the Light of Comparative Akkadian Expressions." *Revue biblique* 86: 231–39.

Paul, Shalom M. 2015. "Two Notes on Biblical and Mesopotamian Imagery." In *Built by Wisdom, Established by Understanding: Essays on Biblical and Near Eastern Literature in Honor of Adele Berlin*, 171–77. Edited by Maxine L. Grossman. Bethesda, MD: CDL Press.

Roberts, J. J. M. 1973. "Job's Summons to Yahweh: The Exploitation of a Legal Metaphor." *Restoration Quarterly* 16: 159–65.

Ruiten, Jacques van. 2002. "Abraham, Job and the Book of *Jubilees*: The Intertextual Relationship of Genesis 22:1-19, Job 1:1-2:13 and *Jubilees* 17:15-18:19." In *The Sacrifice of Isaac: The Aqedah (Genesis 22) and Its Interpretations*, 58–85. Edited by Ed Noort and Eibert Tigchelaar. Leiden: Brill.

Scholnick, Sylvia H. 1977. *Lawsuit Drama in the Book of Job*. Ph.D. Diss., Brandeis University, Waltham, MA.

Seow, C. L. 2012. *Job 1-21: Interpretation and Commentary*. Illuminations. Grand Rapids, MI-Cambridge, England: Eerdmans.

Sommer, Benjamin D. 1998. *A Prophet Reads Scripture: Allusion in Isaiah 40-66*. Stanford, CA: Stanford University Press.

Sparks. Kenton L. 2005. *Ancient Texts for the Study of the Hebrew Bible: A Guide to the Background Literature*. Peabody, MA: Hendrickson.

Sperling, David. 1989. "Biblical *rḥm* I and *rḥm* II." *Journal of the Ancient Near Eastern Society* 19 (Moshe Held Memorial Volume): 149–59.

Talmon, Shemaryahu. 1977. "The 'Comparative Method' in Biblical Interpretation—Principles and Problems." *Vetus Testamentum Supplements* 29: 320–56.

Talon, Philippe. 2005. *The Standard Babylonian Creation Myth* Enūma Eliš. State Archives of Assyria Cuneiform Texts, 4. Helsinki: Neo-Assyrian Text Corpus Project.

Tawil, Hayim ben Yosef. 2009. *An Akkadian Lexical Companion for Biblical Hebrew*. Jersey City, NJ: Ktav.

Tur-Sinai, N. H. 1957. *The Book of Job: A New Commentary*. Revised edition. Jerusalem: Kiryath Sepher.

Van der Toorn, Karel. 1991. "The Ancient Near Eastern Literary Dialogue as a Vehicle of Critical Reflection." In *Dispute Poems and Dialogues in the Ancient and Medieval Near East: Forms and Types of Literary Debates in Semitic and Related Literatures*, 59–75. Edited by G. J. Reinink and H. L. J. Vanstiphout. Leuven: Departement Oriëntalistiek / Peeters.

Weinfeld, Moshe. 1988. "Job and Its Mesopotamian Parallels: A Typological Analysis." In *Text and Context: Old Testament and Semitic Studies for F. C. Fensham*, 217–26 . Edited by W. Claassen. Sheffield: JSOT Press.

Weissbach, Franz H. 1911. *Die Keilinschriften den Achämeniden*. Vorderasiatische Bibliothek, 3. Leipzig: J. C. Hinrichs.

Whitney, K. William. 2006. *Savage Beasts: Leviathan and Behemoth in Second Temple and Early Rabbinic Judaism*. Harvard Semitic Monographs, 63. Winona Lake, IN: Eisenbrauns.

Chapter 10

Method in the Study of Textual Source Dependence: The Covenant Code

DAVID P. WRIGHT[*]

This paper explores aspects of the methodology used to determine dependence of one text on another. It specifically considers as an example the contention that the Covenant Code (CC) is dependent upon the Laws of Hammurabi (LH). I argued for this in detail in a book a few years ago (Wright 2009). In this I concluded that virtually the entirety of CC, not only its casuistic laws (Exod 21:2-22:19), but also the apodictic laws that encircle the casuistic laws (20:23-26; 22:20-23:19), were influenced by the laws, themes, and structure of Hammurabi's text. A recent and substantial review by William Morrow (2013) looked at the evidence in terms of a focused set of criteria for determining textual dependence. This led him to a more circumspect conclusion, that dependence on LH seems evident mainly or only in the assault laws of 21:18-32. In a way Morrow fulfilled a desideratum of Bruce Wells (2006), who, in a response to one of my early publications on this topic, urged a ranking of perceived similarities to determine if the strongest examples demonstrate dependence.[1]

---

[*] David P. Wright is Professor of Bible and the Ancient Near East at Brandeis University, Waltham, Massachusetts.

1 For another long review, see Otto 2010 (this is a response to articles written before the publication of Wright 2009). For short reviews, see Baden 2010; Holtz 2010; Malul 2011; Polak 2010; and Wells 2011. Those who follow my conclusions for the bulk of the casuistic laws include Levinson (2004: 272-325; republished Levinson 2008b: 276-330); Carr 2011: 470-72. They are hesitant, however, to see influence in the apodictic laws. See also Nihan 2013: 127-28 and n. 19 there, for recognition of the possibility of some influence from LH.

The present essay illustrates that an approach to comparative analysis based on strict criteria, such as employed by Morrow, provides a viable entree to the question of CC's textual dependence. It argues the conclusion that a substantial core passage of CC, specifically Exod 21:18-32, is dependent on LH, can serve as a foundation for concluding that other portions of CC, which have fewer but still notable similarities with LH, are likely dependent on that text. This essay also stresses the importance of assessing the nature of differences between texts. This is important because divergences in a target text may arise through hermeneutical innovation of the source text and thus actually point to an intimate relationship between the texts rather than to distance between them. Both Levinson (1998 and 2008a; especially the descriptive bibliography in the latter at 95–181) and Stackert (2007), provide excellent case studies of how hermeneutical innovation operates in the rewriting of biblical law.

To exemplify these issues and approach, this essay briefly outlines the criteria that served Morrow and can serve us as a basis for an assessment of textual dependence. It then examines a portion of the assault laws that Morrow sees as dependent on LH, i.e., the miscarriage, talion, and slave injury laws of Exod 21:22-27. This surveys the similarities between the collections in these laws as well as describes how some of the differences in CC appear to have arisen from the revision of LH. The essay then extends the argument to the debt-slave laws in 21:2-11, which have fewer or different sorts of correlations with LH. It shows that there are substantial parallels in these laws and that several of the chief differences in CC's laws arose from a similar process of hermeneutical transformation. The conclusion of the essay points to other passages in CC that appear to have a connection with Hammurabi's law text in order to show how the argumentation can be further extended.

THE BASIC CRITERIA FOR DETERMINING TEXT DEPENDENCE

Morrow's criteria for determining textual dependence echo guidelines found in a body of literature that has considered the question of textual dependence (see Wright 2009: 24–28, 375 n. 115; Morrow 2013: 311–13). I cite his criteria in full because they provide a basis for gauging similarity between the texts compared later in the course of this essay. The criteria describe different types of similarity between texts and how these different types can be considered both significant and probative. These criteria also provide a measure against or along which other pieces of evidence might be evaluated, such as the creation of difference through interpretive recasting.

According to Morrow (2013: 312, with discussion at 317–23), for a claim of textual dependence to be valid, the supposed dependent text should reflect the following features:

1.1 Translation or Close Paraphrase. The surest indications of literary dependency are parallels that suggest a translation or paraphrase of a pre-existing text. Such parallels manifest philologically controlled features at either the phrase level or clause [as opposed to similarities in isolated words].

1.2 Textual Organization. As explained by Dennis MacDonald, "The more often two texts share content in the same order, the stronger the case for literary dependence."

1.3 Density. Convincing cases of literary dependency involve a convergence of multiple criteria or lines of evidence. That is, a stronger case for literary borrowing emerges when there are several points of contact as opposed to a single isogloss.

1.4 Uniqueness—as opposed to a coincidence that can be explained by other means. For that reason the criterion of uniqueness can also be referred to as "distinctiveness." In the investigation of uniqueness, one must be aware of both the similarities and differences in the texts being compared. A particular principle that may be invoked in the investigation of uniqueness is that of the "blind motif": a literary image or expression that cannot be explained in terms of its own context, but which reflects a process of borrowing from another source or culture.

Employing these as a guide, Morrow concluded that the similarities of Exod 21:18-32—laws about striking and injury, killing one of a lower class, miscarriage, talion, slave injury, and the goring ox—are so close to laws on similar topics in LH 196-201, 206-210, 250-252 that they are likely dependent on those laws. As he summarizes the matter in view of his criteria: "the various convergences between Exod 21:18-32 and LH in terms of textual organization and content are too many to be considered accidental" (Morrow 2013: 331).

The end of his essay turned to the question of opportunity for dependence. Clearly, for a theory of dependence to be entertained, there needs to be cultural, historical, and geographical occasion for transmission. This is not a problem in the case before us. As Morrow notes, "the possibility of dependence on LH is ... enhanced by the prestige, popularity, and wide circulation this Akkadian classic enjoyed throughout the Bronze and Iron Ages in the ANE" (Morrow 2013: 331). Actually, the problem is not the lack of an opportunity for borrowing, but, perhaps, too many opportunities. One track of explanation argues that the similarities arise from legal tradition (oral or written) that was ensconced in Canaan-Syria in the middle to late second millennium and which was later inherited by Hebrew scribes. Another argument, to which I ascribe because it makes sense of a larger set of data about CC, its narrative, and Deuteronomy's textual and ideological dependence on CC, maintains that the textual borrowing occurred in the Neo-Assyrian period, in the window of 740–640 BCE and probably close to 700.[2] Morrow observes that "all the current historical models for accounting for literary borrowing between these two texts have weaknesses," and he ends saying that "the purpose of this review will have been served if it spurs future scholarship to address these problems" (Morrow 2013: 331). Sharing his desire to foster continued scholarship on this matter, I turn to the specific examples of textual comparison.

---

2 There are two main hypotheses for explaining the similarities between CC and LH. One is the maintenance of a text or texts (not simply oral traditions) from second millennium Syria-Canaan into the first millennium. To explain the detail and breadth of the correlations and to work historically, this would have to posit that all of LH, including the prologue and epilogue, were translated into a Northwest Semitic language before 1200 BCE, transmitted for several centuries, and eventually taken up by Israelite or Judean scribes. The recently discovered law fragments from Hazor (Horowitz, Oshima, and Vukosavović 2012), while pointing to the knowledge of cuneiform law texts in the mid-second millennium in Syria-Canaan, do not provide direct support for the first hypothesis because their content matches neither CC nor LH. The other hypothesis is influence from Mesopotamian sources in the late Neo-Assyrian period (740–640 BCE). This is the period with the greatest number of manuscripts of LH next to the Old Babylonian period when LH was created (ca. 1750 BCE). It is possible, given the context of the Neo-Assyrian political domination of Israel and Judah that some scribes in Israel or Judah were trained in Akkadian, became acquainted with LH, and from this produced CC. A variation of this thesis would claim that LH was translated into Aramaic in the Neo-Assyrian period and that this served as a source for CC. There is no clear evidence, however, for such a translation. For detail see Wright 2009: 91–122, 346–59; 2014: 242–43; 2016a.

THE CORE LEGAL CORRELATIONS: MISCARRIAGE, TALION, AND SLAVE INJURY IN EXODUS 21:22-28

To sample the evidence that Morrow finds persuasive, and to serve as a foundation in extending the argument for dependence to other parts of CC, I examine the heart of the passage that he believes is dependent on LH: the laws on miscarriage, talion, and slave injury in Exod 21:22-27 (for detail, see Wright 2009:154-91; 2010; 2014; 2016b). These verses display some of the densest correlations with LH in all of CC. Along the way I draw attention to correlations with LH in the broader passage of assault laws in verses 18-32. The following analysis also describes how many of the differences in verses 22-27 appear to be responses to the context of LH and thereby demonstrate dependence on LH. The discussion that follows moves back and forth between setting out the evidence of similarity and describing the compositional logic responsible for producing several of the different formulations in CC. The latter is generally couched in a perspective that envisages dependence of CC on LH.

The laws on aggravated miscarriage at the beginning of verses 22-27 correlate with Hammurabi's laws about miscarriage in the case of a free woman in LH 209-210 (emphasis of phrases here and in other compared texts in the rest of the essay draws attention to similar wording or functionally similar concepts):

LH 209-210	Exod 21:22-23
[209] **If a man strikes a daughter** of a man (*mārat awīlim*) **and he causes her to miscarry her fetus, he shall weigh out ten shekels of silver for her fetus.**	[22] **If men** struggle and they **knock a pregnant woman and her fetus comes out** but there is no calamity, **he shall be fined as the husband of the woman exacts from him** and he shall pay בפללים (for the fetus?).[3]
[210] **If that woman dies, they shall kill his daughter.**	[23] **If there is calamity,** you shall pay life for life, [24] eye for eye, tooth for tooth, arm for arm, leg for leg, [25] burn for burn, injury for injury, wound for wound.

Both collections have a pair of laws, the first of which deals with miscarriage and the second where the pregnant woman also dies. Besides CC's

---

3   The meaning of the noun פְּלִלִים is not clear. Some think that the reading was originally נְפָלִים, plural of the noun נֵפֶל "stillborn fetus" as found in Ps 58:9; Job 3:16; Eccl 6:3. The plural would match the plural in the phrase earlier in the verse וְיָצְאוּ יְלָדֶיהָ "her children come out."

portrayal of the assault as unintentional, to be discussed later, the main difference between the two texts is in the penalty of the second law. Hammurabi's legislation requires that the daughter of the assailant be put to death because the victim was a "daughter of a man." Instead of this, CC features its talion law.

CC's different formulation can be explained as a reaction to Hammurabi's requirement of vicarious punishment. That CC found vicarious punishment problematic is evident in its goring ox law in Exod 21:28-32, whose three laws correlate with those in LH 250-252:

LH 250-252	Exod 21:28-32
²⁵⁰**If an ox gores a man (***awīlum***)** while passing through the street **and kills (him), that case has no claim.**	²⁸**If an ox gores a man** or woman **and he dies,** the ox shall be stoned, its flesh shall not be eaten, and **the owner of the ox is not liable.**
²⁵¹**If a man's ox is an habitual gorer, and his district has informed him that it is an habitual gorer, but he** did not file its horns and **did not control his ox, and that ox gores a son of a man (***mār awīlim***), he shall pay one-half mina (= thirty shekels) of silver.**	²⁹**If an ox is an habitual gorer,** from previous experience, **and its owner has been warned, but he did not restrain it, and it kills a man** or woman, the ox shall be stoned and its owner shall be put to death. ³⁰If ransom is laid upon him, **he shall pay the redemption price for his life, according to whatever is laid upon him.** ³¹Or (if) it gores a son or daughter, it shall be done to him according to this law.
²⁵²**If it is the slave** of an *awīlum* he (the ox owner) **shall pay one-third mina (= twenty shekels) of silver.**	³²**If the ox gores a male slave** or a female slave, **he shall pay thirty shekels of silver** to his (the slave's) master and the ox shall be stoned.

CC augments its second law with verse 31, which states that a case where a child is a victim is to be handled like the foregoing case, i.e., where an adult is the victim. CC appears to be responding to a variation in the description of the victim in Hammurabi's laws. In LH 250 the victim is just an *awīlum*, "a man." CC's corresponding v. 28 reflects this in its description of the victim as a "man or woman" (CC tends to include females where LH has only males). But LH 251 describes the victim as a *mār awīlim*, "son of a man." This idiom is ambiguous in Akkadian. It may simply mean "a person of the *awīlum* class," and thus be conceptually equivalent to the "man" *awīlum* in

LH 250. The idiom could also mean, literally, "son of a man" and thus be the male equivalent of *mārat awīlim* "daughter of a man" in the miscarriage law of LH 210. The male equivalent in the context of vicarious punishment is in fact found in two other laws in LH. The debt-servitude law of LH 116 states: "If he (a debt-servant whom a creditor beats to death) was a man's (a debtor's) son (*mār awīlim*), they shall kill his (the creditor's) son" (see also LH 230). In the context of LH, the variation in terminology in LH 251 theoretically raises the question as to whether vicarious punishment might also operate in the case of a goring ox. CC accordingly encoded both interpretations in its second law. It portrayed the victim as an adult in its main law (v. 29) and appended the alternative of a child victim (v. 31). Thus CC rejected the possibility of vicarious punishment in two laws from LH where this principle is stated or hinted at: in its ox law, CC countered it explicitly; in the miscarriage law, CC replaced it with the talion law.

CC drew the idea and basic substance of its talion law from Hammurabi's talion laws, which appear just a few paragraphs before its miscarriage law (LH 196-201):

LH 196-201	Exod 21:23b-25
[196]If an *awīlum* (a free man) blinds the eye of a member of the *awīlum* class, they shall blind his eye.	[23b] ... you shall give (= pay) life for life,
[197]If he breaks the bone of an *awīlum*, they shall break his bone.	[24]eye for eye, tooth for tooth,
[198]If he blinds the eye of a commoner or breaks the bone of a commoner, he shall weigh out one mina (sixty shekels) of silver.	arm for arm, leg for leg,
[199]If he blinds the eye of an *awīlum*'s slave or breaks the bone of an *awīlum*'s slave, he shall weigh out half of his value.	[25]burn for burn, injury for injury, wound for wound.
[200]If an *awīlum* knocks out the tooth of an *awīlum* of the same rank, they shall knock out his tooth.	
[201]If he knocks out the tooth of a commoner, he shall weigh out one third mina (twenty shekels) of silver.	

Hammurabi's talion laws are a series of fully formed casuistic laws and deal with several body parts (an eye, bone, and tooth) and with persons of various social statuses (free persons, commoners, and slaves). CC boiled these down into a list of equations in list form to fit the syntax of the apodosis of the second miscarriage law. It kept the "eye" and "tooth" from LH and bifurcated the broken bone into an "arm" and "leg." The principle of equivalence for homicide in Hammurabi's second miscarriage law led CC to add the equation "life for life" at the beginning of the talion list, to apply to a case of homicide. (I will come back to the textual stimulus for the three lesser injuries in verse 25 in a moment.)

CC's reformulation does more than simply replace vicarious punishment in LH 210. CC made its talion law do double duty, as a punishment for the death or injury of the pregnant woman and as a general law for all cases of homicide and injury. It marked it as a general law by writing a long list of injuries, overkill if referring only to a case of miscarriage. It also marked it thus by using the second person verb "you shall give," unusual in casuistic law which generally has third person description. This broadened the applicability beyond those involved in the assault against the pregnant woman and, thus, metonymically brought into consideration cases of assault in addition to that describe in the miscarriage law. The general application of the talion law is also evident in the relationship of the laws on slave injury (vv. 26-27; discussed below). These depend conceptually on the preceding talion law but have nothing to do with miscarriage. They thus indicate that the talion law deals with cases of assault in addition to miscarriage.

A reason for writing the talion law as a general law was to complete the homicide laws of Exod 21:12-14 (cited below). These verses have a noticeable omission. They legislate that one who intentionally kills another is to be executed, but they say nothing about the punishment or obligation that an unintentional killer has. From their silence, one might expect an unintentional killer to get off completely free. The talion laws flesh out this missing requirement. One who kills another unintentionally needs to "give life for life," i.e., to pay the equivalent for the life lost.

That CC has in mind cases of unintentional homicide and injury in its talion law is clear from its contextualizing the assault on the pregnant woman in a fight that does not involve her (v. 22). The men only happen to butt or crash into the woman, and so, according to the homicide law of 21:12-14, the assault has to be considered inadvertent. This contrasts with the miscarriage laws of LH 209-210, which lack this datum and by default represent the attack as intentional. The severity of the penalty in LH 210 also points to intentionality in the assault. CC gets its motif of men fighting from the series on inadvertent assault in LH 206-208 (cited below), which immediately precede the miscarriage laws. These set up their case similarly: "If an *awīlum* strikes another *awīlum* in a fight and injures him (lit., puts a wound on him)...." CC reflects this same motif of a fight in 21:18-19, which directly correlates with LH 206 (see below). In the context of inadvertence, CC's talion penalty "you shall give life for life ...," with the verb נתן, means to pay the equivalent for the life or body part lost. This is consistent with the use of this verb elsewhere in CC to describe payment (21:19, 22, 30, 32) and with a similar use of the verb *nadānum* "give" in LH (e.g., LH 252, reflected in 21:32).

That CC's talion law deals with indemnification in cases of unintentional injury and homicide is supported by the comparative evidence. CC's homicide laws in verses 12–14, along with the laws on striking and injury in verses 18–19 and killing one of a lower social class in verses 20–21, correlate in content with Hammurabi's assault and homicide laws in LH 206-208, which appear just before its miscarriage law:[4]

LH 206-208	Exod 21:12-14, 18-19
[206]If an *awīlum* strikes another *awīlum* in a fight and injures him (lit., puts a wound, *simmum*, on him), that *awīlum* shall swear (saying), "I did not strike him with intent," **and he shall pay the physician.**	[18]**When men fight and one strikes his fellow** with a stone or with a fist (?), and **he (the latter) does not die** but takes to his bed—[19]if he gets up and walks about outside on his staff, then the striker is absolved, but **he must** recompense him for his period of inactivity and **provide for his cure.**
[207]**If he dies from his being struck, he shall also swear (as in the previous paragraph).** If (the victim) is an *awīlum*, he shall weigh out one-half mina (= thirty shekels) of silver.	[12]**He who strikes a man so that he dies** shall be put to death, [13]and he **who did not plan it**, but God directed (the victim) to his hand, I will appoint a place for you to which he may flee. [14]But if a person plots against his fellow to kill him by deceit, you shall take him from my altar to be put to death.

4   Verses 18–19 clearly parallel LH 206, with the common motifs of fighting, injury, and financial responsibility for recuperation. Verses 20–21 parallel LH 208 in dealing with the homicide of someone of a lower class. CC's sociology did not include a commoner. It therefore substituted a slave for Hammurabi's commoner, as it also does in its law about knocking out a slave's tooth (21:27; LH 201; see below). Logically we would expect a case of homicide of a free person to come between verses 18–19 and 20–21, as LH 207 comes between LH 206 and 208. The subcondition "and he does not die" in v. 18 begs for a companion law that conversely states the condition "and he does die," especially before the case of homicide of a slave in verse 20. CC has this law, but put it at the head of its various cases on assault and capital crimes (21:12-14). This relocation freed CC to formulate its homicide law on the basis of a native participial source, to be consistent with the form of other capital cases (21:15-17). Nevertheless, it maintained the concern about intentionality from LH 206-208.

[208]If (the victim who dies when struck) is a commoner, he (the assailant *awīlum*) shall weigh out one-third mina (= twenty shekels) of silver.	[20]If a man strikes his male slave or female slave with a rod and he (or she) dies under his hand, he (the victim) is to be avenged, [21] but if he lingers for a day or two, he (the assailant) shall not suffer vengeance, since he is his (the master's) silver (i.e., property).

The context of a lack of intention in Hammurabi's series is stated in the base law (LH 206) and continues as a premise in LH 207 and 208. The common focus of this series is to prescribe indemnification in cases of unintentional injury and homicide. While CC's main homicide law does not state this up front in verses 12–14, the talion comes back to this issue and completes the legislation. It says that, yes, one who kills inadvertently is still financially responsible for the victim. Presumably in CC's thinking, working out indemnification with the victim's kin would be the mechanism that would allow the killer to leave the altar which provides temporary asylum. CC's talion law also complemented its law about injury in verses 18–19. That law prescribes that the injurer "must recompense him (the victim) for his period of inactivity and provide for his cure." These are monetary payments, and the talion payment of "an eye for an eye" on down the list is a way of describing this financial obligation as a general principle.

LH 206–208 also provides the basis for the trio of lesser injuries at the end of CC's talion law in verse 25 (the burn, injury, and wound). Hammurabi's talion laws did not include such soft tissue traumas. However, these are the types of injuries that can be included under the term *simmum* ("wound, affliction") in LH 206. To flesh out its talion list, CC apparently trifurcated Hammurabi's *simmum* into the trio of soft tissue injuries, similar to how it bifurcated the broken bone in Hammurabi's talion laws into an arm and leg. CC put the soft tissue traumas at the end of its talion list otherwise based on Hammurabi's talion law.

Finally, CC's slave injury law in 21:26-27 correlates with and also drew on Hammurabi's talion laws in LH 196-201:

LH 196-201	Exod 21:26-27
[196]If an *awīlum* blinds the eye of a member of the *awīlum* class, they shall blind his eye. [197]If he breaks the bone of an *awīlum*, they shall break his bone. [198]If he blinds the eye of a commoner or breaks the bone of a commoner, he shall weigh out one mina (sixty shekels) of silver.	
[199]**If he blinds the eye of an** *awīlum*'s **slave** or breaks the bone of an *awīlum*'s slave, he shall weigh out half of his value.	[26]**If a man strikes the eye of his male slave** or the eye of his female slave and **destroys it**, he shall send him away free for his eye.
[200]If an *awīlum* knocks out the tooth of an *awīlum* of the same rank, they shall knock out his tooth.	
[201]**If he knocks out the tooth of a commoner**, he shall weigh out one third mina (twenty shekels) of silver.	[27]**And if he knocks out the tooth of his male slave** or the tooth of his female slave, he shall send him away free for his tooth.

CC's two laws in verses 26–27 have a complete casuistic formulation that matches the full formulation in Hammurabi's talion laws, as opposed to the talion summary at the end of the miscarriage laws in verses 23b–25. This reinforces the conclusion made above that CC's talion list is a summary of a set of talion laws that had full casuistic formulation. That is, the full formulation of verses 26–27 is at home stylistically in casuistic law. One would expect the governing laws about injury to free persons to also have full casuistic formulation. The list formulation in verses 23b–25, which deal with injury to free persons and conceptually govern verses 26–27, therefore looks secondary. Even without LH, one might posit that verses 23b–25 derive from a source with fully formulated casuistic laws. LH happens to provide a text that, when viewed as a source, allows us to make sense of the incongruence in style between verses 23b–25 and 26–27.

The sequence of verses 23b–25 about injury to free persons and verses 26–27 about injury to slaves follows the socially graded pattern set out in Hammurabi's talion laws. Because verses 26–27 change the topic by dealing with a different social class, they could not be summarized in list form but had to remain fully formulated casuistic laws. To create these laws CC took two exemplary cases of bodily injury from LH with different monetary penalties, the cases of an eye and tooth, substituted a slave in place of a commoner in the tooth law (similarly, cf. vv. 20-21 and LH 208, cited above), and gave them a new penalty: the release of the slave. This penalty is a function of another significant modification in CC: changing the assailant from an outside party to the owner of the slave.

The change in assailant is part of a broader hermeneutical transformation whereby CC conflated debt-slaves and chattel-slaves, phenomenologically distinct in LH. Part of the reason for this conflation is to make the laws accord with CC's keen interest in debt-slavery, indicated in part by placement of laws on this topic at the beginning of the casuistic laws (21:2-11). This position and interest correlates with the placement of laws on the poor at the beginning of its final apodictic laws (Exod 22:20-26).[5] CC was apparently interested in applying slave legislation that appears at points in its assault laws that follow, derived from laws on *chattel*-slaves in LH, to the debt-slave (21:20-21, 26-27, 32). This conflation accounts for the tension in the slave homicide law in verses 20–21, cited above, where the owner who beats a slave is liable if the slave dies immediately, but is acquitted if the slave dies a day later. The liability for the death of the slave in verse 20 correlates with the liability of a creditor in the death of a debt-servant in LH 115-116, while the exoneration from liability in verse 21 conforms to the implications about chattel-slave ownership in LH, where such a slave is the owner's property and, therefore, the owner is not liable for killing him or her. CC actually expresses this economic principle at the end of verse 21: the owner has no liability "since he (the slave) is his (the master's) silver (i.e., property)." Because slaves in CC include debt-slaves, who are in principle free persons that are not simply property and for whom there would be liability in cases of homicide and injury, CC shifts the assailant to the owner-master in verses 20–21 and 26–27. This owner-master includes a creditor who has taken in a debt-slave.

This analysis shows that every law or significant legal motif in CC's miscarriage, talion, and slave injury laws has a correlate in Hammurabi's legislation. The major differences—placement of the talion law at the end of the miscarriage law, portraying the assault that causes miscarriage law as an instance of inadvertence, the formulation of the talion laws as a list for those applying to free persons but fully formed casuistic laws for those applying to slaves, and the slave-owner as the assailant in the slave injury

5 The laws on the poor in 23:9-12 are parallel to those in 22:20-26 in the overall structure of the final apodictic laws, and thus augment CC's structural emphasis on the poor. See Wright, 2009: 31–90, 286–321.

laws formed casuistic laws about slaves versus the talion list applying to free people—are all explainable as hermeneutical developments from the context of LH, where CC sought to solve problems it found in LH or sought to formulate more systematic laws that accorded with its ideological perspectives.

EXTENSION TO OTHER CASES: THE DEBT-SLAVE LAWS IN EXODUS 21:2-11

That the miscarriage, talion, and slave injury laws of 21:22-27—or more broadly as indicated by some of the evidence above, and as Morrow concludes, that the larger gamut of assault laws in verses 18-32—are dependent on LH sets the stage for examining the evidence of correlations in other parts of CC with LH and assessing whether these indicate dependence. Methodologically, this approach uses the conclusion about verses 22-27 (and, more broadly, 18-32) as an evidential foundation for explaining the significance of similarity to LH in other passages of CC, even though similarities in such cases may be less dense or qualitatively different from those examined in verses 22-27 (18-32).[6] Moreover, the way that differences in legal formulation in verses 22-27 appear to have arisen as a reaction to LH also provide a model for understanding differences in other passages of CC vis-à-vis LH.

The debt-slave laws of Exodus 21:2-11 are a good example of where the analysis and argument can be extended (for detail, see Wright 2009: 123-53). The foregoing section of this essay noted that these laws are related to the assault laws that deal with slaves (vv. 20-21, 26-27, 32) by CC's conflation of debt-slaves with chattel slaves as part of the revision

---

6 This relates to one of eight criteria set out by Leonard (2008: 246, 253-55) for determining if one biblical text alludes to another. His fifth principle states that "the accumulation of shared language suggests a stronger connection than does a single shared term of phrase." His criterion of narrative tracking, discussed in his essay in this volume ("Identifying Subtle Allusions: The Promise of Narrative Tracking"), also relates to how CC's correlations reflect the same or similar sequences as found in LH. Accordingly, the whole context of a text becomes important for judging textual associations. Criteria for determining allusion between biblical texts to a large extent coincide with those that operate in transcultural comparative study as considered in this essay. But transcultural analysis requires a greater density of correlations, appropriate to the chronological and geological distance of the compared texts.

of Hammurabi's legislation.[7] This indicates at the outset that the debt-slave laws in verses 2–11 are compositionally tied to the production of the assault laws. Therefore it would not be surprising if verses 2–11 also had generative ties to LH. In any case, verses 2–11 have a number of correlations with LH substantial enough that dependence may also be posited for these laws in view of the conclusions already made about the assault laws of verses 22–27 (18–32). Several of the differences in these laws over against Hammurabi's legislation appear to arise from a process of revision akin to that found in verses 22–27. The main difference in the debt-slave laws of verses 2–11 in relation to the assault laws of verses 22–27 (18–32) is that, rather than following the template and content of a relatively circumscribed group of laws in LH, they used a single law—the debt-slave law of LH 117—as a foundation and drew in motifs from other laws in LH at some distance from this, even from the very last law in that collection.

CC's debt-slave law has two parts. One treats the case of a male debt slave (Exod 21:2-6), and the other, a case where a daughter is sold to pay a debt (vv. 7-11). The initial and basic laws in both these sections correlate with Hammurabi's basic debt-slave law (LH 117):

LH 117	Exodus 21:2, 7
[117]If an obligation has come due for a man, and **he sells his wife, son, or daughter,** or he gives any (of them) for dependent debt-servitude, they **shall work** in the house of their buyer or creditor **for three years. In the fourth year their freedom shall be effected.**	[2]**If you acquire** a Hebrew **slave, he shall work for six years. In the seventh he shall go free**, without further obligation. ... [7]**If a man sells his daughter** as a slave-woman, she shall not go free as male slaves go free.

CC's basic laws reflect the essential framework of Hammurabi's rule. Specifically, the protasis of the daughter law (v. 7a) and the apodosis of the male law (v. 2aβb) correlate with the protasis and apodosis of LH 117: "if a man sells his daughter + he shall work for six years; in the seventh he shall go

---

7   While Exod 21:20-21, 26-27, 32 apply to both chattel- and debt-slaves, the main debt-slave law in 21:2-11 applies only to *free* persons enslaved for debt. This is indicated by inclusion of the adjective "Hebrew," an ethnic designation, in verse 2. This is paralleled contextually by verse 7, where the woman is given by her father, a free man. Hebrews so enslaved in the context do not become chattel-slaves, though a male in become a permanent slave in certain circumstances (vv. 5-6). Only foreigners would be chattel-slaves.

free," which is comparable to "if a man...sells his [family member]...they shall work...for three years; in the fourth year their freedom shall be effected."

The treatment of the daughter as a separate case appears to have arisen from a problem inherent in the legislation of LH. In Hammurabi's law, a debtor's dependents—wife, son, or daughter—are all treated the same. They work for three years in the creditor's custody and are released in the fourth. This uniform procedure for resolving a debt, however, would have entailed a practical problem: a creditor might well sexually exploit the daughter of a debtor given to pay off a debt, a woman who would have been unbetrothed and unmarried. (Logically the father would not have legal and economic control of a daughter who was betrothed or married and therefore would not have economic right to deliver her into debt-slavery.) CC separated the case of the daughter from the other family members listed in LH 117. With this, CC circumvented the problem of a creditor having sexual relations with the woman by prescribing that she become his wife. The motivating logic was that sexual intercourse with an unbetrothed and unmarried woman would require the male to marry her. CC, in fact, included a law to this effect near the end of its casuistic laws in 22:15-16:

> [15]If a man seduces a maiden who is not betrothed, and he lies with her, he shall acquire her as a wife by paying the bride price. [16]If her father refuses to give her to him, he shall (still) weigh out silver as the bride price of maidens.

Though this deals with a free woman outside a context of debt, this law could still serve as a legal analogy to debt-slavery in the conceptualization of casuistic legislation, where the introduction of variables in the protasis lead to different legal outcomes (more on this, below). In view of this, the seduction law in 22:15-16 looks like a footnote to the daughter debt-slave law that justifies this treatment of the woman.[8]

8 The seduction law is very close to Middle Assyrian Laws A 56 (whose details are dependent on and filled in from the preceding rape law A 55). According to MAL A 56, one who seduces an unbetrothed and unmarried woman is to pay threefold the price of the woman and marry her. The father may refuse to give his daughter in marriage, but the seducer must still pay the price for the woman. In the larger analysis of sources behind CC, it appears that a law like MAL A 56 (though not necessarily MAL A *per se*) from cuneiform legal tradition provided a catalyst for this legal innovation in CC's debt-slave law. The reason that 22:15-16 is placed near the end of the casuistic laws is that it derives from a source other than LH. In the primary body of casuistic laws in 21:2-22:14, CC basically follows the template of the latter half or so of LH.

To flesh out its law about the daughter (I will return to the case of a male debt slave in a moment), CC included requirements (vv. 8-11) that correlate with other laws in LH about wives and dependent women. The foundation of these other requirements appears to be Hammurabi's laws about taking a second wife when a first wife becomes displeasing (LH 148-149):

LH 148-149	Exodus 21:8, 10-11
[148]If a man marries a woman **and *la'bum*-disease then seizes her, and he decides to take a second** (woman), he may marry (her), but he may not divorce (lit.: forsake) his wife whom *la'bum*-disease seized. **She shall stay in a habitation that he builds** and **he shall support her** (*ittanaššīši*) as long as she lives. [149]If that woman does not consent to dwell in her husband's house, he shall replace the dowry that she brought from her father's house, **and she may leave.**	[8]**If she is displeasing** in the view of her master who has designated her for himself, he shall let her be redeemed. He shall not have power to sell her to a foreign people because he betrayed her. ... [10]**If he takes another (woman), he shall not withhold her** (the first wife's) **food, clothing, and habitation.** [11]If he does not do these three things for her, **she may leave** without further obligation; no (redemption or debt) silver is (due).

CC's laws in verses 8, 10–11 correlate broadly in the motifs of displeasure with a first wife, taking a second wife, the requirement for supporting the first wife, and a legal mechanism that allows the first wife to leave. The reason for taking a second wife in LH 148 is that the first wife has contracted a skin-disease. This implies that the first wife has become displeasing in some way. CC can be seen as broadening the reason for rejection to unspecified displeasure. As a consequence, befitting the context of debt-slavery, CC allows the woman to be redeemed in verse 8. Verses 10–11 follow on this (for verse 9, see below) describing the situation where the displeasing woman stays with the creditor (i.e., is not redeemed). These verses resume the correlations with LH 148-149. CC prescribes in analogy to LH that the woman is to receive support from her husband. LH 148 describes this requirement with the verb "he shall support her" (*ittanaššīši*) and includes the specific requirement that the man provide housing. Another law in LH (LH 178) uses the same verb to describe the support of a dependent woman and describes this support as consisting of *three* items: food, oil, and clothing:

[178]If an *ugbabtum-*, *naditum-*, or *sekretum*-woman, whose father gives her a dowry and writes for her a document, but...did not write for her to dispose of her property as she wishes..., after her father dies, her brothers shall take her field and orchard and give her an allowance of **food, oil, and clothing**....If her brothers do not give her an allowance of **food, oil, and clothing**..., she may give her field or orchard to any cultivator she desires, and her cultivator **shall support her** (*ittanaššîši*).

CC's requirement of *three* modes of support correlates with Hammurabi's trifold requirement. If CC's last term עֹנָתָהּ means "her habitation" (rather than "cohabiting with her"; compare, for example, the noun מָעוֹן "habitation" from the root עון), then CC can be seen as having replaced "oil" in Hammurabi's list of three items with the requirement to provide living quarters from LH 148. Certainly providing housing makes more sense as a basic requirement of subsistence than maintaining conjugal relations.

Verse 9 intervenes in the overall legal context of verses 8–11, which are otherwise based on LH 148-149. This is a digression that entertains the option that the woman is given to the creditor's son as a wife. This has similarities to laws about daughters and daughters-in-law, especially laws about a father choosing a wife for his son, in LH 154-156:

LH 154-156	Exodus 21:8-9
[154]If a man knows (sexually) **his daughter**, they shall make that man leave the city. [155]**If a man designates a bride for his son** and his son knows her, but afterwards he (the father) **lies in her lap...**, **they shall bind that man and throw him into the water.** [156]**If a man designates a bride for his son** and his son does not know her, **and he (the father) lies in her lap, he shall weigh out one-half mina (= thirty shekels) of silver....**	[8]If she is displeasing in the view of her master who has designated her for himself, he shall let her be redeemed.... [9]**If he designates her for his son, he shall treat her according to law pertaining to daughters.**

The protasis of verse 9 ("if he designates her for his son") matches the protases of the daughter-in-law laws in LH 155-156. The meaning of the apodosis of verse 9—treating the woman according to law for daughters—has been disputed and even understood as meaning that the woman becomes a free woman if she is given to his son. But it makes better sense to think that the law is proscribing the father's sexual access to the woman as in laws about a daughter-in-law in LH 155-156, paralleled by the law about a daughter in LH 154. This interpretation is consistent with the implicit motivating concern in the law generally about preventing or legally channeling a creditor's sexual exploitation of women. Verse 9 is saying that, when the woman is transferred to the son, the creditor's sexual access is blocked.

The subsidiary laws in the male debt-slave law (vv. 3-6) are also concerned with the matter of sexual access and they deal in particular with the wife of the debtor. This relates to an ambiguity about the status of the male who is enslaved. LH 117 talks about two males, the father-creditor and his son. The law clearly states that a son, like a daughter, may be delivered to a creditor to pay off a debt. A verb in the protasis of Hammurabi's law, however, may be read to include the creditor as well: "If...he sells his wife, son, or daughter, or he gives (*ittandin*) any (of them) (alternatively: he surrenders himself) for dependent debt-servitude..." (see Wright 2009: 140 and 416 n. 70). However this verb is to be read, CC's male debt-slave law seems to be written to include both the creditor and his son. Verse 3 (cited below) speaks of the male entering servitude with his wife. This points to a mature male who is independent of his father and hence one who holds the debt. Verses 4–6 (cited below), in contrast, speak of the creditor giving a wife to the male debt-slave, the debt-slave's having children with her, and his desire to stay with her. This appears to be a young male who may not yet be in a position to hold a substantial debt, i.e., he is the debtor's son.

If this is the case, then verse 3 can be seen as correlating with and responding to the matter of enslavement of the wife in LH 117:

LH 117	Exodus 21:2-3
[117]If an obligation has come due for a man, and he sells **his wife**, son, or daughter... they shall work...for three years. In the fourth year their freedom shall be effected.	[2]If you acquire a Hebrew slave, he shall work for six years. In the seventh he shall go free, without further obligation. [3]If he came in by himself, he shall go free by himself. **If he is the husband of a woman, she shall go free with him.**

CC allows the wife to enter servitude only when she accompanies her husband, and she is to go free with him. This seems calculated to prevent sexual exploitation. Her husband's presence would deter the creditor's advances. Thus the hermeneutical innovation operative here is consistent with that in the daughter debt-slave law.

The rest of the male debt-slave law (vv. 4-6) correlates with and appears indebted to laws from elsewhere in LH, similar to how the daughter debt-slave laws drew from laws in LH at a distance from the basic debt-servitude law of LH 117. Verses 4–6 entertain a case where a male slave enters as a bachelor, the creditor provides a wife, and they have children. The two alternative cases in verses 4 and 5-6 correlate, respectively, with LH 175 and LH 282, and the correlations are conceptually or topically inverse:

LH 175, 282	Exodus 21:4-6
175 If a palace-slave or a slave of a commoner marries a woman of the *awīlum*-class and she bears (him) children, **the owner of the slave has no claim of slavery on the children of the woman of the *awīlum*-class.**	4If his master gives him a woman and she bears him sons or daughters, **the woman and her children shall belong to her master,** and he (the male debt-slave) shall go free by himself.
282If a slave should say to his master, "You are not my master," he shall prove that he is his slave and his owner shall cut off his ear.	5If the servant should say, "I love my master, my wife, and my children; I will not leave," 6his master shall bring him to the God, and bring him to the door or the doorpost. His master shall pierce his ear with an awl, and he shall thus work for him indefinitely.

LH 175 deals with a male slave marrying a free woman. This situation is essentially the opposite of verse 4. In this verse the male, though a slave, is only temporarily so, and may be freed. His wife is presumably a chattel slave, owned by the creditor. But both laws are similar in that the children inherit the woman's status. In LH 175, the woman's children are free, as she is. In verse 4, the children are chattel-slaves, like the mother.

Verses 5-6 extend the case by adapting LH 282 through conceptual inversion. Though Hammurabi's law deals with a chattel slave and his rejection of his owner's authority, the two laws have the same basic elements in the same order: introduction of the slave's speech, a citation of his speech in which he accepts or rejects the owner's authority, a formal legal process that determines status, culmination of that process that involves physical trauma or disfigurement of the slave's ear. CC turns the slave into a debt-slave, has him express love for his master, and prescribes a less traumatizing mark of servitude. This repurposing of a law unrelated to the new or target context is similar to CC's repurposing the Hammurabi's talion law to serve in the context of miscarriage.

In this regard, it is worth noting that cases of hermeneutical transformation such as this do not come about by unbridled inventive flights of imagination, but reflect a process of differentiation and alternation inherent in casuistic formulation and reasoning. Many of the laws in LH and CC present coherent series of laws in which subsequent laws in a series develop by the introduction of a variable. The assault laws in LH 206-208, cited and discussed in the previous section of this essay, constitute a textbook case: LH 206 starts with a case of inadvertent injury; LH 207 introduces the variable that the victim dies; and LH 208 introduces the variable that the victim is a commoner. The conceptual inversion that we see in CC over against LH in many cases works in terms of the introduction of variables in source laws used. This then produces new laws suited to the context of CC. In this manner laws that appear unrelated to the topic of interest to a passage in CC can be read as analogically applicable and could be used to create new laws to fit the new context.

In summary here, the debt-slave laws of Exod 21:2-11 appear as dependent on LH as the assault laws of verses 22–27 (or verses 18–32 more broadly). There is a substantial basic and pervasive similarity which points to dependence. Moreover, many of the differences appear to arise from employing techniques similar to those found operative in verses 22–27 in the interest of producing more systematic legislation or resolving problems in the presumed source. This process of legal innovation ultimately betrays a genetic tie to the source even though the resulting laws are substantially different. In both cases we have examined in this essay, hermeneutic transformation also entails a hierarchy of influences from LH. Certain source laws provided a legislative foundation, the miscarriage law in LH 209-210 for verses 22–23 and the debt-slave law in LH 117 for verses 2 and 7. Other laws, sometimes from quite a distance and about different topics, were then brought in to augment the foundational laws.

CONCLUSION

The two cases examined in this paper, the miscarriage, talion, and slave injury laws of Exod 21:22-27 (as part of the wider assault laws of verses

18–32) and the debt-slave laws of verses 2–11 are the passages in CC that have the most pervasive correlations with LH. Nevertheless, using these as an evidential basis, the analysis could be extended to other passages of CC where similarities with LH are evident. This includes most of the casuistic laws: on homicide and capital crimes (21:12-17; cf. LH 14, 192-195, 207),[9] animal loss and theft (21:35-22:3; cf. LH 253-266),[10] animal grazing (22:4; cf. LH 57-58), deposit (22:6-8; cf. LH 122-126), animal loss (22:9-12; cf. LH 266-267), and animal rental (22:13-14; cf. LH 244-249, 268-271).[11] Some of these cases are more complex in that they appear to reflect use of auxiliary sources beyond LH (see, for example, n. 8). But they all point to the fact that CC has used sources, primarily LH.

The analysis can also be extended to CC's apodictic laws (20:23-26 and 22:20-23:19; see Wright 2009: 31–90, 286–321). These have various correlations with the prologue and especially the epilogue of LH. Like the prologue and epilogue, CC's apodictic laws provide an envelope around the central casuistic laws. These outer sections are the parts of the two works where the personalities of the deities are on full display, in contrast to their rather theologically dry bodies of casuistic law. It is, in fact, in the apodictic laws where we find what is perhaps the collection's chief transformative hermeneutic: the replacement of the human lawgiver Hammurabi with the deity YHWH. This appears to inform and provide motivation for the use of LH in CC's casuistic laws. The themes of the apodictic laws correlate with the themes of a set of exhortations in the epilogue, including care for the weak members of society, speaking about sovereigns, the cult, and justice. The injunctive formulation of the apodictic laws broadly correlates with the injunctive style of the exhortations in the epilogue. New evidence since my book suggests that the appendix to CC (Exod 23:20-33) continues the thematic reflexes of Hammurabi's epilogue as well as incorporating motifs from Assyrian royal inscriptions about conquest of enemies (see Wright 2014; 2016a). This rewriting of law and other sources points to the highly ideological character and goal of CC. This appears mainly for

9   The section on the miscarriage, talion, and slave injury laws, above, already demonstrated that the homicide laws are conceptually entailed in the topical matter and source analysis for the assault laws of verses 18–32.

10 Exod 21:36, 37 use talion language to describe the replacement of animals and thus show these laws are tied to the systematic thinking that produced the main talion laws in 21:23-25.

11 See the detailed mapping of primary and secondary source correlations in Wright 2009: 360–63. The body of that book discusses all the correlations charted there in detail.

the purpose of creating history, to use Brettler's (1995) characterization of biblical historiography, more than prescribing law. CC adapts its source material to fit Israelite religious and legal perspectives, particularly those it imagined to operate at the earliest stage of Israelite history.

In short, the whole evidential picture of CC must be considered when trying to determine whether any particular passage may be dependent upon LH and related sources. If CC's assault and debt-slave laws are dependent on LH, then one should consider the possibility, for example, that the deposit law in Exod 22:6-8 may in part rely on the deposit law in LH 122-126. One should also consider that the mention of providing justice to a trio of poor people in 22:20, which includes the widow and orphan, and the mention of memorializing the divine lawgiver's name in a cult place in 20:24 are also tied, respectively, to the mention of providing justice to a trio of poor people, including the widow and orphan, and of the memorialization of Hammurabi's name in the temple, found in cols. 47:59-62 and 47:93-48:2 of the epilogue.

REFERENCES

Baden, J. 2010. Review of Wright, *Inventing God's Law*, in *Review of Biblical Literature* 7.

Brettler, M. Z. 1995. *The Creation of History in Ancient Israel*. London: Routledge.

Carr, D. 2011. *Formation of the Hebrew Bible: A New Reconstruction*. New York: Oxford.

Holtz, S. 2010. Review of Wright, *Inventing God's Law*, in *Catholic Biblical Quarterly* 72: 820–22.

Horowitz, W., Oshima, T., and F. Vukosavović. 2012. "Hazor 18: Fragments of a Cuneiform Law Collection from Hazor." *Israel Exploration Journal* 62: 158–76.

Leonard, J. M. 2008. "Identifying Inner-Biblical Allusions: Psalm 78." *Journal of Biblical Literature* 127: 241–65.

Levinson, B. M. 1998. *Deuteronomy and the Hermeneutics of Legal Innovation*. Oxford: Oxford University Press.

Levinson, B. M. 2004. "Is the Covenant Code an Exilic Composition? A Response to John Van Seters." Pp. in *In Search of Pre-Exilic Israel*, edited by John Day, 272–325. Supplements to the Journal for the Study of the Old Testament, 406. London: T&T Clark.

Levinson, B. M. 2008a. *Legal Revision and Religious Renewal in Ancient Israel*. Cambridge: Cambridge University Press.

Levinson, B. M. 2008b. *"The Right Chorale": Studies in Biblical Law and Interpretation*. Forschungen zum Alten Testament, 54. Tübingen: Mohr Siebeck.

Malul, M. 2011. Review of Wright, *Inventing God's Law*, in *Bulletin of the Anglo-Israel Archaeological Society* 29: 155–59.

Morrow, W. 2013. "Legal Interactions: The *Mišpāṭîm* and the Laws of Hammurabi." *Bibliotheca Orientalis* 70: 309–31.

Nihan, C. 2013. "Révisions scribales et transformations du droit dans l'Israël ancien: le cas du talion (*jus talionis*)." In *Loi et Justice dans la Littérature du Proche-Orient ancien*, edited by Olivier Artus, 123–58. Beiheft zur Zeitschrift für Altorientalisiche und Biblische Rechtsgeschich, 20. Wiesbaden: Harrassowitz.

Otto, E. 2010. "Das Bundesbuch und der 'Kodex' Hammurapi: Das biblische Recht zwischen positiver und subversiver Rezeption von Keilschriftrecht." *Zeitschrift für Altorientalisiche und Biblische Rechtsgeschichte* 16: 1–26.

Polak, F. 2010. Review of Wright, *Inventing God's Law*, in *Review of Biblical Literature* 5.

Stackert, J. 2007. *Rewriting the Torah: Literary Revision in Deuteronomy and the Holiness Legislation*. Forschungen zum Alten Testament, 52. Tübingen: Mohr Siebeck.

Wells, B. 2006. "The Covenant Code and Near Eastern Legal Traditions: A Response to David P. Wright." *Maarav* 13: 85–118.

Wells, B. 2011. Review of Wright, *Inventing God's Law*, in *Journal of Religions* 11: 558–60.

Wright, D. P. 2009. *Inventing God's Law: How the Covenant Code of the Bible Used and Revised the Laws of Hammurabi*. Oxford: Oxford University Press.

Wright, D. P. 2010. "Miscarriage, Talion, and Slave Injury in the Covenant Code and Hammurabi's Laws." In *Gazing on the Deep: Ancient Near Eastern and Other Studies in Honor of Tzvi Abusch*, edited by J. Stackert, B. N. Porter, and D. P. Wright, 539–64. Bethesda: CDL Press.

Wright, D. P. 2014. "The Origin, Development, and Context of the Covenant Code (Exod 20:23-23:19)." In *The Book of Exodus: Composition, Reception, and Interpretation*, edited by Thomas Dozeman, Craig Evans, and Joel Lohr, 220-44. Formation and Interpretation of Old Testament Literature. Supplements to Vetus Testamentum, 164. Leiden: Brill.

Wright, D. P. 2016a. "The Covenant Code Appendix (Exod 23:20-33), Neo-Assyrian Sources, and Implications for Pentateuchal Study." In *The Formation of the Pentateuch: Bridging the Academic Cultures of Europe, Israel, and North America*, edited by J. Gertz, B. M. Levinson, D. Rom-Shiloni, and K. Schmid, 47-85. Tübingen. Mohr Siebeck.

Wright, D. P. 2016b. "Source Dependence and the Development of the Pentateuch: The Case of Leviticus 24." In *The Formation of the Pentateuch: Bridging the Academic Cultures of Europe, Israel, and North America*, edited by J. Gertz, B. M. Levinson, D. Rom-Shiloni, and K. Schmid, 651-682. Tübingen. Mohr Siebeck.

Chapter 11

To Refer or Not To Refer: That is the Question

PETER MACHINIST[*]

I. INTRODUCTION

It should be no surprise that ancient Near Eastern "literary" texts, or what the late A. L. Oppenheim famously called texts of the "stream of tradition" (Oppenheim 1977: 13–23), exhibit references to one another or to statements or turns of phrase taken from otherwise non-surviving sources, whether written or oral. No surprise, because, on the one hand, such reference is a phenomenon arguably endemic to the very act of writing, indeed of communication altogether. And no surprise, on the other hand, because many of these Near Eastern texts are what may be called "traditional": texts composed and re-composed sometimes over centuries, thus in a process of continual intra-textual, as well as inter-textual reference. Moreover, the composers/transmitters, where we can observe them, were largely, if not exclusively, scribal elites, for whom the ability to undertake, and more, to perform, textual reference was a primary means of manifesting their self-identity and self-esteem.

Although the referencing at issue could theoretically involve oral and written (on whatever materials) communications, in practical fact, the modern study of the ancient Near East must begin and end with what has survived: communications that were written. There certainly must have been oral communication, indeed a great deal of it given the restricted state of literacy in the ancient Near East, but this is to be surmised mainly, if not exclusively, on the basis of the written material. Focusing, thus, on

*   Peter Machinist is Hancock Research Professor of Hebrew and Other Oriental Languages at Harvard University, Cambridge, Massachusetts.

this material, we may observe that the textual referencing it exhibits can be found in many shapes and sizes. The theories to account for these have become legion, especially since the end of the Second World War, with particular impetus from a succession of French literary critics (Cheney 2012). At the risk of great oversimplification, let us briefly consider four pairs of distinctions, in part overlapping, that may serve as useful guides to the kinds of connections we encounter.

The first is between written texts and visual art or image. (Of course, one could consider connections between specimens of visual art exclusively, and the appeal to other artistic works has been the backbone of visual artistry and art criticism throughout history. But in this essay, as in the volume in which it appears, written texts remain the base.) Here the connection may be immediate: a relief or sculpture with an inscription or the reverse, forcing the viewer to relate them in some way. This relationship could be direct, wherein the inscription explains the relief or an element thereof explicitly, or it may be indirect, indeed far from transparent: thus a scene on a seal impression rolled on a cuneiform tablet that may have nothing directly to do with the legal contract written on the tablet. Alternatively, the relationship between a written text and visual art may not be immediate, that is, the two may not be physically connected, and so the relationship between them not obvious. One example, again Mesopotamian, is the frequent appearance in cylinder seals and larger visual art of a brawny male human figure holding, if not crushing a bull. This has often been connected by modern scholars with the story of the hero Gilgamesh killing the Bull of Heaven, but no written caption to the visual art is extant that makes that connection explicit (e.g., Steymans 2010). The connection is certainly not implausible, particularly because the Gilgamesh story is the best known example of human hero and bull of what survives from Mesopotamia. But, of course, that cannot exclude other possible stories not now extant, nor the possibility that the visual scene represents a general motif of the confrontation between humans and animals, not one of its particular instantiations as represented by Gilgamesh. And even if the Gilgamesh connection were accepted, the visual scene may not be an echo of the specific written stories that we have in Akkadian and Sumerian, which, in fact, show that not simply Gilgamesh, but his companion, Enkidu, were together responsible for the killing of the Bull (George 2003: 47–54 [Standard Babylonian, tablet VI]; 166–175 [Sumerian]).

A second pair of distinctions that provide a perspective on textual referencing in the ancient Near East (and beyond) involves that between historical/genetic and functional/typological. Historical or genetic connections are similarities and differences that can be interpreted, if not explained, as actual connections in time and space between a particular text or image and another, whether an individual text or image or a plurality of them. In other words, the author/creator of text/image A uses something from text/image B, or both A and B can actually be connected with a C, or, finally, the author of A can be shown to have been influenced by a variety of other texts, images, or a general stock of motifs and language. To establish such an historical or genetic connection, therefore, a modern interpreter must not only show a very specific set of connections in motif, structure, language, etc., but also establish a plausible historical channel of communication between the target text or image and the claimed influences on it from other texts, images, and motifs. All of this is to be contrasted with textual references that, from the point of view of the outside interpreter, are functional or typological, wherein, for example, a text from the Hebrew Bible echoes in language, motif, idea, etc., something from a culture that can be shown not to have had any historical contact with the Hebrew Bible and the ancient Israel from which it comes. The value to the modern interpreter, then, of appealing to such an historically distant and unrelated phenomenon would lie in the possibility that in its functional or typological similarity to the biblical text, it could help to make sense, to explain the meaning, of the biblical which would not have been possible for the interpreter focusing on that biblical text alone.

The preceding two perspectives on textual/imagistic referencing have hinted at a third: whether references to another text or image or any outside influence are conscious or unconscious. In other words, is the author intentionally referring to another and so prior particular text, image, motif, or literary tradition in the composition of his own text? Or is he using a feature of whose source he is unaware, indeed, may not even be aware that it originates outside of his own immediate context: something that could have been a commonplace phrase in his Zeitgeist? In either case, the reference could be an historical or genetic one, but how can a modern interpreter discern whether it is conscious or unconscious? Are there, for example, explicit linguistic or visual markers in the text pointing to a conscious connection? What kinds of conscious references could be at stake: citations, allusions, reformulations, etc.?

The issue of conscious and unconscious can be framed in another, somewhat different way, as proposed for Hebrew biblical literature by Benjamin Sommer (Sommer 1998: chap. 1, especially 3–15), building on an essay by Jay Clayton and Eric Rothstein (Clayton and Rothstein, 1991). Their distinction is between "influence" and "allusion," on the one hand, and "intertextuality," on the other. Of course, these terms are well represented in the history of literary criticism, even if with wildly varying definitions. But let us see what Sommer, and Clayton and Rothstein, have to offer. For them "influence" and "allusion" comprise an older and often practiced method in literary criticism, "asking how one composition evokes its antecedents, how one author is affected by another, and what sources a text utilizes. That approach is diachronic" (Sommer 1998: 6–7)—or in terms of one of our preceding distinctive pairs, it is historical/genetic: it looks for specific and chronologically prior sources that serve the author as his background. Therefore, like another of our pairs, "influence" and "allusion" focus on the author and how he views and uses his antecedents, emphasizing the possibility that his reference is conscious. Against this approach, for Sommer, and Clayton and Rothstein—who themselves acknowledge other scholarly predecessors—stands "intertextuality". Here the focus is not on what an author does to produce the text or image, but on the text and image itself and how readers or onlookers understand it. In this act of understanding, readers may make connections to specific texts, images, motifs, literary traditions and/or to "commonplace phrases or figures from the linguistic or cultural systems in which the text exists... connections [that] do not arise exclusively from an intentional or signaled use of an earlier text, such as citation...." (Sommer 1998: 7). And different readers/onlookers may make different connections. Moreover, diachrony is not important: the focus is not on whether the connected texts, images, commonplaces were created before the text at issue; all that is necessary is that they be in the mind of the reader or onlooker as he or she confronts the text. Consciousness of particular or general connections, therefore, is now a matter of the reader/onlooker, not of the author. In sum, the view of "intertextuality" advocated by Sommer, Clayton, and Rothstein is a post-modernist one, for it is the reader/onlooker who controls the network of connections that a given text or image evokes, not the author of that text/image. The question that remains, however, is whether there are any limits to the connections a reader/onlooker can make—any criteria for evaluating what constitute appropriate connections. It is a question, to be sure, that bedevils much post-modernist literary interpretation as a whole.

In this essay, we will focus on texts, not visual images, on written texts, not oral, and on connections between texts that would appear to be historical/genetic and reflect "influence/allusion" rather than "intertextuality". It remains to be seen whether in the four case studies that follow—all of them well known from previous scholarly studies—the connections are conscious or unconscious ones, thus involving either specific texts, like citations, allusions, reformulations, etc., or more generalized, commonplace phrasing and/or ideas. We will in the process have to ask what purposes these connections serve in making up the meaning of the four texts at issue.

II. CASE STUDIES

1. AN IDIOM FOR "TO SLANDER"

Hayim Tawil offers, inter alia, the following three texts, from Akkadian, biblical Aramaic, and biblical Hebrew (Tawil 2009: 17, 347, 452):

> Akkadian (*akālu karṣa*)
> *bēlīmi ana* LU₂.MEŠ *sarrūti ša ikkalūnim karṣīya ana pāni šarri bēlīya lā tešemme.*
> "My lord, now, do not listen to the liars who are slandering me before the king, my lord" (Amarna EA 161:7-8) (Rainey 2015: I, 798-99).

> Biblical Aramaic (אכל קרצין)
> ואכלו קרציהו די יהודיא
> "And they slandered the Jews" (Dan 3:8; 6:25).

> Biblical Hebrew (אכל בשר) ("to eat flesh")
> בקרב עלי מרעים לאכל את-בשרי צרי ואיבי לי המה כשלו ונפלו
> "When evildoers attack me to slander me—they are to me my enemies and my foes—they stumble and fall" (Ps 27:2).

These three examples all turn on the same idiomatic phrase, literally, "to eat the *karṣu* (Akkadian)/*qarṣîn<qəraṣ* (Aramaic) or *bāśār* (= 'flesh' in Hebrew)," meaning "to slander, denounce". *karṣu* seems to indicate some kind of clump, from the verb *karāṣu* (Akkadian) or *qāraṣ* (biblical Hebrew), meaning, it appears, "to press together tightly." In this sense, it occurs in the Hebrew Bible with eyes to mean "squint" (Prov 6:13; 10:10; Ps 35:19) or with lips to mean "to purse" (Prov 16:30). In these occurrences, the squinting or pursing is said to be done by evildoers who want to commit deception. It is also found, both in the Hebrew Bible and in Akkadian (Job 33:6 and *CAD* K: 209-210a s.v. *karāṣu*), with clay, to refer to the "squeezing" or, better, "pinching off" a portion of clay by which God or the gods created humans. In that usage, it would appear that the clay could well be the basis for, and thus equivalent to, human flesh. "Eating the clay or flesh" would

then be understood as a negative, something injurious to human beings, and so could then be extended, in a metaphorical way, to the injury caused by slander. In turn, the extension might be understood to connect with the squinting of eyes and pursing of lips that mark the deception of the evildoer.

In the three examples above, it is obvious that the one in biblical Aramaic is a simple cognate of the Akkadian, whereas the biblical Hebrew represents a translation—an interpretative effort to find an equivalent of the Akkadian idiom in Hebrew by equating *bāśār* with *karṣu*.[1] The Hebrew example, therefore, is one step removed from the Akkadian. All of this presumes that the Akkadian is the original, and the two West Semitic examples, from Aramaic and then Hebrew, are the derivatives. But how can we know this, particularly if we rely just on the Akkadian example given, which is from an Amarna letter written by Aziru, the ruler of the Levantine state of Amurru, to his putative overlord, the Egyptian Pharaoh? The Amarna example, to be sure, is much earlier than the two West Semitic texts, but theoretically, it could still reflect a West Semitic idiom, since, as is well known, the Akkadian of these Levantine princelings shows in different ways much West Semitic interference.

Two arguments, however, speak against this in the present instance. The first is another Amarna letter, from Lab'ayu, the ruler of the Palestinian city-state of Shechem, to the Pharaoh, in which he uses a similar idiom, substituting *qabû* for *akālu*: *qabi qarṣīya (šīrti) ina pāni šarrīma bēlīya*: "I have been slandered before the king, my lord" (EA 252:13-14; Rainey I: 1022–23). Here the idiom *qabû qarṣa* (note the noun is written with *q* instead of *k* as in biblical Aramaic) is glossed in the scribe's local West Semitic language as *šīrti*, which Tawil plausibly explains (Tawil 2009: 452) as a first singular passive of the West Semitic root *šwr/šrr* "to treat disloyally, slander."[2] The

---

1 The relation between the Akkadian and Aramaic words may even be closer if we follow Stephen Kaufman's view (1974: 63), repeated in Tawil (2009: 452), that *qəraṣ* in biblical Aramaic is always in the plural, like Akkadian *karṣu*, but unlike the biblical Hebrew *bāśār*, which is in the singular. It is true, as Kaufman notes (1978: 63), that in almost all the Aramaic dialects, with just a few exceptions in Jewish Aramaic, the noun is in the plural, but so far as I can tell, the Akkadian texts, as cited in *AHw*: 450b, and *CAD* K: 222b-223, could be either plural or singular, although the consistent lack of plene spelling (e.g., *kar-ṣu-u*) suggests that the Akkadian word is a singular.

2 *AHw*: 1193 categorizes *šīrti* as a G or D form of *šāru* II, though the two examples it cites are both from the Amarna letters, namely, Nos. 252, as given here, and 286, where it appears as the finite D form both as *ú-ša-a-ru* (line 21) and as *ú-ša-wa-ru* (line 24). (Rainey 2015 I: 1106, however, reads them both the same: *ú-ša-à-ru*.) *AHw* says nothing explicit about the origin of this word, whether it

use of a gloss, evidently, suggests that the idiom *qabû qarṣa* is not native to this West Semitic scribe, even if the writing as *qarṣu* instead of *karṣu*— so echoing the biblical Aramaic and Hebrew forms—may reflect a West Semitic phonological adaptation. In addition, the idiom *qabû/akālu karṣa* is attested in Mesopotamian sources well outside of the Amarna corpus, from Old, Standard, and Neo-Babylonian texts in addition to grammatical texts of the scholastic tradition (*AHw*: 450b; *CAD* K: 222b–223; Tawil 2009: 17, 347, 452). This range of attestation, much more than what is extant for the ancient West Semitic languages, is thus a second argument that Mesopotamia is indeed the source of the idiom.

What, finally, about the usage of the idiom? Do the examples above show a conscious effort to react to Mesopotamian Akkadian in some way? If we assume that the Amarna texts are not examples of a West Semitic idiom intruding into Akkadian, but offer genuine Akkadian phrases, then here the local Levantine scribe is simply using what is part of the Akkadian language that he learned. In the case of the Daniel texts, one might argue that given the fact that they are set in Babylon, at the court of Nebuchadnezzar, the author might have availed himself of an Akkadian idiom, here directly transcribed, in order to lend verisimilitude to the scene. This is possible, because the idiom appears as part of a description of what the Babylonian courtiers have said in their "slandering" of Daniel and other Jewish captives. Relevant here may be the fact that there were other possible words for "to slander," as evidenced in the biblical lexicon, that our Daniel author could have chosen—options that look more straightforward and, in any case, are evidently not Mesopotamian-linked: the *hiphil* of *lšn*, the *piel* of *rgl*, and several nouns for "slanderer" (*rākil, nirgan*) and "slander" (*dibbâ*). That our author chose not one of these, but a Mesopotamian idiom raises the possibility that he wanted that Mesopotamian flavor and/or a means of heightening the seriousness of the "slander" that the Babylonian courtiers pronounced. A conscious reflection on Mesopotamian origins may also be at work in the sole biblical Hebrew occurrence of our idiom, Ps 27:2. Unlike the Amarna and Daniel occurrences, this psalm does show a difference from the Mesopotamian, since the object of the verb *'ākal* is not *qarṣu*, but *bāśār*. What is the point here? It could reflect a deliberate change in order

---

is Akkadian or West Semitic, but *CAD* Š/2: 140 does, labelling it West Semitic, although it regards the meaning as uncertain. It goes on to state that the attested forms are passives, and for attestations it cites three Amarna letters: not only 252 and 286, as above, but also 180, referring for the latter to a note by W. L. Moran (1975: 161–62: n. 180).

to clarify what the original *qarṣu* is, or to substitute something that was understood to make better sense. Unfortunately, there is not enough context in the psalm to be certain. And even if we could explain the *bāśār* as a substituted word, it remains undecided whether this was the work of the author of Psalm 27 or something already in the lexical tradition that was available to him or her. In the end, therefore, the appearance of the idiom "to eat *qarṣu*/flesh" in non-Mesopotamian contexts, including the Hebrew Bible, may reflect some conscious borrowing, but the case remains open, and the safer conclusion may be that by the time of these occurrences, the idiom, though ultimately Mesopotamian, was already too well embedded in the languages of the texts involved to be regarded as something special and unusual.

2. THE RHETORIC OF DESTRUCTION: ISAIAH 1:7 AND ITS NEO-ASSYRIAN CONGENER

ארצכם שממה
עריכם שרפות אש
אדמתכם לנגדכם
זדים אכלים אתה

"Your country is a devastation;
Your cities burned with fire;
Your land, in your very presence,
Aliens consume it."

These lines are part of a passage in the First Isaiah describing the destructive invasion of Judah by a foreign enemy.[3] Although not named, there is general agreement from the context that the enemy referred to is the Assyrian army, and probably more specifically, the Assyrian king Sennacherib in his third campaign, which Isaiah elsewhere, along with other biblical and Assyrian sources, depicts as broadly destructive across Judah and the Levantine coast.[4] The words and images used here, particularly *šamāmâ*, *śārap 'ēš*, and *' ākal*, are not unfamiliar from the Akkadian

---

3 The following discussion is a revision of Machinist 1983: 724–25, where fuller textual references may be found.

4 The biblical and non-biblical sources, textual and archaeological, for this third campaign have engendered an immense secondary bibliography. Three recent volumes include Gallagher (1999), Grabbe (2003), and Kalimi and Richardson (2014).

expressions for the conquest and destruction of enemies that are common to the Assyrian royal inscriptions. Here is one example, from the reign of Aššurnaṣirpal II (883–859 BCE):

> *āla appul aqqur ina išāti ašrup akulšu*
> "The city I devastated, destroyed, burned with fire, consumed it"
> (Machinist 1983: 724 and n. 23; Grayson 1991: 201–2, ii 1; 216, iii 54).

How, then, to understand the parallel: biblical Hebrew and Akkadian Assyrian? In the first place, we should note just how close the relationship is between the terms: Hebrew *śārap 'ēš* and *'ākal* are direct cognates of Akkadian *ina išāti šarāpu* and *akālu*, respectively, just like biblical Aramaic *'ăkal qarṣîn* and Akkadian *karṣa akālu* in our previous case study, while Hebrew *šəmāmâ* is semantically, though not morphologically, related to the two Akkadian verbs, *napālu* ("to devastate") and *naqāru* ("to destroy"). To be sure, the Hebrew terms are found, individually, in other biblical texts to describe destruction, many of which are not associated with the Sennacherib campaign nor even with the Assyrians.[5] But this leads to the second point: that the concatenation of these terms together in the same Isaiah passage is not found elsewhere in the Hebrew Bible, but it does match almost completely the Assyrian example above and in the same order. Indeed, this example is only one of many, scattered throughout the Assyrian royal inscriptional tradition from Tiglat-pileser I (1114–1076 BCE) through Sargon II (721–705 BCE). Again, there are some variations that should be noted. So the four Akkadian verbs are not found in all the occurrences: sometimes either *napālu* or *naqāru*—both, as just noted, corresponding to Hebrew *šəmāmâ*—is absent; and in other cases *akālu* can also be absent; in still other cases, another phrase can inserted at the end, namely, *karmē turru* "to turn (the conquered city) into a ruin hill" (Machinist 1983: 724, n. 24; Grayson 1991: e.g., 209–10, ii 100). As for *ina išāti ṣarāpu*, it appears to be replaced in the royal inscriptions after Sargon II by the phrase, *ina girri qamû* (Machinist 1983: 724, n. 24). These variations, however, do not appear to be significant. *Ina girri qamû*, in particular, may be different in vocabulary, but it continues the same meaning and image conveyed by *ina išāti ṣarāpu* "to burn with fire." We are left, therefore, with the distinct impression that *napālu*, *naqāru*, *ina išāti ṣarāpu/ina girri qamû*, and *akālu* constitute a conventional formula in the Assyrian inscriptions

---

5 For a list of examples, see Machinist (1983: 724: nn. 25–26). In n. 26, observe that Joel 2:3 has two of the terms, *'ākal 'ēš* and *šəmāmâ*, but not the others nor in the same order as in Isa 1:7.

for the destruction of the enemy. The closeness of this formula, then, to Isa 1:7 in wording, meaning, image, and order; the uniqueness of the Isaiah passage in the Hebrew Bible in its display of the formula, even if individual terms in it can be found in other biblical passages; and the fact that Isaiah applies the formula to the Assyrians themselves—all together argue that the relationship between Isaiah and the Assyrian formula is no accident. It may be suggested, in sum, that while Isaiah drew on older phraseology known in Israelite tradition for his description of the Assyrians, his selection and arrangement of that phraseology show the effect of Assyrian royal idiom—an idiom that our prophet learned in some way from the Assyrians who had become the imperial overlords of Judah several decades earlier (see further below).

Yet we must still ask: why did Isaiah use this idiom as he did? Let us begin by observing the location of the idiom: part of the first unit of chapter 1 of the Isaiah book, verses 2-9—that is, the first unit after the introductory rubric in verse 1 to the whole book. The unit describes, as already mentioned, a destructive invasion by the Assyrian army into Judah and Jerusalem, which are identified in verses 1 and 8. The invasion is presented as punishment from Yahweh for Judah/Israel's rebellion against him. The proclamation of this rebellion begins the unit, and, though vehemently expressed, that proclamation is unspecific in detail (vv. 2-4). The punishment, on the other hand, is presented at greater length and is specific, depicted as having already arrived and that in two ways: as the excruciating and unhealed bruising of a human body (vv. 5-6),[6] and then as the desolation of the land with the survival of just a few landmarks, principally Jerusalem (= "daughter Zion" in v. 8) (vv. 7-9).[7]

---

6 This can be understood as a metaphor for the destruction of the whole population and its land, but also as a depiction of the more actual wounds and mutilations on the bodies of the victims of the punishing invasion. The latter are often described in the Neo-Assyrian royal inscriptions, particularly of Aššurnaṣirpal II (Grayson 1991: e.g., 201–2, i 116–ii 1). Cf. the celebrated study of A. T. Olmstead (1918).

7 The survival of Jerusalem from the Assyrian invasion, is, of course, evidenced elsewhere in the Hebrew Bible, including Isaiah, and in Assyrian sources. See the discussions in the volumes mentioned above in n. 4. In the present instance, it is verse 9 that turns a negative picture of Jerusalem's devastated survival in verse 8 into a more positive one with "a few survivors" (*śarîd kim'at*), but note how even this is qualified. The uncertainty continues, in the present form of the Isaiah text, with the mention of Sodom and Gomorrah at the end of verse 9. Here they are an image that the Judahites who are speaking reject: God's allowing us "a few survivors" has saved us from the destruction meted

In this context, it may be suggested, our Assyrian idiom is used to heighten the severity of the Assyrian destructiveness—the severity expressed by citing, supposedly, the very words of the destroyers. Yet the fact that these words in Isaiah are spoken—or better, appropriated—by Yahweh, and not by their original Assyrian royal authority, can be understood as Yahweh's appropriation of that authority: his control of the Assyrians. They are his agents of destructive punishment, as is made clear later in the First Isaiah, especially Isa 10:5-15, where Yahweh is presented as not only using Assyria to punish Israel and Judah, but then as eventually turning around to punish Assyria itself for having exceeded and corrupted the role he gave it (see Machinist 2016).

3. A PUBLIC SPECTACLE: ISAIAH 46:1-2 AND A MESOPOTAMIAN RITUAL

כרע בל קרס נבו 1a

היו עצביהם לחיה ולבהמה b

נשאתיכם עמוסות אשמ לעיפה c

קרסו כרעו יחדו 2a

לא יכלו מלט משא b

ונפשם בשבי הלכה c

1a "Bel bowed down; Nebo was stumbling.
  b The idols (embodying) them were attached to (= borne by) animal and beast.
  c The(se) objects that you carried were loaded as a burden on the weary (creatures).
2a They stumbled, they bowed down all together.
  b They were not able to deliver (from) a burden//deliver (= bring to pass?) an oracle;
  c (Instead) they themselves proceeded along in captivity."

This short text, on which much commentary has been expended, describes the physical images of the two major Babylonian gods of the first millennium BCE, namely, Bel (the principal title, becoming an alternative name, of Marduk) and his son, Nebo (Hebrew for Babylonian Nabu). The images move along in some kind of procession, apparently strapped to animals

---

out to Sodom and Gomorrah. But then in the following section, verses 10–18, it is these same Judahites whom Isaiah addresses as Sodom and Gomorrah in their brazen disobedience of Yahweh's will, thus leaving open the question of whether they will indeed share the fate of those two cities of yore.

(v. 1b), probably either cattle or donkeys depending on the weight of the images, and also carried by humans, probably either Babylonians or Babylonian slaves (v. 1c); or perhaps we should understand these two parallel cola (1b and c) as the carrying animals being led by the humans. The procession is not explicitly identified until the last colon, verse 2c, which suggests that the images have been taken by an invader who is leading them out of the city(ies) and sanctuary(ies) where they are normally worshipped. The structure of these two verses is in six short cola, the first four of which are in chiasm: 1a-1b::1c-2a. The chiasm is heightened by the fact that 2a has the two verbs of 1a in reversed order. Notice further that in the Tiberian Masoretic text the verbs in 1a are in the singular, one for each of the deities, while in the chiastic 2a they are in the plural, connected, it appears, with the plural nouns *'ăṣabbêhem* and *nəśû'ōtêkem* of the preceding two chiastic cola, 1b::1c. Moreover, in 1a the second verb is a *qal* participle, *qōrēs*, while the first is a *qal* perfect, but in the chiastic 2a, both verbs are now *qal* perfects. This has occasioned, on the part of a number of commentators (e.g., *BHS ad loc.*; Blenkinsopp 2002: 264; Paul 2012: 88, 276; opposed: Hermisson 1998: 86), the emendation of the "aberrant" *qal* participle to a *qal* perfect, *qāras*. But though there is some versional evidence for this—so, for example, the Septuagint (noted, e.g., Goldingay & Payne 2006: 69)—the emendation is not necessary. The participle suggests that the bowing down or falling at the start of the narrative, in 1a, is not complete: Bel has bowed down, but Nebo is in the process of stumbling. By the time of the repetition, in the chiastic 2a, the actions are complete: both in unison (*yaḥdāw*) have fallen. Furthermore, if at the beginning, 1a suggests that it was the *gods* Bel and Nebo who were bowing/stumbling, the following 1b and its chiastic 1c shift to describing them as *'ăṣabbêhem* and *nəśû'ōtêkem*, so that by the chiastic repetition in 2a, it is clear that there is no question of real deities here.[8] What bowed down and stumbled were *inanimate objects—idols*, as expressed by *'ăṣabbêhem*, one of several pejorative terms in

---

8 The two plural suffixes here, *-hem* and *-kem*, are to be interpreted differently: *-hem* is an objective suffix, "the idols (embodying) them," while *-kem* is subjective, "the things/objects that are carried by you (= that you carried)." The *-kem* does not refer to the idols as personified, which are thus carrying the gods Bel and Nebo, but, as noted in our main discussion, to the Babylonians carrying these idols; see below n. 12 for further discussion. In any case, as a second person plural suffix, *-kem* has disturbed some interpreters (see references in Koole 1997: 498), because it does not conform to the third person suffixes and verbs around it. But the disturbance is deliberate, signifying an abrupt break as Isaiah turns directly to the Babylonian carriers to satirize their action.

the biblical lexicon for a divine image (see Meyer ThWAT VI, 298–301, and more generally, e.g., Berlejung 1998: 286–413; Dick 1999: chap. 1; Levtow 2008: 40–85; Bonfiglio 2015; Dohmen 1987).

The final two cola (2b-c) are in what can be called antithetic parallelism, though not as closely aligned between themselves in syntax as the preceding four-colon chiasm.[9] This parallelism expresses the significance of the falling down of the images, namely, that they cannot function as deities offering help, saving from disaster their human worshippers, including those carrying them, because as inanimate objects, they are powerless to prevent themselves from being hauled off by their captors. The point here seems to be made in a pun in verse 2b on the noun *maśśā'* and its two different meanings: "burden/load" and "utterance/oracle". The pun appears to work in three different, yet overlapping perspectives. First, the supposedly divine images cannot relieve the weary animals and humans of the *maśśā'* = "burden," mentioned earlier in 1b-c, of carrying them; all that the images represent, then, is an oppressive weight. Second, the images cannot bear their "burden," meaning their Babylonian worshippers, and "save" (*mallēṭ*) them from disaster. This point becomes clear in the succeeding verses to 46:1-2, namely, 3 and 4, which offer a deliberate contrast to 1 and 2, using some of its same language, though not *maśśā'*, to describe Yahweh as the god who has been able to bear Israel—those "loaded" (*ha-'ămûsîm*) and "borne" (*han-nəśû'îm*) by him since birth—and to "save" (*wa-'ămallēṭ*) them from destruction. A third possible perspective on *maśśā'* in verse 2b extends the second one just proposed. Here, the images of Bel and Nebo, being only inert physical objects, cannot "deliver," that is, bring to pass any favorable *maśśā'* = "utterances or oracles" they might have been expected to pronounce through their human intermediaries for the deliverance of the Babylonians from danger.[10] In sum, the prominence of *maśśā'* in the final two cola, verse 2b-c, connects with the preceding four chiastic cola, verses 1a-b-c-2a, picking up and drawing out the meaning of words of the same root, *nəśû'ōt* and *maśśā'*, in verse 1c, even as its images and language echo in the following verses 3-4. One last note: the six cola are all in a third-person narrative, with the exception of verse 1c, which breaks the sequence

---

9   Yet note the pronounced alliteration in both of *h(eh)*, *k(af)*, *l(amed)*, *m(em)*, and *š(in)*.

10   The suggested meaning of *mallēṭ* here as "to bring to pass" is admittedly tentative, since it does not appear to occur as such elsewhere in the Hebrew Bible. But if we understand the basic meaning of the verb, "to deliver/save," as indicating "to remove from trouble and so to open up a new possibility," then the meaning "to bring to pass" seems to fit into this sense.

to address in the second person plural the apostrophized audience of this prophetic text, namely, those Babylonians or Babylonian slaves attending to the transport of the idols, indeed Babylonians in general. The break is obviously meant to be dramatic, stressing the impact of the fate of the idols on the welfare of the Babylonians.

So much for the internal analysis of Isa 46:1-2. But we need to go further with meaning and place these verses in wider contexts, both biblical and non-biblical, and thus raise the issue of referencing among texts. On the biblical side, two themes and their associated language are prominent. The first is the critique of the physical images of deities—idols in the biblical conception. The focus on this in 46:1-2 is echoed in the immediate literary vicinity in 46:5-7 and 45:16-17, 20, and then elsewhere in Second Isaiah, in 40:18-20 and especially 44:9-20. It is also noteworthy outside of Isaiah, as in Hos 13:2, Hab 2:18-19 and Jer 10:2-13, the latter particularly close to Isa 44:9-20 in its detailing of idol-making. These passages tend to contrast the powerlessness, indeed lifelessness of the idols—sometimes, as here in 46:2, who cannot save[11]—with the living and all-powerful creative and punishing capability of the god of Israel. This capability of God, one should note, is also marked in our text, in a deliberate contrast with 46:2. Thus, whereas 46:2 declares that the idols cannot "save" (*mallēṭ*) a favorable future for their human worshippers, in 46:3-4 it is the god of Israel who says, "I am the one who saves" (*ʾămallēṭ*) the remnant of Israel.

The second prominent theme in 46:1-2 concerns the root *nśʾ* and its nominal form *maśśāʾ*. This concern is interwoven with the first theme on idols, and like it occurs or is echoed in meaning in other biblical texts. Thus, in the following verses 3 and 4, the god of Israel not only "saves" Israel, over against the failure of the idols in verses 1 and 2, but he "bears (*ʾesbōl*) the house of Israel born from the womb" (*han-nəśûʾîm minnî-rāḥam*), as against the Babylonians who "carry/bear" (*nəśûʾōtêkem*) idols (46:1c). Something of the same contrast is found in the preceding chapter (Isa 45), which satirizes Babylonian worshippers "carrying their wooden idol" (*han-nōśəʾîm ʾet-ʿēṣ pislām*) and "praying to a god who cannot save" (*û-mitpaləlîm ʾel-ʾēl lōʾ yôšîʿa*) (45:20).[12] As for *maśśāʾ*, it is a term especially striking in the

---

11 In these other Isaianic passages, different verbal roots for "save" are used: *yšʿ* in 45:17,20; 46:7; *nṣl* in 44:17.

12 See Blenkinsopp (2002: 266). One may note that the phrase in Isa 45:20, *han-nōśəʾîm ʾet-ʿēš pislām* – which applies there to humans, more specifically, to Babylonians – helps to clarify the meaning of *nəśûʾōtêkem* in 46:1c as also referring to human carriers, again Babylonians or Babylonian slaves, of the images of Bel and Nebo.

prophetic books, where it describes and serves as the rubric for statements of divine judgment and prediction, mediated by the prophets, about and to both Israel and various foreign groups (e.g., Isa 13:1; 15:1; Jer 23:33-40; Ezek 12:10; Nah 1:1; and Mal 1:1). These texts, thus, furnish a background for the use of *maśśā'* in Isa 46:1-2 as a divine oracle, and yet against them and their depiction of Yahweh in control of the *maśśā'* he sends, 46:1-2 presents a sharp contrast, for here it is two foreign deities which cannot control their *maśśā'*—cannot bring to pass an oracle of future deliverance.

There is yet one more point, and that concerns the play on meanings and perspectives of *maśśā'* in our 46:1-2. While none of the other texts mentioning *maśśā'* seems to be quite so complex in this regard, Jer 23:33-40 does offer some analogy. This is a difficult text, and it has challenged interpreters since antiquity, with no certain resolution (e.g., McKane 1980; Holladay 1986: 647–53; Lundbom 2004: 212–21; Allen 2008: 269–70, 272–74). But its central point, I think, is clear, and is the one relevant to our present concern. The point has to do with a debate in this passage over the meaning of *maśśā'*, more specifically, *maśśā' Yahweh*. For the populace of Judah whom Jeremiah addresses, perhaps in the early stages of the Babylonian conquest, the phrase refers to the favorable prediction that Yahweh will save his people from disaster and restore them to their previous security and abundance. This view is displayed in the first part of Jer 23:9-20 as well as elsewhere in that book (e.g., Jer 7:4; 8:10-11; 14:13; 27:16; 28:1-4). The prophet Jeremiah, however, hears a different message from God, namely, that Judah will suffer disaster at the hands of the Babylonians for its sins. This different message is also on display in various parts of the book (e.g., Jer 7; 14:14-16; 28:5-17), as well as in 23:33-40 in particular, where Jeremiah castigates the Judahites, and especially his fellow prophets, for propagating what he terms as a lie, a perversion of God's words (23:36—*wa-hăpaktem 'et-dibrê 'ĕlōhîm ḥayyîm Yahweh ṣabā'ôt 'ĕlōhênû*).[13] Indeed, in 23:33-40 the confrontation reaches one of its high points, with the phrase *maśśā' Yahweh* rejected vehemently by Jeremiah, quoting God, because it has become the label used by the populace for their favorable prophecy. The phrase, in other words, which essentially must be a neutral designation for any legitimate "oracle" from Yahweh, has become, in Jeremiah's eyes, debased by widespread misuse, and therefore, he proclaims as a command from God that it is henceforth forbidden. In other words, just as in our

---

13 The word *šeqer* "lie" runs throughout Jeremiah as a principal term for the work of his opponents and particularly for this false prophecy; e.g., 6:13; 8:10; 9:2; 14:14; 20:6; 27:15. A prominent study of it is Overholt (1970).

main text Isa 46:1-2, *maśśā'* is mentioned in Jer 23:33-40 to show how it has been misapplied by its human exponents: in the case of Isaiah, that Bel and Nebo, or rather their idols, cannot sustain *maśśā'* for Babylonia; in the case of Jeremiah, that it is not the *maśśā'* that Yahweh in fact has in store for Judah.

It is clear, then, that Isa 46:1-2 has a background furnished by other texts in the Hebrew Bible. But none of these, with the exception of the succeeding verses, 46:3-4, and perhaps the preceding 45:20, seems to be echoed in particular in our text, since the relationships are not specific or exclusive enough to warrant such a deliberate connection. Rather, we appear to be in the presence of broader rhetorical and conceptual traditions in Israel regarding divine images/idols and the term *maśśā'*, to which 46:1-2 is responding. What, then, about the wider non-biblical context in which we could place our passage?

The explicit mention of the deities Bel and Nebo and of the movement of their images on animals and with humans in some kind of procession has made clear the Babylonian setting of the text, and modern interpreters have generally focused on one or both of two ways in which this setting may be defined.[14] The first is a procession as part of a festival—the most common choice being the New Year's festival (*zagmukku*/*akītu*), when the divine images were paraded out of their normal sanctuaries to the festival house (*bīt akīti*) in the outskirts of Babylon. The second setting involves a specific historical event—a disaster in which the divine images of Bel/Marduk, Nebo, and other gods were taken from their native sanctuaries either by Babylonians to protect them from an enemy or by the enemy itself. Interpreters have proposed different disasters scattered across the history of the sixth and fifth centuries BCE, thus in the Neo-Babylonian to the Achaemenid Persian periods. Of these options, the most obvious and so most popular, given the other indications in the Second Isaiah, is the end of the reign of the last Babylonian king, Nabonidus, and the conquest of his kingdom by the Achaemenid Persian ruler, Cyrus II—all in the middle decades of the sixth century BCE. More specifically, it has been proposed, Isa 46:1-2 reflects the actions of Nabonidus as he gathered the images of some of the major Babylonian deities to Babylon to protect them and the city from the impending invasion by Cyrus and, thereafter, as Cyrus conquered Babylonia and returned these images to their native sanctuaries.

---

14   A brief survey is in Blenkinsopp (2002: 266–68); also Machinist (2003: 251–52). Cf. Hermisson (2003: 95–96, 98–102, 103–4, 105–6).

How to resolve, then, this Babylonian setting for our 46:1-2? The last two cola (2b-c), telling, as we have noticed, of the disastrous capture of the images, clearly suggest an outside attack on Babylon and/or its environs. We appear, thus, to have a pointer toward the Nabonidus-Cyrus setting outlined above. Yet this setting does not seem not quite right. For in the other sources on Nabonidus and Cyrus (see Machinist 2003: 248, 4), the images of Marduk and Nabu/Nebo appear to play roles other than what one might conclude from Isa 46:1-2. Thus, there is no mention in these sources of Marduk, that is, his image, being gathered by Nabonidus to Babylon or restored by Cyrus to his native sanctuary, since Marduk was already in Babylon, the site of his principal sanctuary, and Cyrus tells us that he conquered Babylon with the direct help of Marduk, whose servant he proclaims himself. As for Nabu/Nebo, his principal sanctuary was, indeed, outside of Babylon, in Borsippa, but the Babylonian Chronicle says explicitly that the gods of Borsippa and two other Babylonian cities were not brought into Babylon. Consequently, Cyrus did not need to restore them to Borsippa. In short, it appears that our Isaiah passage has erred in its historical reference, unless one assumes that the passage comes from before the Cyrus conquest and represents a mistaken prediction about Cyrus. Yet this last assumption raises its own problem. For as the final verbs in our passage suggest—the perfect forms *qārəsû, kārə'û, yākəlû*, and *hāləkâ* in verse 2—the action looks to be in past time: Bel and Nebo have finally bowed down and have been taken into captivity. As a whole, then, 46:1-2 appears to be formulated as a reminiscence of actions *after* they have taken place. Moreover, the Babylonian gods here being satirized do not include the one that, in fact, Nabonidus elevated to supreme position in the pantheon, the moon-god Sin (Nanna-Suen). There may be an allusion to Sin elsewhere in the Second Isaiah (47:11 and perhaps 13; Machinist 2003: 256–57), but it is not certain, and even if correct, does not suggest the importance of this deity in Nabonidus' program. Now, as the evidence makes clear (Machinist 2003: 245–50 and references there), Nabonidus' exaltation of Sin was a highly controversial step, which met with real opposition among other Babylonian elites, for whom the two gods in our passage, Bel/Marduk and Nebo/Nabu, remained central. Our passage, to be sure, satirizes, not exalts, Marduk and Nabu; nonetheless, it operates from the context of their primacy in Babylonia—a primacy that was restored after the capture of Nabonidus by Cyrus. This primacy, thus, appears to be another mark for the lateness of Isa 46:1-2: after, not before, the conquest by Cyrus.

If an allusion to the Nabonidus-Cyrus period, thus, is difficult to maintain for our Isaianic passage, such difficulties are not evident for the alternative setting proposed for the passage, in the *zagmukku/akītu* or New Year's festival. Here, as we have seen, our verses can easily be understood as a procession, as the divine images are pulled along by animals and humans, and then "go/proceed" (*hāləkâ*) into captivity. But that this procession could reflect the New Year's festival has recently been sharpened by the work of Hanspeter Schaudig. He calls attention to a Mesopotamian omen collection that describes the movement of the principal image of Marduk from his principal sanctuary, the Esagil in Babylon, as the image is paraded from the Esagil to the *akītu* house for the *akītu* festival. The various twists and turns, bowing down, etc. of the image as it is pulled along the processional route are understood to have ominous significance for the welfare of a country as a whole. The literary pattern is as follows: "if the image twists, etc. in one direction, then x will occur (negative or positive) with respect to a particular people or peoples, land or lands (Babylonia or foreign)"; for example, "if Marduk (= its image) turns/twists as it goes out (on procession), then an upheaval of the land will take place" (*šumma Marduk ina āṣīšu zēr nabalkatti māti iššakkan*) (Schaudig 2008: 568, referring to Sallaberger 2000: 238, line 26). The significance of the movement of the image, thus, epitomizes the significance of the *akītu* festival altogether with its marking of the future of Babylonia and its environs. At the same time, as Schaudig observes, the content and context of these omens echo the description of the Bel and Nebo images in our Isaianic verses almost perfectly, with the connection heightened by the fact that two of the principal verbs used in the omens to describe the Marduk image are close to being semantic equivalents of the two verbs used in our verses; i.e., Akkadian *zâru* ("to twist/turn") and *kadāru* ("to bow down/tilt"), where *zâru* corresponds to Hebrew *qāras* and *kadāru* to Hebrew *kāraʿ*. Thus, for Schaudig 46:1-2 appears to recognize that the "bowing down" and "stumbling" of the Bel and Nebo idols are ominous movements portending the disaster that occurs to Babylon(ia), as noted in the last two cola (2b-c).

Schaudig has made a powerful case. But several questions need to be dealt with before we can decide. The first is: how does our Isaianic author use his knowledge of these processional omens; how does the presence of the omens in 46:1-2 correlate with our internal examination of these verses and their biblical background? That examination has suggested that the movements of Bel's and Nebo's images only demonstrate that they are worthless idols. Yet this is not the viewpoint of the Mesopotamian omens themselves, in which "the twisting and turning, the bowing down and tilting, etc." show, rather, the power of the divine images and the gods they embody; i.e., their ability to communicate and control the weal and the woe of their worshippers.

Is there a way, then, to connect these two apparently opposing perspectives? To do so, we have to assume that the biblical author has made an adaptation, has understood the omens differently from did their Mesopotamian originators. The bowing down, the twisting and turning have become a sign not of the affirmation of divine power, but of its ridicule. "Look at these idols," Isaiah seems to be saying, "their bowing and stumbling indicate their dead weight." In other words, Isaiah has preserved the gestures involved in the ominous movements of the divine images, but stripped from them their original explanation. The question is: does the prophet do so without knowing or understanding this explanation, or does he understand it and deliberately ridicules it? We cannot be certain, but the evidence here points to something deliberate. One will notice that in his adaptation, Isaiah has not actually reproduced the full literary structure of the omens: conditional sentences, as noted above, each with a protasis describing the movement of the image and an apodosis giving the significance in terms of weal or woe for people and land. Rather, what 46:1-2 offers is part of the protasis, the bowing down and stumbling in verses 1a and 2a, but not formulated as a protasis, with "if...." Then, Vverse 2b-c, subsequently, takes up the theme of the omen apodoses, in this case the woe, but does not present it as an omen apodosis, that is, as a result produced by the gods through their images; rather, it is set up as a comment on the weakness of the images themselves. In other words, for 46:1-2 the gods do not direct, as they would in the omen collection, that the land of Babylonia will not be saved and they do not communicate this expressly through making their images of bow and stumble. Rather, the statement from Yahweh through Isaiah is that the images themselves are dead weight—their bowing and stumbling serving, indeed, as ominous signs, though not of their power, but rather of the fact that they cannot save either their land or themselves, and will be taken away in captivity. All of this, in short, looks like a deliberate reversal of the omens in content as well as in rhetorical structure, and bespeaks, thus, a real knowledge on Isaiah's part of how this kind of divination works.

If, then, a deliberate reversal of Mesopotamian divination practice is involved, this leads to a second question about the "processional omens" in 46:1-2: how would our Isaianic author have known about them? Schaudig argues that Isaiah's knowledge would not have needed to come from an acquaintance with the texts of these omens. It could easily have resulted from direct or mediated experience of the procession of the divine images in the New Year's festival in Babylon—a procession open to the public, which included not only Babylonians, but various of the exiled populations, among them Judahites (Schaudig 2008: 565, 569, with reference to Blenkinsopp 2002: 107; generally on Judahites in Babylonia, see recently, e.g., Machinist 2003: 255–56; Nicholson 2014: 41–53; Stökl and Waerzeggers 2015; and Pearce and Wunsch 2014: especially 3–29). In the procession, the swaying to and fro of the images would have been evident to all, as would have a general public awareness of their ominous significance. But accepting the possibility of such actual experience of the festival, we do not have to exclude also a more specialized awareness gained from the texts, whether in their original Akkadian or in Aramaic translation, or from some oral explanation of them. Pointing in this direction would be the deliberate reversal we have argued for, of the content and structure of the omens in 46:1-2. In the same direction is the possible, indeed probable awareness of some of the Mesopotamian technical terminology of divination behind the biblical words *kara'* and *qaras*. And elsewhere in Second Isaiah are yet other indications of a specialized knowledge of Mesopotamian divination: in astronomy (47:13) and concerning the principal term for diviner, *bārû* (44:25 as emended) (Machinist 2003: 253 with n. 29; add Cooley 2013: 257–59). All of this suggests that in this prophet we should see a literatus, knowledgeable in both the traditions of his own community and those of Mesopotamia (Eph'al 1990).

To summarize so far: the "processional omens" have a real place in Isa 46:1-2, where they quite probably have been deliberately and artfully adapted from their Mesopotamian context. The omens thus confirm a setting for our passage in the major religious celebration of the Mesopotamian calendar, the *zagmukku/akītu* festival. But still, this setting does not fully explain the disastrous invasion and conquest that are the final point of our passage. Can we rescue the Nabonidus-Cyrus setting here, flawed as it seems to be? Or are we able to go to the other historical possibilities briefly mentioned before? Let us start with the latter, more specifically with the possibility that is most regularly appealed to, the supposed destruction of Babylon and removal of the major divine statue of Marduk from the city's temple quarters—all in the latter 480s BCE by the Achaemenid emperor, Xerxes, supposedly in reaction to a rebellion in Babylonia against Achaemenid rule. The point would be, then, that it is Xerxes' actions against Babylon and its deity which underlie Isa 46:1-2: the Isaiah verses being composed, or edited, in the time of Xerxes or thereafter, with Xerxes' actions reconfigured and retrojected as Second Isaiah's comments sixty years earlier on the fall of Babylonia to the Achaemenid Cyrus (review of the issue briefly in Blenkinsopp 2002: 267–68, and more elaborately, in Hermisson 2003: 95–96, 99–101, and Kuhrt 2014, with reference especially to Kuhrt and Sherwin-White 1987 and Waerzeggers 2003/2004). But there are serious problems in the ancient sources for this proposal, as argued persuasively by Kuhrt with Sherwin-White (Kuhrt and Sherwin-White 1987; Kuhrt 2014). Thus, while virtually contemporary Babylonian sources note two short-lived Babylonian rebellions in 484 BCE against Xerxes, none of the early sources, Greek or Babylonian, indicates that Xerxes destroyed Babylon or removed the Marduk statue. Rather, these sources suggest that Xerxes maintained Babylon and other Babylonian cities, including their sanctuaries and their cults, although they do point to a radical change in the personnel involved and, at least for Herodotus (1.183), the removal of a statue of a man and the killing of a priest who tried to prevent it from the main temple building in Babylon (Kuhrt and Sherwin-White 1987; Kuhrt 2014; Waerzeggers 2003/2004: 150–63). Xerxes' actions toward Babylon, thus, appear to offer no real parallel to the picture in Isa 46:1-2, and the disjunction is made all the greater by two other features: none of the sources on Xerxes, early or late, talks about Nabu, his images, or his sanctuary, as Isaiah does (Hermisson 2003: 101,104), and, in any case, as we have noted, the surrounding context of chapter 46 in the Second Isaiah locates it in the years of the Nabonidus-Cyrus transition (especially Isa 44:24-45:7; cf. 41:2), thus putting the burden of proof on those who would advocate the period of Xerxes.

So we return to this transition and wonder whether it could still function as the background for the invasion and conquest stated in our Isaianic verses. The key issue here is the verbs, especially the last one, *hālǝkâ*, which is in the perfect, describing the procession into captivity. Above, we took this as a past tense, making our verses a reminiscence of the transition as already completed, that is, of the desperate last actions of Nabonidus in gathering the divine images to Babylon and then the conquest of Cyrus and his return of these images to their native sanctuaries. But as a reminiscence of these actions, our verses would have to contain, as we saw, some major inaccuracies. So if we want to retain the allusion to Nabonidus and Cyrus, the easiest and best solution, it appears, is to reconsider the perfect form. Could it be not a past tense, but a future—the so-called "prophetic" or better predictive perfect, whereby the prophet would announce the coming judgment of Yahweh as something already determined and so fulfilled before it has actually occurred (Franke 1994: 83; uncertain in Hermisson 2003: 93)? In this way, we could return to our earlier suggestion though on a more secure basis; namely, that our Isaianic verses would be

an utterance made not after, but before the conquest of Cyrus and probably before or at least at the start of Nabonidus' gathering of the divine
images, but still when the threat of Cyrus had become real. In short, our
verses would function as a prediction about Cyrus's coming actions—a prediction whose (partial) inaccuracy would have been based on the under-
standable fear that the coming invasion of Cyrus would show him to be like
other foreign conquerors, who normally remove the images of the gods
of the place conquered. For Isaiah, then, the images to be removed would
indeed be of the two principal gods of Babylon, Marduk and Nabu, the two
gods at the center of the New Year's festival; the moon-god Sin was not
at this festival center, even apparently for Nabonidus, and so would have
been ignored here by Isaiah. In final summary, then, our Isaiah passage
appears to proclaim that in the imminent future, there will be a disaster
for Babylon which its gods, Bel/Marduk and Nebo/Nabu, cannot prevent
and from which they cannot even save themselves, and the first signs of
this are the bowing down and stumbling of their images in the very festival
designed to exalt them.

4. PSALM 29 AND THE CANAANITE WORLD

1 הבו ליהוה בני אלים
הבו ליהוה כבוד ועז
2 הבו ליהוה כבוד שמו
השתחוו ליהוה בהדרת קדש
3 קול יהוה על המים
אל הכבוד הרעים
יהוה על מים רבים
4 קול יהוה בכח
קול יהוה בהדר
5 קול יהוה שבר ארזים
וישבר יהוה את ארזי הלבנון
6 וירקדים כמו עגל לבנון
ושריון כמו בן ראמים
7 קול יהוה חצב להבות אש
8 קול יהוה יחיל מדבר
יחיל יהוה מדבר קדש
9 קול יהוה יחולל אילות
ויחשף יערות
ובהיכלו כלו אמר כבוד
10 יהוה למבול ישב
וישב יהוה מלך לעולם
11 יהוה עז לעמו יתן

יהוה יברך את עמו בשלום

1 Grant to Yahweh, o divinities,
  Grant to Yahweh glory and strength,
2 Grant to Yahweh the glory of his name,
  Prostrate yourselves to Yahweh, in (his) holy splendor.[15]
3 The voice of Yahweh is on the waters.
  El of glory thunders mightily.[16]
  Yahweh is on many waters.
4 The voice of Yahweh is in power.
  The voice of Yahweh is in splendor.
5 The voice of Yahweh breaks cedars.
  And Yahweh breaks the cedars of Lebanon.

15 As against Cross's well-known interpretation of *hadrat* (<*hădārâ) here as "(the-
    ophany) of holiness," based on a presumed Ugaritic cognate (Cross 1950: 20–21;
    173: 152–53, n. 28, supported by Freedman and Hyland 1973: 243–44), Pardee
    (2005: 166–67) sides with those who argue that the one Ugaritic occurrence was
    due to an ancient spelling mistake. In its stead, he advocates keeping the more
    standard understanding as "splendor, glory, etc.," with *hadrat*, thus, a variant
    form of the root *hdr*. In this way, it would take its place with parallel words in
    the psalm, including *kabod* "glory" (vv. 1b, 2a, 9c) and *hādār* itself (v. 4b).
16 The hiphil *hir'îm* appears to function as an elative, supplying a heightened
    meaning to the thundering. On this form in biblical Hebrew with its compara-
    tive Semitic base, see Speiser (1967: especially the example at the end of 493).
17 The phrase *ḥōṣēb lahăbôt 'ēš* has perplexed interpreters, because if translated
    literally, it does not seem to make sense: "he cuts down/up flames of fire."
    Three ways of understanding it seem possible. In the first, *lahăbôt 'ēš* serves as
    some kind of adverbial accusative, describing the means by which Yahweh cuts
    down. It would thus be comparable to Hos 6:5: *ḥāṣabtî ban-nəbî'îm* ("he (=God)
    has cut (them) down by means of the prophets"), which, however, makes this
    instrumental use explicit with the preposition *bə-*. As a second possibility, the
    literal translation could be retained, if we understand "cutting (up) flames of
    fire" to mean "splitting the fire into different flames, which shoot out in var-
    ious directions of destruction." This more or less correlates with the views of
    Pardee (2005: 167–68) and Mittmann (1978: 180–81), who think of the voice of
    Yahweh here striking rocky, perhaps specifically flinty, objects, which would
    then give off fiery sparks. A third suggestion comes from Barth (1902: 22), who
    finds that the Arabic cognate, *ḥaṣaba*, can mean besides "to cut down" also
    "to ignite/light/set to fire" (German: "entzünden"). The verse, thus, would be
    translated: "The voice of Yahweh ignites flames of fire" (German: "entzündet
    Feuerflammen"). All three interpretations could fit, but probably the second
    and third are to be preferred to the first. In any case, it is clear that *ḥṣb* in
    our verse designates the destructive power of Yahweh, in this instance against
    natural elements; one may compare Isa 51:9c, where, in the *piel*, *ḥṣb* is used for
    Yahweh's slaying of the sea monster, Rahab.

6   And he makes Lebanon dance/leap about like a calf,
    Siryon like a young wild ox.
7   The voice of Yahweh cuts up flames of fire,[17]
8   The voice of Yahweh causes the wilderness to writhe,
    Yahweh causes the wilderness of Qadesh to writhe,
9   The voice of Yahweh makes female deer give birth,
    And he strips the forests bare,
    And in his temple everyone exclaims, "Glory!"
10 Yahweh has sat down on the Flood,
    And Yahweh has sat down as king forever.
11 Yahweh gives strength to his people,
    Yahweh blesses his people with well-being.

This must be one of the most discussed texts in the history of modern biblical interpretation. The story begins in the 1930s, following the discovery of ancient Ugarit and its Ugaritic language, and involves the effort to locate the psalm in the broader Canaanite world that the excavations at Ugarit decisively opened up. The initial and still most important step was taken by H. L. Ginsberg in four publications of the mid- and latter 1930s, which he resumed and added to in 1969 (Ginsberg 1936a: 35–36, 129–31; 1936b; 1938; 1939; 1969). His work, in turn, was picked up, enlarged, varied, and challenged in a myriad of other studies, which show no sign of closure. Our present discussion cannot review all this scholarship, Ginsberg and post-Ginsberg, on the Canaanite connection of Psalm 29, let alone examine in detail many other facets of the psalm, like the state of its text and its structure. Apart from some comments on these matters, we will rather focus on what the nature of the Canaanite connection may be.

Obviously, the working assumption is that there is a connection, and today that assumption, at least among critical biblical scholars, would not be challenged (e.g., Gaster 1946–1947; Cross 1950; 1973: 151–56; Margulis 1970; Craigie 1972; Freedman and Hyland 1973; Pardee 2005; Smith 2014). The reasons are several and compelling, and may be briefly summarized. The geographical setting of the psalm, for one thing, is not in ancient Israel/Judah, but in Syria—the northern region of ancient Canaanite culture and the major region, it appears, of the Canaanite storm god, Ba'al/Hadad, who, as we will see, is understood by many scholars to furnish the background of our psalm. More specifically; the psalm talks about Yahweh,

18 The terrestrial meaning of *mayîm rabbîm* in this verse as the Mediterranean fits the geographical journey of Yahweh that our psalm traces; on this meaning, see, e.g., Ginsberg 1939: 97; 1969: 45; Dahood 1966: 176; Loretz 1984: 34–36; Pardee 2005: 165, n. 33. At the same time, the phrase has a mythological

the God of Israel, moving in dramatic fashion across the "many waters"—probably, as most would argue, the Mediterranean.[18] From there, he moves inland through the Lebanon and Anti-Lebanon mountains, including the wilderness/desert area somewhere around Qadesh.[19] Finally, he comes to rest—specifically, sits down on his throne—in his sanctuary (*hêkāl*; v. 9c), the location of which is unspecified except that it is connected with the (Primeval) Flood (*mabbûl*; v. 10a). Second, Yahweh himself is described like the Canaanite god Ba'al (Hadad) as the god of the storm, who brings his rain and fierce wind, thunder, and fire from the "many waters" through Syria, shaking the mountains and wilderness, stripping the forests bare, and unsettling wild animals. The emphasis on Yahweh's thunder as his "voice"—*qôl* in repetitive intensity is mentioned seven times—directly echoes, as again many interpreters have observed, the same idiom for Ba'al/Hadad in Canaanite texts of the second millennium BCE. (Ginsberg 1936a: 129–30; 1938: 472–73; Pardee 2005: 167 and n. 41; Dobbs-Allsopp 2015: 156–57). Third, our psalm places Yahweh within a circle of subordinate and adoring deities, the "sons of gods" (*'ēlîm*) who are called upon, in the opening verse 1–2, to give him their praise. This circle or "council" of deities is a well-known feature of Canaanite religion and the phrase *banê 'ēlîm,* one of several for it, is found in the Ugaritic texts, although, to be

---

meaning in the Hebrew Bible, treated by May (1955) (though without reference to our psalm!), which refers to the cosmic waters that need to be tamed by a god who brings order to the universe. Both meanings, as discerned by Loretz, Pardee, and others, appear to be involved in the present verse. The phrase itself seems to be found only in the Hebrew Bible, among ancient Near Eastern texts, though its reference to cosmic waters that can be in conflict with the god of order is, of course, a widespread ancient Near Eastern theme, attested, especially, in Ugaritic and cuneiform texts for such gods as Ba'al/Hadad, Marduk, as well as Yahweh.

19 On *midbar Qādēš* as located in Syria, connected in some way with Syrian Qadesh, and not, thus, with the Qadesh-Barnea of the Sinai wanderings of the Israelites, see, e.g., Ginsberg 1936a: 130; 1938: 473–74; 1939; 1969:45 n. 2; Dahood 1966: 178; Loretz 1984: 87–92; Pardee 2005: 168–70. While there is some disagreement on precisely where in Syria to situate *midbar Qādēš*, its association in our psalm with the Cedars of Lebanon, Mts. Lebanon and Siryon, its appearance in Ugaritic, and the fact that it is never used explicitly for a site in the Sinai—all suggest that it should be in Syria, at least here in the psalm. For a dissenting view, based in part on an unconvincing reading of *'ylt* in verse 9a as the place name, *'Ēlôt* (corresponding to Elat), instead of *'ayyālôt* "female deer," see Margulis 1970: 338–40, 341–42, 346–47.

20 Besides our verse, *banê 'ēlîm* occurs in the Hebrew Bible otherwise only with certainty in Ps 89:7. Normally in the Bible the term would be *banê (ha)'ĕlōhîm*.

sure, not restricted to them.[20] Finally, there are the grammar and poetic style of Psalm 29. Most striking here are two features. The first is the use of the enclitic *mem* in v. 6 (*way-yarqîdēm*), a feature well known in the Ugaritic texts and found especially in what appears to be older biblical poetry (the classic study is Hummel 1957). The second feature, within a style that is built on groups of bi- and tri-cola, is the so-called climactic or staircase parallelism of cola in verses 1a-b-2a (-b), that is, cola in the schema a-a'-a''(-b), which again is quite noticeable in Ugaritic literature and in apparently older biblical poetry.[21]

While certain features of those just mentioned may not be distinctively Canaanite, together they present a persuasive case for a Canaanite background to Psalm 29. The question remains, however, as to what kind of relationship the psalm has to this background. Two major alternatives have been advanced. The first, by Ginsberg himself (1936a: 129–31; 1938)—but note also that Gaster developed his own ideas independently even slightly before, as Ginsberg eventually realized (Gaster 1946–47: 57 n. 13; Ginsberg 1939: 96 n. 2)—sees the psalm as a whole as a Canaanite composition which has been adapted by an Israelite author principally through substituting the name Yahweh for the original Ba'al. Actually, Ginsberg conceived of the author, principally because of the psalm's geography in central and southern Syria, as a Phoenician, of the first millennium BC, not a Canaanite of the Late Bronze Age as represented by Ugarit in coastal northern Syria. But no features of Psalm 29 seem to be distinctively Phoenician in the first millennium BC, and, in any case, Phoenicia itself may be understood as a descendant of Late Bronze Canaanite culture. Indeed, Late Bronze Canaan quite probably contained several, interrelated cultural traditions, from the

On the phrase here see, e.g., Ginsberg (1936a: 129; 1938: 472) and Loretz (1984: 75–78), and for the broader background of the divine council in biblical and other ancient Near Eastern religions, there are such works as Mullen 1980. Freedman and Hyland (1973: 242 and n. 7), among others, have suggested that instead of *'ēlîm* here, one should read the singular *'ēl* (= the god El) + enclitic *mem*, but in light of *banê 'ēlîm* in Ps 89:7, this seems unnecessary.

21 On climactic/staircase parallelism in Psalm 29, see, e.g., Ginsberg 1936b: 180–181; Cross 1950: 19–20; 1973: 151–55; Dahood 1966: 175; Freedman and Hyland 1973: Loretz 1984: 25–32 and passim; Pardee 2005: 160 within 154–55,158–63, and, more generally with bibliography, Dobbs-Allsopp 2015: 80–81, 388 n. 384. As these and other studies show, however, there is some disagreement on how to characterize this parallelism in verses. 1–2, indeed, on how to divide and arrange the poem into cola altogether.

22 See Smith 2014: 49–50, who in discussing the studies of Ginsberg (1936a and 1938) and Pardee (2005) suggests that the Ba'al behind Psalm 29 is from the middle to southern Levant, more specifically of the Lebanon.

Ugarit area as well as from areas to the south of it, and our psalm may reflect more than one of these.[22] There is no substantial reason, therefore, why the term Canaanite cannot be used for the cultural background Ginsberg proposed. Now Ginsberg's position was at first widely accepted, although occasionally with some concern about the amount of Israelite "rereading" of this putative Canaanite original (Cazelles 1961). But about 1970, doubts about the process involved became more explicit and were extended into an alternative view, to wit, that Psalm 29 was an Israelite composition, which, although referring to Canaanite~Phoenician literary and religious traditions, was not a simple re-layering of an original Canaanite~Phoenician text (e.g., Margulis 1970; Craigie 1972; 1983: 243–46; Wagner 1996; Pardee 2005, with a concise and lucid summary of the debate by Smith 2014: 48–50).

Without treating this debate in full, one may highlight several factors that point in the direction of the Ginsberg view. First, there is nothing in Psalm 29, apart from the mention of the name Yahweh, which explicitly refers to an Israelite setting. Rather, the bulk of the details of the psalm, as we have seen, look toward a Canaanite world and its storm god, Ba'al/Hadad. To be sure, we might question, in part with some interpreters, whether the last two verses and perhaps even verse. 9c reflect the Israelite author (e.g., Cross 1973: 152 and n. 23, 155 and n. 44 on vs. 11, with response by Fitzgerald 1974: 62–63, n. 8; Craigie 1983: 248–49 on v. 10; Pardee 2005: 171 on vv. 10-11). But the case here is not, or not fully, probative. Verse 9c speaks of the worshippers in Yahweh's temple proclaiming his glorious epiphany, but while an Israelite/Judahite audience could well understand this as the Jerusalem temple, the text does not make that explicit, and the sentiment involved, with the emphasis on the deity's appearance in literally a brilliant manifestation (*kābôd*), is one widely known in the ancient Near East and elsewhere (most recently Aster 2012, with 286–87 on v. 1). Verse 10, in turn, speaks of Yahweh taking up his throne presumably in his temple, but here the throne appears to be the *mabbûl*, a rare word that elsewhere in the Hebrew Bible appears only in Genesis and indicates the Primeval Flood of Noah (Gen 6:7; 7:6, 7, 10, 17; 9:11, 15, 28; 10: 1, 32; 11:10). Cognates for this word in Akkadian and Eblaite have been suggested, but are uncertain, and it would appear that at least in the meaning of a Primeval Flood *mabbûl* is on present evidence unique to biblical Hebrew (cf. Gesenius 18 [2013]: 623b; Pardee 2005: 170–71; the first full study was that of Begrich 1928/1964: 39–54). If that Primeval Flood meaning is at work here in our verse, then *mabbûl* could indicate an Israelite author. On the other hand, the idea behind the verse, of Yahweh enthroned on a body of water conceived of as a dangerous divine/cosmic phenomenon that had to be vanquished or otherwise neutralized—this is not unique to the Hebrew Bible and the present psalm (cf. the view of Craigie 1983: 248–49). A parallel—not, to be sure, exact, but yet quite relevant—is to be found, not in the Canaanite world, but in the Mesopotamian creation myth, Enuma eliš. In the first part of that text, the god Ea defeats and kills the older deity, Apsu, who is the embodiment of the fresh waters, and to complete his victory, "he founded upon the Apsu his dwelling" (*ú-kin-ma eli apsî šu-bat-su*) (Lambert 2013: 54–55, line I 71; for similar texts see Gaster 1961: 445–46). While such a formulation does not occur in the extant Ugaritic corpus, we have what appears to be an analogous event in the Ba'al and Anat Cycle: Ba'al, once he defeats and neutralizes his enemy Yamm/Nahar, the god embodying the sea/river(s), builds a dwelling for himself as a sign of his victory and newly displayed power (among the many discussions, e.g., Cross 1973: 112–16, 155–63). Completing the broader ancient Near Eastern, if not specifically, Canaanite background of verse 10 is the grammar: Yahweh "sits down on the Flood," wherein "sits down on" > "enthroned" is expressed by *yāšab lə*, as in Ps 9:5 and in the Ugaritic corpus, not by the usual *yāšab bə* or *'al*.[23] We may look finally at verse 11, which talks about Yahweh strengthening and blessing his people (*'ammô*). For various modern interpreters (e.g., Cross 1973: 155 and n. 44; Craigie 1983: 248–49; and Pardee 2005: 171; cf. Fitzgerald 1974: 62–63 n. 8), this indicates an Israelite author, because speaking about Yahweh and "his people" should refer to the covenant between Yahweh and Israel, echoing similar expressions elsewhere in the Hebrew Bible. But the identification of Israel here is still not explicit, and the concept of a deity and his/her people does not appear to be exclusive to Israel in the ancient Levantine, or, more broadly, ancient Near Eastern

23 For the occurrences of *yāšab lə/bə/'al*, see Gesenius 18 (2013: 505a) and the discussion in Cross (1973: 147–48 and nn. 3–4, 155 and n. 43). Other translations, like the locative "at the Flood" (e.g., Pardee 2005: 155, 170–71), appear to me less likely.

24 Cf. Zevit 1977 for a text that possibly comes from ancient Syria of the first millennium BCE, which describes a covenant between the god Aššur and his divine entourage, and the human community to whom the text is directed. In addition, Gaster (1961: 446) points to lines from one of the concluding episodes of the Babylonian creation myth, Enuma eliš, in which various of the gods praise Marduk, following his victory over Tiamat, and adjure him to fulfill his role as protector of the people and land. Gaster's translations, however, must be modified and supplemented on the basis of the most recent and authoritative edition of Enuma eliš, by W.G. Lambert 2013: 117, 119. Here are Lambert's translations of the pertinent lines from tablet VI, with my interpretive comments:

arena.[24] And even if one were to attribute the verse to an Israelite author, it looks somewhat tacked on to the preceding verses, not directly echoing any of their sentiments concerning the power of the deity in the storm. Verse 11, in other words, could well have been an Israelite addition to a text that was originally foreign, and that, in fact, is the opinion of many of the modern interpreters who assign it to an Israelite author (e.g., Cross 1973: 151–52 and n. 23).

If, in sum, the presence of Israelitisms, or more exactly biblicisms, in Psalm 29 is at best very limited and non-essential, apart from the use of the name Yahweh, there is another feature of our text that strengthens dramatically the case for its Canaanite origin. This was first explored by Aloysius Fitzgerald in a short article published in 1974, which has largely been neglected in subsequent published scholarship (Fitzgerald 1974). Fitzgerald proposed to substitute Ba'al for each of the eighteen occur-rences of the name Yahweh in the psalm—that number itself a striking testimony to the focus of the psalm on the character of Yahweh. The result, as he easily demonstrated, was a conspicuous increase in the allit-eration of the text, focusing on the repetition of **b** and **l**, and as he properly observed, alliteration is a marked feature of biblical and Ugaritic poetry. In Fitzgerald's words: "There is not a single line where the name 'Yahweh' fits better, and in most lines it does not fit at all" (Fitzgerald 1974: 61). Only in three places, Fitzgerald noted, could the retention of the name Yahweh produce "noteworthy alliterative connections" (vv. 2b, 9a, and 9b—the last, however, emended by Fitzgerald and relocated in the psalm over against the Tiberian Masoretic text). Nonetheless, these three con-nections, Fitzgerald went on, are not probative: in verse 2b, Ba'al works better than Yahweh, while in the other two, 9a and the modified 9b, either Ba'al or Yahweh would fit (Fitzgerald 1974: 62). Here is a modified ver-sion of the chart drawn up by Fitzgerald of Psalm 29 with Ba'al in place of Yahweh. The text used is the Tiberian Masoretic from the *BHS ad loc.* with-out Fitzgerald's emendation and relocation of 9b as well as of 3a-b and 8; to

> VI 107 Let him (=Marduk) shepherd the black-heads (= humanity, focused on the Babylonians), his creatures,
>
> 108 Let them tell of his character to future days without forgetting.
>
> 135 Marutukku (=one of Marduk's honorific names): he is the support of land, city, and its peoples,
>
> 136 Henceforth let the peoples ever heed him,
>
> 149 Who, as his name says, is a protecting angel (*lamassu*) for god and land.

keep his changes would not strengthen, but, I think, muddy and so weaken his argument for an original Ba'al in the psalm. The transliteration of the consonants without the accompanying vowels makes the heightened alliteration clear, and one will note that this alliteration extends to the last verse, 11—the verse which on other grounds as just discussed may be, but is not certainly, an Israelite addition:

1 *hbw **lb'l** bny 'lym*
   *hbw **lb'l** kbwd w'z*
2 *hbw **lb'l** kbwd šmw*
   *hšthww **lb'l** bhdrt qdš*
3 *qwl **b'l** 'l mym*
   'l hkbwd hr'ym
   ***b'l** 'l mym rbym*
4 *qwl **b'l** bkḥ*
   *qwl **b'l** bhdr*
5 *qwl **b'l** šbr 'ryzm*
   *wyšbr **b'l** 't 'rzy hlbnwn*
6 *wyrqdym kmw 'gl lbnwn*
   wśryn kmw bn r'mym
7 *qwl **b'l** hṣb lhbwt 'š*
8 *qwl **b'l** yḥyl mdbr*
   *yḥyl **b'l** mdbr qdš*
9 *qwl **b'l** yḥwll 'ylwt*
   wyḥśp y'rwt
   wbhyklw klw 'mr kbwd
10 ***b'l** lmbwl yšb*
   *wyšb **b'l** mlk l'wlm*
11 ***b'l** 'z l'mw ytn*
   ***b'l** ybrk 't 'mw bšlwm*

Fitzgerald, it must be said, has uncovered a most important facet of our psalm, and its significance would appear to be what he himself recognized: the name Ba'al was an original and integral part of the text, which Yahweh was not, and therefore our present text is an Israelite appropriation of the Ba'al original with the major, if not the only change being the substitution of Yahweh. In short, Fitzgerald's discovery would appear to confirm Ginsberg's initial conclusion about the origin of Psalm 29.

Fitzgerald's discovery, it should be added, provides the kind of specific technical evidence that the other features of the psalm do not have: the latter show some kind of close Canaanite connection, but in the end leave open the question of whether that connection is one of a borrowing of a whole text as a base. Text borrowing, on the other hand, is the logical, perhaps even the only explanation for the natural fit of the name Ba'al in all those places in the text where Yahweh now occurs. And once the shift to Yahweh occurred, then other features of the psalm that had referred to Ba'al/Hadad directly or indirectly could now be understood as part of Yahweh's realm and cult. Thus, for example, the temple of the god unnamed in verse 9c would become, depending upon the local setting of the psalm, the Jerusalem Temple or a northern sanctuary like Bethel.

The kind of borrowing at issue here is, of course, not unique. A partial analogy may be discerned in Urartu/Biainili, Assyria's great imperial rival of the first millennium BCE. As Paul Zimansky has recently observed (2007: 264), the first Urartian royal inscription that we know is by Sarduri, whose reign was about the third quarter of the ninth century BCE. At the time, there was apparently no established royal inscriptional tradition in Urartu, and this monumental text, in six copies, was written in cuneiform in the format of Urartu's Neo-Assyrian counterparts, more specifically, that of the early ninth-century Assyrian king, Aššurnaṣirpal II. Sarduri's scribe, as Zimansky points out, took over the Assyrian royal titulary and made only simple substitutions of personal and geographical names as well as changes in the section describing the royal building project to fit the local Urartian context. What was the aim of this borrowing of a specific text or textual model? Here, it seems, the Urartian and Psalm 29 examples diverge. For the Urartian Sarduri, the aim was not to satirize or otherwise to criticize the Assyrian model—no indications of that in Sarduri's inscription can be discerned—but to accept the Assyrian model because perceived as the only available means for imperial public display, and in the process, therefore, to set out the claim that Urartu should be accepted as an imperial power on the level of its Assyrian opponents. In the case of Psalm 29, also, it looks impossible to detect any satirical orientation toward the putative Canaanite model text. But here, the aim does not appear to be one of equivalence: of proposing that Yahweh was simply another powerful storm god on the level of Ba'al/Hadad. The fact that Yahweh is depicted as sovereign in Ba'al's homeland of Syria as well as the hostile reception of Ba'al and his cult in a number of other biblical texts (e.g., Hos 2:18; 1 Kgs 18:17-40; 2 Kgs 10:18-28) suggests that a hostility, albeit implicitly, exists as well in Psalm 29: that it is not a matter of Yahweh being an equal storm god to Ba'al/Hadad, but a replacement for him—a replacement who has usurped or absorbed Ba'al's powers everywhere, both in his homeland of Syria and in Israel/Judah, and so removed Ba'al as a presence in the cosmos. And yet, there is some irony in all of this, for the replacement involved implies that it was carried out in a context in which Yahweh and Baʿal were understood as rivals, and thus as potential equivalents, even by some syncretistically as two names for the same divine phenomenon (see further below with Hos 2:18 [Heb.]). In Psalm 29, however, it appears that the decision has been for exclusion, not for syncretism (cf. the people's cry after Yahweh's, and Elijah's, victory over Baʿal and his prophets in the Mt. Carmel contest: *Yahweh hûʾ hā-ʾĕlōhîm* "Yahweh it is, who is god!" [1 Kgs 18:39]).

There is one other significance to the conclusion that Psalm 29 may be a rather straightforward adaptation of a Canaanite text, and it was already seen by earlier interpreters (especially Cross 1950: 19), namely, that with this psalm we have found a hitherto unknown type of Canaanite literature—a hymn to a deity celebrating his power and sovereignty. Such hymns, shorter or longer extending into epic poetry, are known, say, from Mesopotamia.[25] They are not attested, however, in the Canaanite literary corpus, though the theme of the celebration of a god's power can be found in the context of a literary narrative like the Baʿal and Anat Cycle, or briefly alluded to in a diplomatic letter, so from Amarna.[26] Yet if Ginsberg, Fitzgerald, and others are right about Psalm 29, we must now assume that the corpus did have such hymns, which are still awaiting discovery.

III. REFLECTIONS

The subject of textual referencing in literature is vast, and the present study has offered only a very limited, culturally specific purview of it. The four well-known case studies we have considered all involve connections between particular passages in the Hebrew Bible and phenomena outside of that Bible: from Mesopotamia: (No. 1—"to eat *karṣu*/flesh"); (No. 2—Isa 1:7); and (No. 3—Isa 46:1-2); or from the Canaanite world: (No. 4—Psalm 29). The extra-biblical phenomena cover: conventional language which the Bible appears to use, that is, language not from a particular text, but from a specific linguistic tradition (No. 1); a particular non-Israelite

---

25 The most famous Mesopotamian example, of course, is Enūma eliš with its exaltation of Marduk: see Lambert (2013: Parts I–II). A biblical example is Exodus 15 to Yahweh, which is treated, along with the whole category of exaltation of deity texts, by Mann (1977).

26 The Amarna letter is EA 147, addressed to the Egyptian Pharaoh by Abi-milku, vassal ruler of Tyre. In it, Abi-milku compares the Pharaoh to Baʿal as follows:

who gave forth his voice in the sky like Baʿal, such that all the land was frightened by his voice. (Rainey 2015: I, 742–43, lines 13–15)

literary tradition which the biblical authors recognize as such, but one not attached to any single specific text (No. 2); a particular custom or ritual and perhaps the textual embodiment of this (No. 3); and a specific text or textual genre (No. 4). In all four cases, the argument is that the connections should be regarded as references made by the biblical authors to the outside phenomena: references that are historical/genetic to specific conventional language, textual idioms, customs or rituals, or individual texts or textual genres. Apart possibly from No. 1, the references should be understood as conscious or deliberate, though of varying kinds: from an awareness of a literary tradition without a particular text (No. 2), through awareness of a particular custom with or without a particular text (No. 3), to an awareness of a particular text or textual genre (No. 4).

The question, of course, is: how do we know that we have such references—that the connections are historical and perhaps deliberate? The question is made difficult by the fact that in all our cases there is no explicit marker in the biblical passage that another text or tradition is being cited. The only exception—and it is at the most partial—is No. 3, Isa 46:1-2, which mentions Bel and Nebo as the divine protagonists; yet even here they are not labelled "Babylonian" or the like and their particular setting, in the New Year's festival and/or the events of Nabonidus's and Cyrus's reign, is not named, perhaps because the biblical author thought all that was obvious. This lack of explicit labelling, it must be observed, applies to the Hebrew Bible generally: not always, when we might have expected it, do we have references to an external source like "the Scroll of the Upright" (*sēper hay-yāšār*: Josh 10:13; 2 Sam 1:18) or the "Annals of the Kings of Israel" (*sēper dibrê hay-yāmîm lǝ-malkê yiśrā'ēl*: e.g., 2 Kgs 13:8). And while sometimes these labels are accompanied by the lines quoted from the compositions to which they refer—so for the *sēper hay-yāšār*—this is not consistently the case (e.g., 2 Kgs 13:8) (for a general discussion, see recently Stott 2008).

By way of compensation for the lack of specific marking labels, there are other features we can turn to in order to ascertain a reference. Most obvious, of course, is the degree of similarity that can be shown between the biblical passage and its putative connection. Can one go beyond similar themes or concepts to the language and imagery involved? This, as we have seen, is the case in No.1, with the idiom for "to slander," which in the Daniel passages shows a virtually exact copy of the Akkadian original. It is also to be found in No. 2, in the idiom for military destruction of enemy territory. In No. 3, the two words *kāra'* and *qōrēs* appear to reflect a special technical usage from Babylonian divination, while in No. 4, there are elements of grammar, parallelistic style, and idiom, not to mention the stylistic fit of the name Ba'al, that tie Psalm 29 to a Canaanite text or textual model.

Despite the language similarity, if not identity, we can still ask how distinctive is the connection: is it unique to the particular biblical passage and the other text, or is the connecting element(s) shared by other texts as well? The latter, for example, is exemplified in No. 2, where, as discussed, the individual nouns and verbs for destruction are found in a number of other biblical passages that do not apparently evoke the Neo-Assyrian world. Nonetheless, in that instance, we were able to go beyond these individual elements to demonstrate that the particular choice of them and not other words for destruction, as well as their particular ordering together revealed a connection to the Neo-Assyrian royal inscriptional tradition that was, indeed, distinctive.

There is a third feature that can help to tie passages together. This concerns other indications in the texts that provide a background, a context for the particular passages to be connected. So in No. 2 the proposal of a Neo-Assyrian idiom for military destruction in Isa 1:7 is strengthened by the orientation of the surrounding verses to the same kind of destruction quite probably at Assyrian hands, though this is not made explicit. It is also strengthened by the fact that Neo-Assyrian references occur in many other parts of First Isaiah, such as 10:5-15 and 36–39 (see, e.g., Machinist 2016; Gallagher 1999; Grabbe 2003; and Kalimi and Richardson 2014). No. 3 is similar, with its evocation of a Babylonian setting by the mention of the deities, Bel/Marduk and Nebo, and the references in other chapters of Second Isaiah, not to mention other biblical books, to the Neo-Babylonian period (e.g., Isa 44:28-45:7; 47; 48:14-22; Jer 50-51). And in No. 4, Psalm 29, the proposal of the god Ba'al as original coheres with the other Canaanite imagery, grammar, and style in this text.

Finally, we should mention the deliberate reversal of theme or language as one observes it from the outside phenomenon—text, textual or linguistic tradition, or custom—to the biblical passage. The more this can be demonstrated in precision and detail, the more convincingly it affirms not only that biblical and non-biblical are historically related, but that the connection is a deliberate, conscious one to the outside phenomenon. The latter, then, would be viewed as the source for the biblical passage, rather than assuming that both derive independently from a common source. So in No. 2, Yahweh displaces the Assyrian army and its king and god as the cause of military destruction; in No. 3, Babylonian custom and probably the textual tradition of divination are treated satirically; and in Psalm 29 of No. 4, Yahweh takes over from Ba'al the Canaanite imagery and poetics. With No. 1, however, the case for deliberate reversal does not seem to be as clear. The examples in No. 1 from Amarna in Akkadian and the biblical Daniel in Aramaic are, as we have observed, (almost) exact duplicates of the apparent Mesopotamian original, which betray no satirical comment on that original. And for the example of Ps 27:2, there is no critical comment also, though its difference from the Mesopotamian form may reflect in some way a conscious change.

In sum, then, the more specific and involved the detail is between the two phenomena, biblical and non-biblical, and the greater the verbal and conceptual play, the more likely is it that their connection was historical and even conscious for the biblical receiver. The case, we must now add, is strengthened if we can explain two other aspects: the channel(s) by which the biblical would have known the non-biblical, and the nature of the audience to which the biblical, as compared with the non-biblical, was directed. The importance particularly of the first aspect cannot be overstated. Without an ability to show that the cultures of the two texts, traditions, or customs were actually in contact, and to explain, then, how the particular connection could have been transmitted from the non-biblical side to the biblical, there can be no persuasive conclusion that the connection was historical. Of course, this demonstration and explanation are not easily found. Indeed, we cannot avoid some speculation—but speculation, the hope is, that will fit the historical facts that can be known and avoid unnecessarily complex and ad hoc explanations. For all four examples, fortunately, the larger background of cultural contact can be demonstrated. Nos. 1, 2, and 3 assume direct or indirect contact between Israel and Mesopotamia. For No. 1, this is a contact that could easily go back to the Late Bronze Age of the second half of the second millennium BCE, when Mesopotamian Akkadian, albeit in local West Semitic forms, is well attested (cf. the Amarna examples). For Nos. 2 and 3, the background is the first millennium Neo-Assyrian and Neo-Babylonian empires, which battled with, conquered, and eventually ruled Israel and Judah and those Israelite and Judahite groups whom the empires deported. No. 4, as we have discussed, is based on cultural contact between Israel and Judah with the Canaanite world not simply in their midst, but to the north of them, in Syria. Here too the historical evidence is secure.

If the general cultural contacts, thus, are clear, it is more speculation than demonstration to say what the specific channels of communication were for the connections at issue. And speculating on these channels involves speculation also on the audiences at which the biblical passages were aimed. So for No. 1, it may be that the Mesopotamian idiom for slander, being attested in the West Semitic world already in the Late Bronze, became embedded in broader West Semitic literary traditions, and it was on these that ultimately the biblical authors drew. But a more direct recognition of the Mesopotamian origin of the idiom may eventually have come to the biblical authors, if we accept the possibility that the use of the idiom in the book of Daniel reflects a knowledge of Babylonian speech. Presumably, then, the author at least of this part of Daniel had a Babylonian background, deriving directly or indirectly, perhaps, from the Babylonian exile. In turn, the audience at which Daniel was aimed must have included people of the same background.

For No. 2, as we have seen, the author must have been acquainted with the diction of the Neo-Assyrian royal inscriptions, and several different channels of acquaintance are possible: he could have read or had read to him actual inscriptional texts in Akkadian; he could have read or had read to him such texts in translation, with the most likely choice, Aramaic, which increasingly became a language of administration and a lingua franca in the Neo-Assyrian empire (Tadmor 1991); or he could have heard, without reference to any text, the idiom for military destruction in Akkadian or translation. An underlying issue here, which has continued to be debated without final agreement, is the extent of Akkadian knowledge, oral and written, in Judah and Israel during the Neo-Assyrian period. It was doubtless not large and certainly not distributed beyond the ruling elites, but a few data suggest that it should not be dismissed, either: the Neo-Assyrian policy of installing royal inscriptional stelae in all parts of the realm to broadcast the sovereignty of the empire to their subjects, the extant finds of which include a few pieces from Israel and neighboring Philistia, though not Judah; Neo-Assyrian inscriptional phrases and concepts and an awareness of the genre of royal inscriptions elsewhere in the book of Isaiah and beyond in the Hebrew Bible, as we have signaled, which may add up to enough of a dense and intricate picture to conclude that the picture at least in part was based on a knowledge of written Akkadian texts; finally, the interaction of local Judahite and Israelite officialdom

27 The complex of issues summarized in this paragraph is being addressed in an increasingly abundant scholarship. Among the studies are: Aster 2007a, 2007b; Cohen 1979; Hartenstein 2009; Horowitz, Oshima, and Sanders 2006: especially 19–22, with review of the volume by Cohen 2008: especially 84; Levine 2005 (with reference to his earlier articles); Levinson 2009; Machinist 1983, 2016; Morrow 2010; Otto 1999, with the critical review of Morrow 2005; Radner 2006; Steymans 1995; and Wright 2009: especially 96–106.

with their Assyrian masters, including ambassadors at the Assyrian capitals, who would have picked up some Akkadian and knowledge of Assyrian official inscriptions and reliefs.[27]

Our example No. 3, Isa 46:1-2, fits nicely with the view that its biblical author, presumably the so-called Second Isaiah, was in Babylonian exile. As we have discussed, the text here conveys an immediacy of observation and a knowledge of Babylonian ritual actions and terminology, including the *akîtu* festival, that make the best sense if the author were an actual or near witness to what he writes; the text also conforms to other testimony in the Second Isaiah to a serious knowledge of Babylonian culture of the Neo-Babylonian period (Eph'al 1990: Machinist 2003: 253 with n. 29; Cooley 2013: 257–59).

Moreover, there is growing non-biblical evidence, which can be joined to the biblical, that illuminates Judahite life in Babylonian exile, and while this evidence points especially to the Judahites in rural or small town Babylonian settlements, it also indicates that they could be found in the larger cities as well, including Babylon, where they would have been exposed to the public side of the *akîtu* festival and, for the Judahite royals, to the royal court (e.g., Machinist 2003: 244–45, 255–256; Nicholson 2014: 41–53; Stökl and Waerzeggers 2015; Pearce and Wunsch 2014: especially 3–29). It is this Babylon milieu, accordingly, in which the Second Isaiah could easily have fitted, even if explicit evidence for him there is lacking. Overall, then, our chapter (46:1-2) is part of a web of evidence that is too strong to deny a setting in Babylonia and in Babylon for our prophet, as some modern scholarship has done (Barstad 1997; Tiemeyer 2011). On the other hand, other Second Isaiah chapters do suggest a location also in Judah, but at a later point in the prophet's career, which should be placed in the period of return from Babylonian exile (Blenkinsopp 2002: 102–04; Machinist 2003: 245 and n. 16).

What, lastly, about the channel by which the author of No. 4, Psalm 29, acquired his knowledge of Canaanite lore and literature? Given the liturgical ambience of the psalm as a hymn of praise and exaltation of the deity whose resting point, at the end of his atmospheric journey, is his sanctuary, the author should be a specialist in cultic poetry—one who was attached to the sanctuary of the god, or perhaps to the royal court in authority over the sanctuary, as is generally supposed for most of the biblical psalms and, of course, exhibited in a number of the psalmic titles. If the psalm is supposed to come from Judah, then the best candidate for the sanctuary, clearly, is the temple of Yahweh in Jerusalem, where the royal court also resided. If it is a northern, Israelite psalm, then, presumably, it would have concerned the royal court at Samaria and/or, apparently, a sanctuary there, or one or both of the other two major northern sanctuaries of the monarchic period, Dan and Bethel. All of these locations would have given access, in one way or another, to Canaanite cultural traditions, but the presence of such traditions in Israel and Judah throughout their history makes fixing a particular date rather uncertain.

Nonetheless, let us see if we can be more specific. If the underlying concern of Psalm 29 is with the replacement of Ba'al by Yahweh, then we must ask: what kind of presence did Ba'al have in Israel and Judah, and was there a period when the replacement issue was of special concern? Without examining in detail all the abundant evidence and scholarly studies on these questions—and the almost dizzying variety of answers offered—we may focus on a few salient points. The first is that Ba'al was indeed a deity known in Israel and Judah, as well as in the immediately surrounding cultures (e.g., Smith 2002: 43–47, 65–101; Zevit 2001: 592–96, 603–09, 648–53; Norin 2013: 180–267, 274–76, with summary on 241–43, 264–67, 274–76; Day 2000: 68–85, 102). The primary evidence is from the Hebrew Bible, and it can be divided into five categories: (1) Ba'al as a singular noun without the definite article, thus as the proper name of the god, who sometimes appears with the epithets, Ba'al Pe'or, Ba'al Berit, or Ba'al Zebub (< Zebul), each denoting, it appears, a particular manifestation of Ba'al at a particular site of worship; (2) Ba'al as a singular noun but with the definite article, thus perhaps as a title for the god ("the lord") or a label for an object, especially an image, associated with him; (3) Ba'al in the plural with the definite article (*hab-bə'ālîm*), indicating either the group of local manifestations of the deity ("Ba'al of X" and "Ba'al of Y") or, more generally and normally in a pejorative way, non-Israelite (male) deities and/or their images; (4) Ba'al as part of human personal names, like Jerub-ba'al, or in the substituted dysphemism, *bōšet*, thus Iš-bošet (for Iš-ba'al); and (5) Ba'al as part of geographical names, like Ba'al-ṣapon, probably connected in some way with a cultic site or region of Ba'al. This biblical evidence is supported by some non-biblical epigraphic attestation of human personal names with the element Ba'al, the primary source being the capital of the northern kingdom of Israel, Samaria, during the first half of the eighth century BCE (see, e.g., Smith 2002: 65–66; Norin 2013: 265–66, 274).

---

28 For a nuanced effort to understand the historiography of the Deuteronomistic corpus and its use as a witness to the religion of ancient Israel, see Zevit 2000: 438–79.

Of these biblical attestations of Ba'al, it is well accepted that their usage, particularly their pejorative usage, was colored by the views of the biblical authors/editors involved, particularly the attestations in the Deuteronomic/Deuteronomistic corpus that refer to the generalizing "the Ba'als".[28] The pattern of attestations, therefore, may not be fully representative of the broader history of Ba'al belief and worship in Israel and Judah, and yet there are too many attestations scattered over a number of biblical texts, several within credible historical narratives (see below), to say that they are simply fictional creations of the biblical authors, and not rooted in external reality—a reality attested to, moreover, by the non-biblical evidence, small as it may be. To be sure, it is the case that some of the attestations may not be of the god Ba'al, but of Yahweh, the God of Israel, for whom *ba'al* would then be an alternative name or the epithet "lord". This is marked clearly by the passage, referred to above, in the latter eighth century BCE prophet, Hosea (2:18), where Yahweh, through Hosea, commands Israel that in the future, "You will call [me] my husband (=*'îšî*, literally 'my man'); no longer will you call me my spouse/lord (= *ba'lî* = my Ba'al)." Even so, this text does not deny the reality of the god Ba'al.

When we gather up the biblical and non-biblical attestations of Ba'al, they appear to point, as a number of scholars have concluded (e.g., Smith 2002: 65–75; Norin 2013: 265–67, 274–76), much more to northern Israel than to southern Judah as the locus of Ba'al recognition and worship. Two periods in the history of the north stand out in our sources, principally the biblical sources, as candidates for the kind of Ba'al-Yahweh tension depicted in Psalm 29. The first is the middle decades of the ninth century BCE, during the period of Omride rule in northern Israel and its destruction and aftermath at the hands of Jehu, together with the accompanying removal of Omride influence, represented in the person of Queen Athaliah, in Judah. Challenging and ending Omride rule and influence turned out to be a bloody affair, and its most prominent proponents, according to the biblical narrative, were the prophets Elijah and Elisha and the army general Jehu, who succeeded the Omrides as king of northern Israel. The narratives in 1–2 Kings center the bloodbath on the cult of Ba'al and his personnel, brought into prominence in the Omride court by the Tyrian princess, Jezebel, with her marriage to the Omride Ahab. The entourage of Ba'al prophets was slain by Elijah in the contest at Mt. Carmel (1 Kgs 18:17-40), and the cult of the god altogether, its personnel, worshippers, and the Omride court, were extirpated by Jehu in his successful overthrow of Omride rule (2 Kgs 10). A corresponding bloodbath occurred in southern Judah perpetrated by and then against Athaliah, the royal Omride princess married to the Judahite king Jehoram, and her entourage. While the biblical accounts certainly exhibit the influence of their authors, ultimately Deuteronomistic, there is no reason to reject their basic historicity as this involved the overthrow and replacement of the Omrides in north and south and the role of the Ba'al cult as a visible element in the Omride program that was attacked and decimated by the victorious opposition. Particularly striking in this regard is the biblical depiction of Elijah's Mt. Carmel contest. As generally recognized, this was at heart a contest over which god, Yahweh or Ba'al, was the real storm god, controlling the winds and the rains and the fertility therefrom—exactly the issue that is at the core of Psalm 29. The psalm, therefore, makes excellent sense as a composition originating during the revolt against the Omrides in north and/ or south, or, perhaps better, following their destruction—in either case as part of a proclamation of the (coming) triumph over the Omrides and their Ba'al religio-political program.

A second possible setting for our psalm, in the context of Ba'al-Yahweh tension, may be placed in northern Israel about a half to a full century later than the Omride overthrow. The appearance of several personal names with Ba'al in the Samaria ostraca of the first half of the eighth century BCE is one clue. More direct is a text already mentioned, which comes from somewhere after the middle of the century. This is a harangue given to the northern prophet, Hosea, about Israel's adulterous faithlessness to Yahweh in her turning to Ba'al (2:4-15 [Heb]) and then the prophet's word-play promise that in the future, Yahweh and Israel will reconcile: "And in that day, says Yahweh, you will call me, 'my husband (*'îšî*)'; no longer will you call me 'my master (*ba'lî*).'" Here we may infer that the issue was not only the worship of Ba'al, but, it appears, the worship of a kind of syncretistic Ba'al-Yahweh. Hosea sets himself decisively against both choices: the people must worship only Yahweh, who can have no equal or alternative manifestation in Ba'al. Now this view would not be incompatible with the understanding of Psalm 29 that we have been exploring, though, as we have noted, syncretism is not stipulated as such in our psalm. In any case, this verse and its surrounding context in the book of Hosea are to be understood as set in the wake of the Omride bloodbath and destruction, to which the prophet makes explicit reference in the first chapter concerning the "blood of Jezreel" (1:4-5). Hosea, thus, addresses a situation vis-à-vis Yahweh and Ba'al that was not completely resolved and eliminated by the work of Jehu and his anti-Omride allies, and that would be appropriate for a psalm like 29.

We have traveled along a sinuous, densely laden path through the thicket of what Sommer, Clayton, and Rothstein have called "influence" and "allusion" in the Hebrew Bible and some of its Near Eastern cultural neighbors. Our four case studies may be a modest sampling, but what emerges from them with no little clarity is how intricate and far-reaching "influence" and "allusion" could be. They were not simply fun and games—the leisurely and ultimately pointless luxury of an excessively learned authorship, although in places they could partake of this—but much more, a device to promote, even to create meaning. They stand, in other words, as a demonstration that the messages of the biblical passages in question would not be nearly so variegated, so nuanced, and yet so forceful were they not in some way appropriations of and often reactions to another text, or tradition, or custom. If such "influence" and "allusion" are a foundational feature of all human communication, they had a particular visibility in the ancient Near East and the Hebrew Bible that belonged to it, where writing was not only restricted, but also traditional: the point even in innovation was not to break, at least openly, with the works of the past, but to find some continuity with them. "Influence" and "allusion" in this context thus become not a possibility, but a necessity.

REFERENCES

AHw. 1965–1985. *Akkadisches Handwörterbuch, unter Benutzung des lexikalischen Nachlasses von Bruno Meissner (1868-1947)*, edited by Wolfram von Soden, 3 vols. Wiesbaden: Harrassowitz.

Albani, Matthias. 2000. *Der eine Gott und die himmlischen Herrschaften.* Arbeiten zur Bibel und ihrer Geschichte, 1. Leipzig: Evangelische Verlagsanstalt.

Allen, Leslie. 2008. *Jeremiah.* Old Testament Library. Louisville/London: Westminster John Knox Press.

Aster, Shawn Selig. 2007a. "Transmission of Neo-Assyrian Claims of Empire to Judah in the Late Eighth Century B.C.E." *Hebrew Union College Annual* 78: 1–44.

Aster, Shawn Selig. 2007b. "The Image of Assyria in Isaiah 2:5-22: The Campaign Motif Reversed." *Journal of the American Oriental Society* 127: 249–78.

Aster, Shawn Selig. 2012. *The Unbeatable Light: Melammu and Its Biblical Parallels.* Alter Orient und Altes Testament, 384. Münster: Ugarit-Verlag.

Barstad, Hans. 1997. *The Babylonian Captivity of the Book of Isaiah: "Exilic" Judah and the Provenance of Isaiah 40-55.* Institute for Comparative Research in Human Culture Series B/CII. Oslo: Novus.

Barth, Jacob. 1902. *Wurzeluntersuchungen zum hebräischen und aramäischen Lexicon.* Leipzig: J. C. Hinrichs.

Berlejung, Angelika. 1998. *Die Theologie der Bilder: Herstellung und Einweihung von Kultbildern in Mesopotamien und die alttestamentliche Bilderpolemik.* Orbis biblicus et orientalis,162. Fribourg: Academic Press/Göttingen: Vandenhoeck & Ruprecht.

BHS. 1983. *Biblia Hebraica Stuttgartensia.* Edited by Karl Elliger and Wilhelm Rudolph. Stuttgart: Deutsche Bibelgesellschaft.

Bonfiglio, Ryan. 2015. "Images and the Image-Ban in the Hebrew Bible and Israelite Religion." *Oxford Biblical Studies Online.* www.oxfordbiblicalstudies.com.

Blenkinsopp, Joseph. 2002. *Isaiah 40-55.* Anchor Bible, 19A. New York: Doubleday Random House.

CAD. 1956–2010. *The Assyrian Dictionary of the Oriental Institute of the University of Chicago.* Edited by Ignace J. Gelb, A. Leo Oppenheim, Erica Reiner, Martha Roth, et al. 26 vols. Chicago: The Oriental Institute of the University of Chicago.

Cazelles, Henri. 1961. "Une relecture du Psaume XXIX?" In *À la rencontre de Dieu: mémorial Albert Gelin*, 119–28. Bibliothèque de la Faculté Catholique de théologie de Lyon, 8. Le Puy: Éditions Xavier Mappus.

Cheney, P. 2012. "Intertexuality." In *The Princeton Encyclopedia of Poetry and Poetics*, 4th edition. Edited by Roland Greene, et al., 716–18. Princeton: Princeton University Press.

Cohen, Chaim. 1979. "Neo-Assyrian Elements in the First Speech of the Biblical Rab-Šaqê." *Israel Oriental Society* 9: 32–48.

Cohen, Yoram. 2008. Review of: *Cuneiform in Canaan: Cuneiform Sources from the Land of Israel in Ancient Times*, by Wayne Horowitz, Takayoshi Oshima, and Seth Sanders. *Bulletin of the American Schools of Oriental Research* 349: 83–86.

Clayton, Jay, and Eric Rothstein. 1991. "Figures in the Corpus: Theories of Influence and Intertextuality." In *Influence and Intertextuality in Literary History*, edited by Jay Clayton and Eric Rothstein, 3–36. Madison: University of Wisconsin Press.

Cooley, Jeffrey L. 2013. *Poetic Astronomy in the Ancient Near East.* HACL 5. Winona Lake, IN: Eisenbrauns.

Craigie, Peter C. 1972. "Psalm XXIX in the Hebrew Poetic Tradition." *Vetus Testamentum* 22: 143–51.

Craigie, Peter C. 1983. *Psalms 1-50.* Word Biblical Commentary, 19. Waco, TX: Word Books.

Cross, Frank Moore, (Jr.). 1950. "Notes on a Canaanite Psalm in the Old Testament." *Bulletin of the American Schools of Oriental Research* 117: 19–21.

Cross, Frank Moore, (Jr.). 1973. *Canaanite Myth and Hebrew Epic.* Cambridge: Harvard University Press.

Dahood, Mitchell. 1966. *Psalms I: 1-50.* Anchor Bible, 16. Garden City, NY: Doubleday.

Day, John. 2000. *Yahweh and the Gods and Goddesses of Canaan.* Journal for the Study of the Old Testament Supplement, 265. Sheffield: Sheffield Academic Press.

Dick, Michael, editor. 1999. *Born in Heaven, Made on Earth: The Making of the Cult Image in the Ancient Near East.* Winona Lake, IN: Eisenbrauns.

Dobbs-Allsopp, F.W. 2015. *On Biblical Poetry.* Oxford/New York: Oxford University Press.

Dohmen, Christoph. 1987. *Das Bilderverbot: Seine Entstehung und seine Entwicklung im Alten Testament.* 2nd edition. Bonner biblische Beiträge, 62. Frankfurt: Athenaum.

Eph'al, Israel. 2010. "Yiša'yāhû 40: 19–20: Lə-šə'ēlat riq'ō hal-ləššônî və-hat-tarbûtî šel Yiša'yāhû Haš-šēnî." *Shnaton* 10: 31–35, XI–XII.

Fitzgerald, Aloysius, F.S.C. 1974. "A New Note on Psalm 29." *Bulletin of the American Schools of Oriental Research* 215: 61–63.

Franke, Chris. 1994. *Isaiah 46, 47, and 48. A New Literary-Critical Reading*. Biblical and Judaic Studies from the University of California, San Diego, 3. Winona Lake, IN: Eisenbrauns.

Freedman, David Noel, and C. Franke Hyland. 1973. "Psalm 29: A Structural Analysis." *Harvard Theological Review* 66: 237–56.

Gallagher, William R. 1999. *Sennacherib's Campaign to Judah: New Studies*. Studies in the History and Culture of the Near East, 18. Leiden: Brill.

Gaster, T. H. 1946–1947. "Psalm 29." *Jewish Quarterly Review* 37: 55–65.

Gaster, T. H. 1961. *Thespis. Ritual, Myth, and Drama in the Ancient Near East*. revised edition. Garden City, NY: Doubleday.

George, Andrew R. 2003. *The Epic of Gilgamesh: The Babylonian Epic Poem and Other Texts in Akkadian and Sumerian*. Revised edition. London/New York: Penguin Books.

Gesenius 18. 2013. *Wilhelm Gesenius Hebräisches und Aramäisches Handwörterbuch über das Alte Testament, 18*. Edited by Rudolf Meyer, Herbert Donner, Udo Rüterswörden und Johannes Renz. Berlin/Heidelberg: Springer-Verlag.

Ginsberg, H. L. 1936a. *Kitbê 'Ûgārît*. Jerusalem: Mosad Bialik.

Ginsberg, H. L. 1936b. "The Rebellion and Death of Baʿlu." *Orientalia* (NS) 5: 161–98.

Ginsberg, H. L. 1938. "A Phoenician Hymn in the Psalter." In *Atti del XIX Congresso Internazionale degli Orientalisti. Roma, 23-29 Settembre 1935*, 472–76. Rome: Tipografia del Senato.

Ginsberg, H. L. 1939. "Šēm Qadmôn lə-Midbar Sûrîyâ." *Yediot: Bulletin of the Jewish Palestine Exploration Society* 6: 96–97.

Ginsberg, H. L. 1969. "A Strand in the Cord of Hebrew Hymnody." *Eretz-Israel* 9 (W.F. Albright Volume): 45–50.

Goldingay, John, and David Payne. 2006. *A Critical and Exegetical Commentary on Isaiah 40-55*, vol. II: *Commentary on Isaiah 44.24-55.13*. The International Critical Commentary. London/New York: T & T Clark.

Grabbe, Lester L., editor. 2003. *"Like a Bird in a Cage": The Invasion of Sennacherib in 701 BCE*. Journal for the Study of the Old Testament Supplement Series, 363. Sheffield: Sheffield Academic Press.

Grayson, A. Kirk, 1991. *Assyrian Rulers of the Early First Millennium BC*, vol. 1: *1114-859 BC*. The Royal Inscriptions of Mesopotamia, Assyrian Periods, 1. Toronto/Buffalo: University of Toronto Press.

Hartenstein, Friedhelm. 2009. "Unheilsprophetie und Herrschaftsrepräsentation: Zur Rezeption assyrischer Propaganda im antiken Juda (8./7. Jh. v. Chr.)." In *Israel zwischen den Mächten. Festschrift für Stefan Timm zum 65. Geburtstag*, edited by Michael Pietsch and Friedhelm Hartenstein, 121–43. Alter Orient und Altes Testament, 364. Münster: Ugarit-Verlag.

Hermisson, Hans-Jürgen. 2003. *Deuterojesaja, 2. Teilband, Jesaja 45,8-49,13*. Biblischer Kommentar: Altes Testament, XI/2. Neukirchen-Vlyun: Neukirchener Verlag.

Holladay, William L. 1986. *Jeremiah 1. A Commentary on the Book of the Prophet Jeremiah. Chapters 1-25*. Hermeneia. Philadelphia: Fortress Press.

Horowitz, Wayne, Takayoshi Oshima, and Seth Sanders. 2006. *Cuneiform in Canaan: Cuneiform Sources from the Land of Israel in Ancient Times*. Jerusalem: Israel Exploration Society/The Hebrew University of Jerusalem.

Hummel, Horace D. 1957. "Enclitic *Mem* in Early Northwest Semitic." *Journal of Biblical Literature* 76: 85–109.

Kalimi, Isaac, and Seth Richardson, editors. 2014. *Sennacherib at the Gates of Jerusalem: Story, History and Historiography*. Studies in the History and Culture of the Near East, 71. Leiden: Brill.

Kuhrt, Amélie. 2014. "Reassessing the Reign of Xerxes in the Light of New Evidence." In *Extraction and Control. Studies in Honor of Matthew W. Stolper*, edited by Michael Kozuh, Wouter F. M. Henkelman, Charles E. Jones, and Christopher Woods, 163–69. Studies in Ancient Oriental Civilizations, 68. Chicago: The Oriental Institute of the University of Chicago.

Kuhrt, Amélie, and Susan M. Sherwin. 1987. "Xerxes' Destruction of Babylonian Temples." In *Achaemenid History II: The Greek Sources. Proceedings of the Groningen 1984 Achaemenid History Workshop*, edited by Heleen Sancisi-Weerdenburg and Amelie Kuhrt, 69–78. Leiden: Nederlands Instituut voor het Nabije Oosten.

Lambert, Wilfred George. 2013. *Babylonian Creation Myths*. Mesopotamian Civilizations, 16. Winona Lake, IN: Eisenbrauns.

Levine, Baruch. 2005. "Assyrian Ideology and Israelite Monotheism." *Iraq* 67: 411–27.

Levinson, Bernard M. 2009. "The Neo-Assyrian Origins of the Canon Formula in Deuteronomy 13:1." In *Scriptural Exegesis: The Shapes of Culture and Religious Imagination. Essays in Honour of Michael Fishbane*, edited by Deborah A. Green and Laura S. Lieber, 25–45. Oxford: Oxford University Press.

Levtow, Nathaniel B. 2008. *Images of Others: Iconic Politics in Ancient Israel*. Biblical and Judaic Studies from the University of California, San Diego, 11. Winona Lake, IN: Eisenbrauns.

Loretz, Oswald. 1984. *Psalm 29. Kanaanäische El- und Baaltraditionen in jüdischer Sicht*. Ugaritisch-Biblische Literatur, 2. Soest, Germany: CIS-Verlag.

Lundbom, Jack R. 2004. *Jeremiah 21-36*. Anchor Bible, 21B. New York: Doubleday Random House.

Machinist, Peter. 1983. "Assyria and Its Image in the First Isaiah." *Journal of the American Oriental Society* 103: 719–37.

Machinist, Peter. 2003. "Mesopotamian Imperialism and Israelite Religion: A Case Study from the Second Isaiah." In *Symbiosis, Symbolism, and the Power of the Past: Canaan, Ancient Israel, and Their Neighbors from the Late Bronze Age Through Roman Palaestina*, edited by William G. Dever and Seymour Gitin, 237–64. Winona Lake, IN: Eisenbrauns.

Machinist, Peter. 2016. "'Ah, Assyria...' (Isaiah 10:5 ff.). Isaiah's Assyrian Polemic Revisited." In *Not Only History. Non Sola Storia. Studies in Honour of Mario Liverani*, edited by G. Bartolini and Maria Giovanna Biga, 183–217. Winona Lake, IN: Eisenbrauns.

Mann, Thomas W. 1977. *Divine Presence and Guidance in Israelite Traditions: The Typology of Exaltation*. Johns Hopkins Near Eastern Studies. Baltimore: Johns Hopkins University Press.

Margulis, Baruch. 1970. "The Canaanite Origin of Psalm 29 Reconsidered." *Biblica* 51: 332–48.

May, Herbert G. 1955. "Some Cosmic Connotations of *Mayim Rabbîm* 'Many Waters.'" *Journal of Biblical Literature* 74: 9–21.

McKane, William. 1980. "משא in Jeremiah 23 33–40." In *Prophecy. Essays Presented to Georg Fohrer on His Sixty-Fifth Birthday 6 September 1980*, edited by J.A. Emerton, 35–54. Beihefte zur ZAW, 150. Berlin: Walter de Gruyter.

Meyers, Carol. 1987. "עצב *'āṣab*." In *Theologisches Wörterbuch zum Alten Testament*, Band VI, edited by G. J. Botterweck and H. Ringgren, 298–301. Stuttgart: Kohlhammer-Verlag.

Mittmann, Siegfried. 1978. "Komposition und Redaktion von Psalm XXIX." *Vetus Testamentum* 28: 172–94.

Moran, William L. 1975. "The Syrian Scribe of the Jerusalem Amarna Letters." In *Unity and Diversity: Essays in the History, Literature, and Religion of the Ancient Near East*, edited by Hans Goedicke and J. J. M. Roberts, 146–66. Baltimore: Johns Hopkins University Press.

Morrow, William. 2005. Review of *Das Deuteronomium. Politische Theologie und Rechtsform in Juda und Assyrien*, by Eckart Otto. *Bibliotheca orientalis* 62: 204–13.

Morrow, William. 2010. "'To Set the Name' in the Deuteronomic Centralization Formula: A Case of Cultural Hybridity." *Journal of Semitic Studies* 55: 365–83.

Mullen, E. Theodore, Jr. 1980. *The Divine Council in Canaanite and Early Hebrew Literature*. Harvard Semitic Monographs, 24. Chico, CA: Scholars Press.

Norin, Stig. 2013. *Personennamen und Religion im alten Israel, untersucht mit besonderer Berücksichtigung der Namen auf El und Baʿal*. Coniectanea biblica, Old Testament, 60. Winona Lake, IN: Eisenbrauns.

Olmstead, Albert T. 1918. "The Calculated Frightfulness of Ashur Nasir Apal." *Journal of the American Oriental Society* 38: 209–63.

Oppenheim, A. Leo. 1977. *Ancient Mesopotamia. Portrait of a Dead Civilization*. Revised edition. Chicago: University of Chicago Press.

Otto, Eckart. 1999. *Das Deuteronomium. Politische Theologie und Rechtsform in Juda und Assyrien*. Beihefte zur ZAW, 284. Berlin: Walter de Gruyter.

Overholt, Thomas W. 1970. *The Threat of Falsehood. A Study in the Theology of the Book of Jeremiah*. Studies in Biblical Theology 2nd Series, 16. Naperville, IL: Allenson.

Pardee, Dennis. 2005. "On Psalm 29: Structure and Meaning." In *The Book of Psalms: Composition and Reception*, edited by Peter W. Flint and Patrick D. Miller, Jr., 153–83. Vetus Testamentum Supplement Series, 99. Leiden: Brill.

Pearce, Laurie, and Cornelia Wunsch. 2014. *Documents of Judean Exiles and West Semites in Babylonia in the Collection of David Sofer*. Cornell University Studies in Assyriology and Sumerology, 28. Bethesda, MD: CDL Press.

Radner, Karen. 2006. "Assyrische *ṭuppi adê* als Vorbild für Deuteronomium 28, 20–44?" In *Die deuteronomistischen Geschichtswerke: Redaktions- und religionsgeschichtliche Perspektiven zur "Deuteronomismus"-Diskussion in Tora und Vorderen Propheten*, edited by Markus Witte, Konrad Schmid, Doris Prechel, and Jan Christian Gertz, with Johannes F. Diehl, 351–78. Beihefte zur ZAW, 365. Berlin: Walter de Gruyter.

Rainey, Anson. 2015. *The El-Amarna Correspondence. A New Edition of the Cuneiform Letters from the Site of El-Amarna Based on Collations of All Extant Tablets*. 2 volumes. Edited by William Schniedewind and Zipora Cochavi-Rainey. Handbook of Oriental Studies, 110/1–2. Leiden: Brill.

Sallaberger, Walther. 2000. "Das Erscheinen Marduks als Vorzeichen: Kultstatue und Neujahrfest in der Omenserie *Šumma ālu*." *Zeitschrift für Assyriologie* 90: 227–62.

Schaudig, Hanspeter. 2008. "'Bēl Bows, Nabû Stoops!' The Prophecy of Isaiah xlvi 1–2 as a Reflection of Babylonian 'Processional Omens.'" *Vetus Testamentum* 58: 557–72.

Smith, Mark S. 2002. *The Early History of God: Yahweh and the Other Deities in Ancient Israel*, 2nd edition. The Biblical Resource Series. Grand Rapids: William B. Eerdmans/ Dearborn: Dove Booksellers.

Smith, Mark S. 2014. "Canaanite Backgrounds to the Psalms." In *The Oxford Handbook of the Psalms*, edited by William P. Brown, 43–56. Oxford/New York: Oxford University Press.

Sommer, Benjamin D. 1998. *A Prophet Reads Scripture: Allusion in Isaiah 40–66*. Stanford: Stanford University Press.

Steymans, Hans Ulrich, editor. 1995. *Deuteronomium 28 und die adê zur Thronfolgeregelung Asarhaddons: Segen und Fluch im Alten Orient und in Israel*. Orbis biblicus et orientalis, 145. Fribourg: Academic Press/Göttingen: Vandenhoeck & Ruprecht.

Steymans, Hans Ulrich. 2010. *Gilgamesh: Ikonographie eines Helden/Gilgamesh: Epic and Iconography*. Orbis biblicus et orientalis, 245. Fribourg: Academic Press/Göttingen: Vandenhoeck & Ruprecht.

Stökl, Jonathan, and Caroline Waerzeggers, editor. 2015. *Exile and Return: The Babylonian Context*. Beihefte zur ZAW, 478. Berlin: Walter de Gruyter.

Stott, Katherine M. 2008. *Why Did They Write This Way? Reflections on References to Written Documents in the Hebrew Bible and Ancient Literature*. The Library of Hebrew Bible/Old Testament Studies, 492. New York/London: T & T Clark.

Tadmor, Hayim. 1991. "On the Role of Aramaic in the Assyrian Empire." In *Near Eastern Studies Dedicated to H.I.H. Prince Takahito Mikasa on the Occasion of His Seventy-Fifth Birthday*, 419–26. Bulletin of the Middle Eastern Culture Center in Japan, 5. Wiesbaden: Harrassowitz.

Tawil, Hayim. 2009. *An Akkadian Lexical Companion for Biblical Hebrew: Etymological-Semantic and Idiomatic Equivalents with Supplement on Biblical Aramaic*. Jersey City, NJ: KTAV Publishing House.

Tiemeyer, Lena-Sofia. 2011. *For the Comfort of Zion: The Geographical and Theological Location of Isaiah 40–55*. Vetus Testamentum Supplement Series, 139. Leiden: Brill.

Waerzeggers, Caroline. 2003–2004. "The Babylonian Revolts Against Xerxes and the 'End of Archives.'" *Archiv für Orientforschung* 50: 150–78.

Wagner, Andreas. 1996. "Ist Ps 29 die Bearbeitung eines Baal-Hymnus?" *Biblica* 77: 538–39.

Wright, David P. 2009. *Inventing God's Law. How the Covenant Code of the Bible Used and Revised the Laws of Hammurabi*. Oxford: Oxford University Press.

Zevit, Ziony. 2001. *The Religions of Ancient Israel. A Synthesis of Parallactic Approaches*. London/New York: Continuum.

Zimansky, Paul. 2007. "Writing, Writers, and Reading in the Kingdom of Van." In *Margins of Writing, Origins of Cultures*, 2nd edition, edited by Seth Sanders, 263–82. Oriental Institute Seminars, 2. Chicago: The Oriental Institute of the University of Chicago.

Chapter 12

Gauging Egyptian Influences on Biblical Literature

MICHAEL V. FOX[*]

I. PARALLELOMANIA

"Parallelomania"—the title of Samuel Sandmel's 1961 SBL presidential address—was a one-word warning against the abuse of literary, sociological, and historical comparisons in Bible studies. Sandmel's governing principle was the determinative force of context: "Two passages may sound the same in splendid isolation from their context, but when seen in context reflect difference rather than similarity" (1962: 2). This warning is to the point, except that it makes a false dichotomy between difference and similarity. Both features lie in any comparison, and discovery of difference is one of the rewards of the comparative approach. The essence of Sandmel's warning was developed by Shemaryahu Talmon in a 1978 critique of the use of the comparative method in Bible studies. Talmon's article has since been disputed, but its analysis is penetrating and its critique pungent, and I take it as my starting point.

Talmon posits an "unbridgeable dichotomy" between what he calls, tendentiously, the "atomistic" approach and the "holistic" approach. The atomistic approach observes relations between isolated components of two cultures in order to describe cross-cultural patterns. The holistic approach insists on the individuality of cultures and "tries first to understand a

* Michael V. Fox is Jay C. and Ruth Halls-Bascom Professor Emeritus in the Department of Hebrew and Semitic Studies at the University of Wisconsin-Madison.

cultural configuration in its entirety" and also "emphasizes the individuality and dissimilarity conferred upon these identified components by their very existence within specific organic cultural totalities" (1978: 328). The abstraction of a concept or an aspect of culture from its wider framework, and its contemplation in isolation, more often than not will result in distortion; its intrinsic meaning ultimately is decided by the context, and therefore may vary from one setting to another" (1978: 356). Hence the elucidation of ideas and texts must come from within the biblical books themselves. Moreover, since every *Gattung*, Talmon believes, had a specific *Sitz im Leben*, "the identification of a *Gattung* evidenced in the literature of one society also in the creative writings of another requires the additional proof that in both it had the same *Sitz im Leben*" (1978: 352).

II. PRINCIPLES OF A HOLISTIC COMPARATIVE APPROACH

Talmon's critique of the comparative method (better: approach) seems like common sense, but it holds certain distortions. In response, I propose the following principles:

1. A truly holistic approach views a biblical text in its broader culture-world, namely the ancient Near East. It is atomistic to limit oneself to a biblical context (though atomism too can serve certain purposes, as in a close reading).The context of biblical literature was not only the Bible. If we had more Hebrew texts, the local (Israelite) context might look much different. (This happened with the discovery of Kuntillet 'Ajrud texts with its war hymn to El and Baal.) To get a sense of the local context of biblical texts, we must broaden the picture to include neighboring cultures. The validity of this picture does not assume "borrowing," as if features of Israelite literature that it shares with neighboring cultures must have been taken from the outside. This might happen, but it also might be that as a participant in an international culture Israel inherited and shared many of its, social, religious, legal, and literary usages and assumptions. For example, the creation myth that features Yahweh as divine warrior defeating Leviathan was not borrowed from Ugaritic literature, nor does it show Canaanite "influence." It was as native Israelite as any other biblical creation account, for Israel's culture *was* Canaanite.
2. The starting point for the study of the Bible is, of course, the Bible, but nothing says we have to stop there. There are numerous

relevant contexts. One is the surrounding literary environment, including writings *and oral* works available to the author. In any case, strictly speaking, the literary context of a book was not the Bible, for there was no Bible when its books were written. There were oral compositions as well as written books and collections with a proto-canonical status.

3.   Talmon declares that "[a] *Gattung* cannot be contemplated in isolation from the overall socio-cultural web of a society" (1978: 352). It is true that a *Gattung* may have different roles in different societies, but its role in one society provides a reasonable hypothesis for its role in another. Moreover, a *Gattung* may have different functions in a single society. The *Sitz im Leben* of the book of Proverbs was, in the first instance, the royal court; the *Sitz im Leben* of Ben Sira was an individual scholar's home or school. The Instruction of King Amenemhet certainly arose in the royal court but it came to be a very popular school text. The Instruction of Amenemope at least presents itself as, and probably was, paternal instruction, which came to be used in the schools.[1]

III. APPLICATIONS

My main role in the panel was to address the questions presented by the editor of this volume: "When you intuit that there is or may be an Egyptian 'connection' for a particular biblical text, how do you determine the nature of the connection? What are you looking for?" In the following, I concentrate on Wisdom Literature, the genre for which Egyptian parallels have been adduced most extensively, and will reflect on some of the claims of Egyptian influence I have asserted or denied—or both—in earlier publications. I summarize the arguments for the literary connections but leave much out, because my purpose is to probe the type of reasoning used and its validity. Full argumentation is available in the publications cited. I do not offer a systematic evaluation of the comparative method. For such an evaluation, I recommend the thoughtful handbook by Malul (1990).

---

1   There is evidence that some Egyptian instructions were indeed father to son teachings, as they present themselves. See Fox 1996 and my "Three Theses on Wisdom," forthcoming 2015.

A. A STRONG PARALLEL: WISDOM INSTRUCTIONS[2]

Comparison of Egyptian and Israelite literature begins with the praise of Solomon's achievements in 1 Kgs 5:9-12, which says that Solomon's *hokmah* was superior to the wisdom of the Easterners and the Egyptians, that he was famous among the nations, and that he spoke 3000 *meshalim* and 1005 songs. Wisdom here refers to literary productivity (apparently oral literature—for Solomon "spoke" it—that was later transcribed). Regardless of its historical accuracy, this notice is significant for the attitude it reveals. It shows that an Israelite (deuteronomistic) historian classed Solomon's wisdom in the same genre as the wisdom of the other nations and regarded it as measurable by the same criteria. Moreover, the author believed that he knew what the wisdom of Egypt was, at least generally, and also expected his audience to find that claim believable. Another author, the Deuteronomist, even considers it plausible to claim that the other nations would know and admire the superlative Israelite instruction—Torah—and think of it in terms of wisdom (Deut 4:6).

Observe also that this ancient comparison in 1 Kgs 5:9-12 assumes *analogy* rather than *homology,* to use a distinction from evolutionary biology. Analogies are resemblances resulting from similar adaption to similar needs, such as the wings of bats and birds. Homologies are resemblances due to common genetic derivation, such as the bird's wings and the lizard's front legs. In human culture, homology may come about by either direct development or influence. "Parallel" is loosely used for both kinds, though on the face of it, it should refer to similar but independent phenomena, such as African and Israelite proverbs.

Of all genres of Hebrew literature, the one with the clearest connections to neighboring cultures is Wisdom Literature, particularly didactic Wisdom Literature, which I would term "Ethical Instructions," following a usage in New Kingdom Wisdom, *sb'yt mryt*.[3] (Earlier, wisdom books are just called "instructions," a word used of various types of teachings.) These books are instruction in the ethical and practical arts of living.

1. The Instruction of Amenemope

The strongest case for literary dependence (and not merely vague "influence") is that of Proverbs on the New Kingdom Instruction of

---

2 The translations in the present article are my own. For full translations of the Egyptian texts, see Lichtheim 1973, 1976, and 1980.

3 See Fox, 2015.

Amenemope.[4] Most striking is the claim that Prov 22:17-23:11 is derived from Amenemope by a combination of translation and revision. Adolf Erman (1924) effectively made the case simply by pointing out parallel passages. Most scholars accepted this view, but there has been opposition. Alternative proposals underscore the differences between the two texts and conclude that the parallels are merely similar literary responses to similar situations, or that they are just examples of the diffuse influence of Egyptian Wisdom on Proverbs (Krispenz 1989: 129-31; Whybray 1994: 133). The alternative explanations, however, do not account for the fact that the Amenemope parallels are concentrated in a short unit of Proverbs, and, moreover, that this unit has no parallels to other Wisdom books (except insofar as Amenemope drew on *them*), even though in total quantity those books far surpass Amenemope. The relation between Amenemope and Prov 22:17-23:11 is special, in fact, unique.

Many scholars have affirmed the dependence of Proverbs Part III on Amenemope (most recently Washington 1994, Emerton 2001, and Shupak 2005). I have supported the case by tracing the working method of the editor of this passage (Fox 2014). Basically my argument is that the well-recognized parallels do not occur at random. They appear in sequence, with the order in Proverbs lining up with the order in Amenemope—not all at once but in five cycles or "sweeps." This arrangement testifies to a particular working method, one suited to (and almost necessitated by) the use of a scroll. In each sweep the editor started from near the beginning of the book and moved forward, picking up material from his source text, Amenemope, and working it into the target text. Nearing the end of the source scroll, he moved back toward the beginning of the book and again moved forward. Every sweep proceeded sequentially, with only slight variations. (The editor may look back a few lines, to a place that would easily be in view in the open section of the source papyrus, or he may move ahead to pick up thematically related material from a later passage, then return to the approximate place he had reached earlier.)

Below I present a chart of the first two sweeps to exemplify the argument I used (for the full argument, see Fox 2014). I designate the passages in Proverbs by chapter:verse, in Amenemope by column.line. Note that the citations from Amenemope are cited according to their locations in the major extant papyrus of Amenemope, BM 10474. These locations are a proxy for their relative placement in the hypothesized intermediary text used by the editor of Proverbs. The correlations below support the

4 The following is a partial summary of a theory developed in Fox 2014.

hypothesis that the organization of the text used by the MT editor was close to that of BM 10474. To be sure, the intermediary text may already have had a slightly different order, but major omissions and re-orderings are unlikely. The jump from 7.12 to 27.16, for example, cannot be due to an omission in the intermediary text, or its predecessors, because some of the intervening material appears in later sweeps (e.g., 22.28; 15.16; 17.1). Moreover, in the seven other witnesses (which all hold only small sections of Amenemope), none have intentional gaps in the sections they preserve.[5] The division into thirty numbered chapters, shows that the book's sequence was important, and this would have made any substantial rearrangements unlikely as long as the numeration was maintained. (This number thirty was known to the Hebrew editor [see n. 8], though he did not maintain the numeration or the sequence.) Finally, the coherence of the resulting Hebrew text favors a single editorial effort—that of the Hebrew editor who used a text of Amenemope very close to BM 10474.

SWEEP I[6]			
Amenemope	column. line	chapter: verse	Proverbs
Give your ears, that you may hear the things that are said;	3.9	22:17b	Words of the Wise. Incline your ear and hear my words,
apply your heart to interpret them.	3.10	22:17c	and direct your heart to my knowledge
They will be a mooring post for your tongue.	3.16	22:18b	that they may all be secure on your lips.
		22:19	In order that your trust may be in Yahweh, I have taught them to you, even you, today.
Look to these thirty chapters.	27.7	22:20a	Have I not written for you <thirty>,[7]

5 For further information on the sources and their dating, see Laisney 2007: 5-6.
6 For exegesis and details of the comparison, see Fox 2000.
7 Neither the ketiv nor the qeré are valid. The ketiv שׁלשׁום is used only in combination with (א)תמול. The qeré שׁלישׁים supposedly means "noble," but שׁליש, a type of warrior, never has that connotation. We should read שְׁלשִׁים, a reference to the thirty maxims in Prov 22:17-24:10. There are various ways of counting them, but most counts agree on the basic components and find thirty, or approximately thirty, components. See ABP II, 710-12.

SWEEP II			
to return an (oral) response to one who says it, to bring back a (written) message to the one who sends it.	1.5-6	22:21	to teach you the truest of words, (whereby) to give answer to those who send you.
Beware of robbing the lowly,	4.4	22:22a	Do not rob a lowly man because he is lowly,
of oppressing the weak.	4.5	22:22b	and do not oppress the poor man at the gate.
but the Moon declares his crime.	(4.19)	22:23	For Yahweh will strive on their behalf, and will steal away the life of those who steal from them.
Do not join quarrel with the hot mouthed man, nor assail him by words. Do not consort with the heated man, or approach him for conversation. Do not share a portion with the heated man or consort with a contentious man.	5.10-11 11.13-14 15.13-14	22:24-25	Do not consort with an ill-tempered man, lest you learn his ways and get yourself snared.
Do not displace the stone on the boundary of the fields. Beware of encroaching on the boundaries of the fields,	7.12 8.9	22:28	Do not encroach on the ancient boundary, which your ancestors made.
As for the scribe skilled in his office,	27.16	22:29a	Have you seen a man adept in his work?
he will be found worthy to be a courtier.	27.17	22:29bc	He will stand before kings. He will not stand before the lowly.

The Hebrew editor begins by writing an introduction to the instruction. It begins with the title "Words of the Wise," which ascribes the teaching to follow to unknown sages of the past. The editor opens the scroll and starts at Amenemope 3.9, right after the titulary (which may have been skipped in the Semitic source text as irrelevant). The editor calls upon the reader to give ear and keep these words in the belly, which is a distinctly Egyptian notion, then the editor interprets the metaphor of "mooring post" to make it more easily comprehensible to a reader who lives away from a river—in Jerusalem, perhaps. The editor adds a theme of his own: trust in Yahweh. The editor ends this sweep by using the number "thirty" to count the components of his instruction. (Thirty is a significant number in Egyptian but not in Hebrew.) The editor is now at the end of the scroll. While still writing the exordium—in fact, in the middle of a sentence—the editor rolls back to 1.5-6 of Amenemope and picks up the theme of "answering," which is used in writing Prov 22:21b. Advice about "answering," which is to say reporting back on a mission, is important in Amenemope and, to a degree, elsewhere in Proverbs, but not in this unit. The editor has rather mechanically borrowed the topic from his source without actually applying it in his own instruction. Continuing to move forward, at 4.4-5 the editor finds the idea to use in his next maxim: the admonition against harming the poor. The Moon (meaning the god Thoth, the arbiter of justice) is easily translated into Yahweh, the vindicator of the helpless. Reaching 5.10-11, the editor jumps ahead to combine this passage with 11.13-14 and 15.13-14 to compose a warning against consorting with contentious men (Prov 22:24-25). This is one the rare violations of sequence. Its motive is clear: to draw together passages with the same theme. The third to fifth sweeps in 22:17-23:11 (on which see Fox 2014: 85–89) draw in material for use in Part IIIa. After 23:11, the editor ceases to use Amenemope. Instead, in Part IIIb, 23:12-24:2, he draws on other Wisdom books, definitely Ahiqar (see Fox 2009: 767–69) and probably Anii (see Fox 2009: 742–43). We can visualize the editor (alone or together with someone who was reading aloud) holding a scroll and rolling forward and back and searching for materials that serve his purposes. This is creative editing or, we could as well say, authorship.

The case for direct derivation is reinforced by the coincidence of two independent variables: sequence and theme. The unpredictable coincidence of sequence is beneath the surface. It is significant that there is no inherent relationship among the passages selected from Amenemope, because the coincidence cannot be explained as the response of two unrelated texts to similar needs of reason or rhetoric. In other words, the relation is homological, not analogical.

It is not only in Prov 22:17-23:11, where Proverbs is dependent on Amenemope, that we find such homological dependence. The prologue of Proverbs (1:1-7) is structured on Amenemope's prologue (1.1-3.7, apart from the titulary), especially in form. Both prologues are extended series of infinitives of purpose dependent on nominal titles ("Proverbs of Solomon" // "The ethical instruction of Amenemope," etc.) and state the pedagogical goals of the books they introduce. There is nothing quite like these prologues elsewhere in Wisdom Literature, even in the books with expansive introductions (such as Ptahhotep), and there is only one clear parallel outside Wisdom Literature (for details, see Fox 2000: 71–73). There are, moreover, significant parallels to Amenemope are not limited to Prov 22:17-23:10. This shows that Amenemope had a broad circulation among the Israelite sages and was not known only to the editor of 22:17-23:10.[8] One type of parallel is especially significant, because it involves a paradigm characteristic of Amenemope *and only* Amenemope: the quadripartite comparison, Better A with A′ than B with B′ (see Fox 2009 on 15:16-17). Examples of this quadripartite comparison are Prov 15:16 and 17, which are based on Amenemope 9.5-8:

> Proverbs 15:16-17:
> (16)   Better a little with the fear of the Lord,
>   than a great storehouse with turmoil in it.
> (17)   Better are provisions of greens where there is love
>   than a fattened ox where there is hatred.

> Amenemope 9.5-8:
> (5)   Better is poverty in the hand of the god,
> (6)   than wealth in the storehouse.
> (7)   Better are (mere) loaves of bread when the heart is pleasant,
> (8)   than wealth with vexation.

Other proverbs built on this paradigm are Prov 16:8 and 17:1.The wide distribution of parallels to Amenemope suggests that editors of several collections of Proverbs had access to Amenemope. It appears that the book of Amenemope had become part of Hebrew literature.

2. The Path of Transmission

To strengthen a hypothesis of literary influence we should try to discover the way that the source could have reached the receiver. In tracing modern literary influence we usually have this information fully available. For the

---

8   In the following, parentheses mark parallels that are thematic but not verbal. Prov 1:1–6 // Amen. 1.1–12; Prov 11:1 // (Amen. 17.18–19); // Prov 12:22 // Amen. 14.2–3; Prov 15:16–17 // Amen. 9.5–8; 16.11–14; Prov 16:8 // Amen. 9.5–6; Prov. 16:11 // Amen. 18.2–3; Prov 17:1 // Amen. 9.7–8; Prov 20:22 // (22.11–16); Prov 25:21–22 // Amen. 5.5–6; 22.3–8; Prov 27:1 // Amen. 19.13; (22.5–6); (23.8–9).

ancient Near East we have nothing similar and must bridge the gap by sur-mises. Such surmises are not mere guesses. They are hypotheses that show how the transference could have occurred and are plausible to the extent that they rest on known facts, such as known channels of communication and historical contact. Bernd Schipper (1999) showed that the most feasi-ble setting for Egyptian cultural influence on Israel was the Saitic period, 664–525 BCE.

This was an age of commercial and cultural connections between Egypt and Palestine. There was a lingua franca, Aramaic, demonstrably known by some educated Egyptians and Judeans. Furthermore, Amenemope, prob-ably written in the tenth century BCE, was still being copied in the Saitic period. The complete manuscript, BM 10476, was inscribed in the second half of the seventh century BCE, in the Saitic period.[9] Speaking more gen-erally, a chronological gap between an Egyptian source and the Israelite receptor does not hinder hypotheses of dependency. Egyptian texts were being copied and quoted for centuries and millennia after they were written.[10]

In the case of Amenemope and Proverbs we not only can describe simi-larities in content and formulations but also explain how they developed. We can follow the tracks of the author-editor who transformed selections from Amenemope into Prov 22:17–23:10 and see the function of their adap-tation. We can see how an author-editor took the quadripartite "better-than" paradigm and filled it with new content. None of these affinities could arise without knowledge of the source text in the receptor culture.

B. A MISGUIDED PARALLEL: MAʿAT AND WORLD ORDER

External models can be used to clarify and explore biblical phenomena, but they should be based on a correct understanding of the source literature. Scholarship of Israelite Wisdom was led astray by the idea of the world order, which was supposedly the governing principle of Wisdom. This idea came straight from the Egyptian principle of Maʿat, or more precisely, a misunderstanding thereof. It arose, I think, with the seminal studies of

---

9   See Laisney 2007: 6 for discussion and references.

10 This is no exaggeration. The first known Wisdom text, the Instruction of Djedefhar, written about 2530 BCE, was frequently copied and was quoted as late as the first century CE. There area other examples of transmission for a millennium and more.

Gese (1959) and Würthwein (1960), which based themselves on important Egyptological studies by Frankfort (1963 [1948]) and Anthes (1952). This idea dominated Wisdom scholarship for some three decades, including my own first article (Fox 1968). I argued that we could trace the inner history of the book of Proverbs by anchoring the sayings that presume a self-regulating world order (that is, that describe retribution as a "natural" event, without divine interference). From this point, the development of two later stages could be traced.[11]

Like other scholars at the time, I found the Ma'at/world-order principle helpful in explaining the seemingly vague relation of God to recompense in Proverbs and the genre's detachment from the specifics of Israelite history. This order entails rules of behavior, a sort of natural law, which the wise can infer from events by empirical observation and rational deduction (hence the absence of revelation in Proverbs). This world order was created and willed by God.

My argument against this theory is two-fold: (1) Ma'at is not the kind of order the theory assumed; (2) the concept of Ma'at as it actually existed was very foreign to Israelite thought in general and Proverbs in particular and was not found in the Bible.

(1) Ma'at is not order as such. It is, rather, the force that creates and maintains order, namely justice/truth, a concept that we subdivide, perhaps artificially, into two. Ma'at was not a mechanistic, self-regulating force that automatically and indifferently links consequence to deed. Nor did such an idea exist in Proverbs. Both sides of the parallel were scholarly constructs, which is fine, but they were feeble ones, which is not fine. The deepest similarity is that neither Israelite Wisdom nor Egyptian thought contains a belief in a world-order of this sort. I will not try to show this here, because I am now concerned with methodological issues of the proper application of Egyptian parallels in the study of Wisdom Literature (for a fuller discussion of this issue, see Fox 1995).

(2) The concept of Ma'at in its fullness did not and could not exist in Israel, and in fact could hardly have been transposed into Israelite

---

11 The stages were (1) the "Egyptian stage", which drew on Egyptian sources and assumed the working of a world order; (2) the "Yahwistic" stage, which made Yahweh independent of the constraints of an external order, so that he was the direct agent of reward and punishment; and (3) the "theological" stage, which explored the relation between Yahweh and wisdom.

terms. The word Maʿat does have Hebrew counterparts in terms for truth and justice, such as ṣedeq ("justice") and mêšārîm ("rectitude"). But Maʿat is quite different from these concepts. To be sure, Maʿat is order, but an order that was infused into the world in creation by the expulsion of disorder, and it is maintained by the king, both ritually and in his deeds, and by society as a whole. It is not an automaton that enforces justice by impersonal processes. Moreover, Maʿat was the foundation myth of the Pharaonic state and was inextricable from the Egyptian religion and hierarchy. Major features of Maʿat, such as statements that Re lives on Maʿat, or that Maʿat is the daughter of Re, as well as important rituals, such as the daily offering of Maʿat to Re, and prominent images, such as the goddess Maʿat in the prow of Re's boat and the weighing of the heart of the deceased against the Maʿat feather, would make no sense outside of Egypt and could not have been transmitted where Egyptian religion was absent.

Nevertheless, some components of the Maʿat belief do have equivalents in Israel, and influences of the concept of Maʿat on Israelite literature are in principle possible, but only of a very attenuated sort. If a translator from Egyptian into, say, Aramaic, saw the word maʿat in his text, he would probably have translated it qĕshoṭ or ṣidqāʾ. It could then be brought into Hebrew as ʾĕmet or ṣᵉdāqāʾ or mêšārîm, and that would be the end of it. (None of the Egyptian source-passages of sentences in Proverbs or elsewhere in the Bible happen to use this word.) Nothing more of the great religious and political edifice surrounding Maʿat would or could have come with it, and the modern scholar should not import it either.

IV. CRITERIA FOR COMPARISON

In conclusion, in answer to Zevit's question to the panel, "What are you looking for," I'd answer: A strong congruity between source and receptor in specific and independent variables, both in form and content, with unpredictable similarities unique to the texts in question, together with a verifiable path of geographical and temporal transmission. But insisting that all these criteria be met would obscure some real and significant connections between Israel and its environment. It is often legitimate to accept a partial case. I try to calibrate the claims to the strength of the evidence, and then to use the parallels with vigor but not mania.

REFERENCES

Anthes, Rudolph. 1952. "Die Maat des Echnaton von Amarna." *Journal of the American Oriental Society* 14: 1–36.

Brunner, Hellmut. 1963. "Der freie Wille Gottes in der ägyptischen Weisheit." In *Sagesses du Proche-orient ancient*, 103–20. Paris: Presses Universitaires.

Caminos, Ricardo. 1958. *Late-Egyptian Miscellanies*. London: Oxford University.

Emerton, John A. 2001. "The Teaching of Amenemope and Proverbs XXII 17–XXIV 22: Reflections on a Long-Standing Problem." *Vetus Testament* 51: 431–65.

Erman, Adolf. 1924. "Eine ägyptische Quelle der 'Spruch Salomos'." *Sitzungsberichte der Preussischen Akademie der Wissenschaften zu Berlin* (phil-hist. Kl. 15): 86–93.

Fox, Michael V. 1968. "Aspects of the Religion of the Book of Proverbs." *Hebrew Union College Annual* 39: 55–69.

Fox, Michael V. 1985. *The Song of Songs and the Ancient Egyptian Love Songs*. Madison: University of Wisconsin.

Fox, Michael V. 1995. "World-Order and Ma'at: A Crooked Parallel." *Journal of the Ancient Near Eastern Society* 23: 37–48.

Fox, Michael V. 1996. "The Social Location of the Book of Proverbs." In *Texts, Temples, and Traditions: A Tribute to Menahem* Haran, edited by by M. V. Fox et al., 227–39. Winona Lake: Eisenbrauns.

Fox, Michael V. 2000. *Proverbs 1-9*. Anchor Bible, 18A. Garden City, NY: Doubleday.

Fox, Michael V. 2009. *Proverbs 10-31*. Anchor Bible, 18B. New Haven, CT: Yale University.

Fox, Michael V. 2014. "From Amenemope to Proverbs: Editorial Art in Proverbs 22,17–23,11." *Zeitschrift für die alttestamentliche Wissenschaft* 126: 76–91.

Fox, Michael V. 2015. "Three Theses on Wisdom Literature." In *Was There a Wisdom Tradition?* Edited by Mark Sneed. Ancient Israel and Its Literature. Atlanta: SBL Press.

Frankfort, Henri. 1963 [1948]. *Ancient Egyptian Religion*. New York: Harper.

Gese, Harmut. 1958. *Lehre und Wirklichkeit in der alten Weisheit*. Tübingen: Mohr Siebeck.

Krispenz, Jutta. 1989. *Spruchkompositionen im Buch Proverbia*. Frankfurt: Peter Lang.

Laisney, Vincent. 2007. *L'Enseignement d'Aménémope*. Studia Pohl, series maior. Rome: Biblical Pontifical Institute.

Lichtheim, Miriam. 1973–80. *Ancient Egyptian Literature*. Vol. 1, 1980; vol. 2, .1976; vol. 3, 1973. Berkeley: University of California (= AEL).

Malul, Meir. 1990. *The Comparative Method in Ancient Near Eastern and Biblical Legal Studies*. Alter Orient und Altes Testament, 227. Neukirchen-Vluyn: Neukirchener.

Rad, Gerhard von. 1970. *Weisheit in Israel*. Neukirchen-Vluyn: Neukirchener [ET *Wisdom in Israel*; James D. Martin. London: SCM, 1972].

Ruffle, John. 1977. "The Teaching of Amenemope and Its Connection to the Book of Proverbs." *Tyndale Bulletin* 28: 29–68.

Sandmel, Samuel. 1962. "Parallelomania." *Journal of Biblical Literature* 81: 1–13.

Schipper, Berndt U. 1999. *Israel und Ägypten in der Königzeit*. Orbis biblicus et orientalis, 170. Göttingen: Vandenhoeck & Ruprecht.

Schmid, Hans Heinrich. 1968. *Gerechtigkeit als Weltordnung: Hintergrund und Geschichte der alttestamentlichen Gerechtigkeitsbegriffes*. Beiträge zur historischen Theologie, 40. Tübingen: Mohr Siebeck.

Shupak, Nili. 2005. "The Instruction of Amenemope and Proverbs 22:17–24:22 from the Perspective of Contemporary Research." In *Seeking Out the Wisdom of the Ancients. Essays Offered to Honor Michael V. Fox on the Occasion of his Sixty-Fifth Birthday*, edited by Ronald Troxel et al., 203–20. Winona Lake, IN: Eisenbrauns.

Talmon, Shemaryahu. 1978. "The 'Comparative Method' in Biblical Interpretation: Principles and Problems." In *Congress Volume—Göttingen 1977*, edited by J. A. Emerton, 320–56. Supplements to Vetus Testamentum, 29. Leiden: Brill.

Washington, Harold C. 1994. *Wealth and Poverty in the Instruction of Amenemope and the Hebrew Proverbs*. SBL Dissertation Series, 142. Atlanta: Scholars Press.

Würthwein, Ernst. 1960. *Die Weisheit Ägyptens und das Alte Testament*. Marburg: Elwert.

Whybray, Roger N. 1994. *The Composition of the Book of Proverbs*. Journal for the Study of the Old Testament Supplement Series, 168. Sheffield: Sheffield Academic Press.

Chapter 13

Afterword: A Future for Back-referencing

ZIONY ZEVIT[*]

The intention of all participants in this volume was that our work present and represent "best practices" not only in the sense that the texts analyzed and their specific or general precursors, alleged and real, be discussed without special pleading, but also in the sense that the accompanying descriptions of methodologies be clear and that difficulties be marked, not minimized. As a consequence, studies presented in the preceding chapters contribute to a better comprehension of the history of (some parts of) biblical literature based on disciplined methodologies than has been available heretofore. They model methodologies for ongoing and future work.

The larger project envisioned by this volume, however, has not yet been launched. For the historical study of biblical citations, allusions, translations, etc., to develop into an active, productive research paradigm within bibliology, a number of steps are necessary:

1. It is necessary to recognize that the focus of scholarly attention in the investigation of citations, allusions, and the like may be crudely described as "back-referencing," a conscious activity in which some ancient writers engaged often or sporadically or not at all (insofar as we are able to discern), depending on what they were composing and why. Back-referencing served to place an author's work in some relationship to an earlier written work or tradition, or merely to part of it, thereby providing contemporary scholars with a relative chronology. Although essentially a mark of an ancient author's *awareness*, back-references can sometimes be explicated

* Ziony Zevit is Distinguished Professor of Biblical Literature and Northwest Semitic Languages and Literatures at the American Jewish University, Los Angeles.

by contemporary scholars as indicators of *influence* or *authority* or shared *intentionality* or as something else. This topic has not yet been addressed thoroughly in monographic depth.[1]

2. The methodological practices presented in this volume must be summarized, categorized, critiqued aggressively, culled, and synthesized.

3. A protocol for future research must be developed and a set of technical terms for such research adopted formally by scholars working actively in the field. The development of such a protocol can be achieved through focused, roundtable discussions in seminars and work-groups at national and international meetings of scholarly societies in Europe and North America. It could be adopted by means of votes at such meetings or through an electronic ballot. The process of developing such a protocol may be loud and contentious. It certain will be interesting.

The significance of a shared protocol lies in its ability to enhance clear communication and the sharing of knowledge. Moreover, a shared protocol will quickly reveal problematic case studies, some of which will require adjustments to the protocol; it will also reveal substandard work products. Such a protocol (or broad-based consensus on how work should proceed in this area of research) will also help focus disagreements and arguable issues that may be discussed using a common technical vocabulary. Ultimately, the fate of such a protocol will be to disappear as the field develops, scholarly interests change, and new understandings about the studied literary phenomena evolve.

4. At some point, discussions of back-referencing will have to engage seriously with Neo-documentarian approaches to (hypothesized) texts discoverable (or already discovered) within extant texts. In one form or another, documentary hypotheses—with their attendant difficulties—provide the major viable explanations for the composition of Kings, Samuel, Judges, Joshua, (much) prophetic literature, as well as Genesis, Exodus, and parts of Numbers and Deuteronomy. Although the research paradigm focusing on identifying and delineating documents within biblical texts has been quiescent, but hardly defunct, for almost sixty years, it remains the most commonly discussed paradigm in textbooks and

---

1 One major source for lists of expressions, idioms, and themes common to two or more biblical books, and hence to two or more ancient authors, are the commentaries (in Modern Hebrew) of the series *Da'at Mikra* published by Mosad HaRav Kook in Jerusalem. Almost every introduction to a book in this series has such lists, some of which run on for may pages, and for which knowledge of Modern Hebrew is not necessary.

standard introductions, and it has been reinvigorated by a new generation of scholars.

5. Finally, for literary research based on the study of back-referencing to be fully integrated into the broader paradigm of historical research, it must engage seriously with other disciplines that study early-late-later phenomena related to biblical literature: lexicography, linguistics, poetics, orthography, and ancient Near Eastern literature. When drawn appropriately into discussions about literary matters, they make for competent philology.

...

The project envisioned has significance beyond the strict study of biblical literature *per se*. It has much to contribute to Tradition History (but not in its amorphous reconceptualization as Memory Studies) and to Reception History. Beyond the Hebrew Bible/Old Testament, it has implications for the study of Second Temple literature preserved in the Apocrypha and Pseudepigrapha, the Dead Sea Scrolls, for New Testament research, for the study of archaic Christianity and Judaism, and for Tannaitic literature preserved in Rabbinic sources.

Finally, the project should not be comprehended as open ended. The number of data is limited since all are contained in the 929 chapters of the Hebrew Bible. Insofar as the data are limited, once launched, the project, executed by coordinated individuals or teams, could be concluded within a decade.

Index of Modern Authors

Index of Subjects

Index of Biblical Passages

www.ingramcontent.com/pod-product-compliance
Lightning Source LLC
Chambersburg PA
CBHW070507030726
47503CB00004B/1193